INSIGHT GUIDE

LISBON

APA PUBLICATIONS

Part of the Langenscheidt Publishing Group

ABOUT THIS BOOK

Editorial
Project Editor
Pam Barrett
Managing Editor
Cathy Muscat
Editorial Director
Brian Bell

Distribution

UK & Ireland
GeoCenter International Ltd
The Viables Centre, Harrow Way
Basingstoke, Hants RG22 4BJ
Fax: (44) 1256 817988

United States
Langenscheidt Publishers, Inc.
46–35 54th Road, Maspeth, NY 11378
Fax: (1) 718 784 0640

Canada
Thomas Allen & Son Ltd
390 Steelcase Road East
Markham, Ontario L3R 1G2
Fax: (1) 905 475 6747

Australia
Universal Press
1 Waterloo Road
Macquarie Park, NSW 2113
Fax: (61) 2 9888 9074

New Zealand
Hema Maps New Zealand Ltd (HNZ)
Unit D, 24 Ra ORA Drive
East Tamaki, Auckland
Fax: (64) 9 273 6479

Worldwide
Apa Publications GmbH & Co.
Verlag KG (Singapore branch)
38 Joo Koon Road, Singapore 628990
Tel: (65) 865 1600. Fax: (65) 861 6438

Printing

Insight Print Services (Pte) Ltd
38 Joo Koon Road, Singapore 628990
Tel: (65) 865 1600. Fax: (65) 861 6438

©2001 Apa Publications GmbH & Co.
Verlag KG (Singapore branch)
All Rights Reserved
First Edition 1988
Fourth Edition 2001

CONTACTING THE EDITORS
We would appreciate it if readers would alert us to errors or outdated information by writing to:
Insight Guides, P.O. Box 7910, London SE1 1WE, England.
Fax: (44) 20 7403 0290.
insight@apaguide.demon.co.uk

www.insightguides.com

This guidebook combines the interests and enthusiasms of two of the world's best-known information providers: Insight Guides, whose titles have set the standard for visual travel guides since 1970, and Discovery Channel, the world's premier source of nonfiction television programming.

The editors of Insight Guides provide practical advice and general understanding about a destination's history, culture, institutions and people. Discovery Channel and its website, www.discovery.com, help millions of viewers explore their world from the comfort of their own home and also encourage them to explore it first-hand.

This fully updated edition of *Insight Guide:*

Lisbon is carefully structured to convey an understanding of the city and its culture as well as to guide readers through its sights and activities:

♦ The **Features** section, indicated by a yellow bar at the top of each page, covers the history and culture of the country in a series of informative essays.

♦ The main **Places** section, indicated by a blue bar, is a complete guide to all the sights and areas worth visiting. Places of special interest are coordinated by number with the maps.

♦ The **Travel Tips** listings section, with an orange bar, provides a handy point of reference for information on travel, hotels, restaurants, shops, nightlife, excursions, and more.

pieces by **Sharon Behn** (festivals), **Jeremy Boultbee** (fado), **John Dalton** (bullfighting), **Thomas Hill** (history), **Ruth Rosengarten** (*azulejos* and art and architecture), **Roger Williams** (people) and **Jenny Wittner** (shopping).

The Places section of the book has undergone radical restructuring to reflect the many changes that have taken place in Lisbon in the past few years.

Building on earlier chapters by **Deborah Brammer**, Ruth Rosengarten and Alison Friesinger Hill, this section was updated by **Paul and Denise Burton**, two English writers who have lived in Portugal for many years and know Lisbon well. The couple contributed to the most recent edition of *Insight Guide: Portugal*, and have written about walking in the Portuguse countryside.

The Burtons also contributed to pieces on Shopping and Eating in the city – two areas of activity that have changed a lot in the past few years, and contributed a piece on the new Parque das Nações, the former Expo '98 site. They were also responsible for overhauling and extending the Travel Tips section.

For chapters on Excursions outside Lisbon, thanks go to **Martin Howe**, Deborah Brammer and **Brian and Eileen Anderson**.

Most of the excellent photography in this edition came from **Tony Arruza**, **Bill Wassmann**, **Alain Evrard**, **Phil Wood** and **Mark Read**, but there were valuable contributions from other photographers.

Thanks also go to **Sue Platt** for proofreading this latest edition of the book and to **Elizabeth Cook** for compiling the index.

The contributors

This edition of *Insight Guide: Lisbon* was revised and edited by London-based editor **Pam Barrett**, supervised by managing editor **Cathy Muscat** at Insight Guides. This new edition has been completely updated with the invaluable help of a number of people.

In the Features section, **Marion Kaplan** contributed a new essay on modern history, entitled Monarchy to Millennium, and a short feature on Luís Camões, Portugal's most revered poet. Kaplan, who lived for many years in Lisbon and has written extensively on all things Portuguese, also updated the Everyday Life feature, to bring it into the new millennium.

Among revised features from the previous edition, which was edited by **Alison Friesinger Hill**, were

Map Legend

▬ ▬ ▪ ▬	International Boundary
▬ ▬ ▬ ▬	Province Boundary
▬ ▪ ▬ ▪ ▬	National Park/Reserve
▬ ▬ ▬ ▬	Ferry Route
Ⓜ	Metro
✈ ✦	Airport: International/ Regional
🚌	Bus Station
❶	Tourist Information
✉	Post Office
† ⳧	Church/Ruins
†	Monastery
☾	Mosque
✡	Synagogue
🏰 🏚	Castle/Ruins
🏠	Mansion/Stately home
∴	Archaeological Site
∩	Cave
𝟏	Statue/Monument
★	Place of Interest

The main places of interest in the Places section are coordinated by number with a full-colour map (e.g. ❶), and a symbol at the top of every right-hand page tells you where to find the map.

CONTENTS

Maps

TERRA

View from
São Pedro de
Alcantara,
Bairro Alto.

Information panels

Places

A WELCOMING CITY

Its history fascinates, but Lisbon has its eyes fixed on the

future, with modern facilities and exciting architecture

Lisbon has a lengthy history. Julius Caesar made it the western capital of the Roman Empire in 60 BC and, while its fortunes fluctuated over the following centuries, it has been the capital of Portugal since 1255. During the great Age of Discoveries – the 15th and 16th centuries – the city was enriched by the wealth from the colonies and some of its enduring monuments, such as the Mosteiro dos Jerónimos and the Torre de Belém, were built.

Even so, the reviews weren't always positive. In 1661 the English diarist Samuel Pepys wrote: "Dined with Captain Lambert and his father-in-law and had much talk of Portugall from whence he is lately come, and he tells me that it is a very poor, dirty place – I mean the City and Court of Lisbone." And in 1797 another English writer, Robert Southey, reported: "The filth of this city is indeed astonishing; every thing is thrown into the street, and all the refuse of the kitchen, and dead animals are exposed to these scorching suns."

Today the reality is very different in this modern city. Yet a sense of the past lingers as you wander around Lisbon, from the Castelo de São Jorge in Alfama, the city's oldest quarter, to the so-called Pombeline architecture of the Praça do Comercio, constructed under the guiding hand of the Marquês de Pombal after the city was devastated by an earthquake in 1755. Another form of devastation came in 1988, when the Chiado district was ravaged by fire, but that, too, has risen phoenix-like from the ashes.

Historically a haven for exiles, Lisbon continues its tradition of extending a warm welcome to visitors. And it has an eye to the future, too. The new Parque das Nações, the site of Expo '98, is an area of stunning modern architecture and encompasses enough leisure facilities to attract Lisboetas to an outlying part of the city that was once an industrial wilderness. Central areas of the waterfront have also become a lively focus of activity by day and night, with the opening of restaurants, bars and clubs on the dockside.

This guide will introduce you to the city's history, its festivals and its art and architecture, as well as giving you a glimpse into the everyday life of its citizens and a snapshot of their major passions: the soulful music known as *fado*, and the national obsession known as football. The Places section will then take you on guided tours around Lisbon's diverse neighbourhoods, and beyond the city limits to resorts and historical towns and monuments made easily accessible by Portugal's improved and extended motorway system. Finally, the Travel Tips section will provide you with all contact details you'll need. ❏

PRECEDING PAGES: detail of figures on the Monument to the Discoveries; enjoying the festival of Santo António; traditional costumes are worn at all the major festivals; children join in the celebrations.
LEFT: Bacchic tile from the Museu Nacional do Azulejo.

Ilium D. N. consolationis
tam ferri. 122 Templum
thonij de Padua
lum Misericordiæ
ion sancti Spiritu de alsama
em sancti Martini 126
sancti Blasij et sanctæ Luciæ
dum sancti Ludouici
ion sancti Spiritu da pecreira
a D. N. do monte

...issima Lusitaniæ, ad Tagum, totig
...e et Americæ emporium nobilissimum.

Septentrio

Oriens

...idies

Nonnulla
130 Moles lapidum v...
131 Carcer privat, Ciui...
132 Dom, monet, ...
Ducis de Auginco...
Ducis de Graganca.
Marchionis de vila re...
tium Comitis de Porcal...
tium Comitis de Redond...
laicium Comitis de Linf...
dos Canes. 140 *Sace...*
Palma. ⊙ *Pucei p...*

Tagus   fluuius

Decisive Dates

EARLY DAYS

9th–6th centuries BC Phoenician and Greek traders establish settlements.

5th century BC Carthaginians in control of the Iberian peninsula.

130 BC The Roman conquest involving bitter fighting between the Romans and the Lusitani – the strongest indigenous group – which gave the country its early name, Lusitania.

60 BC Julius Caesar makes Olisipo (Lisbon) the western capital of the Roman Empire.

4th century AD Christianity spreads rapidly throughout the Roman Empire. Bishoprics are established at Braga and Évora.

AD 419 The Germanic Suevi spread into Lusitania, but during the next half century they are vanquished by the Visigoths.

711 Moors from Africa occupy Iberia.

718 A victory by the Christians over the Moors at Covadonga starts the reconquest.

883 The area between the Douro and the Minho is recognised as Portucale. Remains under Spanish control but with increasing power and autonomy.

11th–12th centuries A complex succession of civil wars occurs as Henri of Burgundy and his cousin Raymond battle for supremacy.

RECONQUEST AND NATIONHOOD

1143 Afonso Henriques is declared first king of Portugal, but is not recognised by Pope Lucius II.

1147 Aided by Crusaders, Henri's son Afonso Henriques captures Lisbon.

1179 At the age of 70, Afonso Henriques is finally recognised as king by Pope Alexander III.

1249 The Moors are finally expelled from Algarve.

1255 Afonso III transfers the capital of Portugal from Coimbra to Lisbon.

1279–1325 Reign of King Dinis, great reforming king and castle builder; married Isabel of Aragón.

1297 Treaty of Alcañices with Castile establishes borders of Portugal.

1348 Plague – the Black Death – ravages Lisbon.

1355 Inês de Castro is murdered.

1373 First Anglo-Portuguese Alliance is signed with John of Gaunt who had married a Spanish princess.

1385 Defeat of the Castilians at the Battle of Ajubarrota. João I becomes king and founder of the second dynasty, the House of Avis.

1386 Treaty of Windsor is signed (and remains unbroken to this day).

1387 João I is married to Philippa of Lancaster, daughter of John of Gaunt.

THE AGE OF DISCOVERIES

1415 Ceuta, on the North African coast, is taken by a Portuguese force including Henry the Navigator. Madeira discovered.

1427 The Azores discovered.

1434 Gil Eanes discovers West African lands beyond Cape Bojador.

1460 Death of Henry the Navigator.

1481 João II comes to the throne.

1487 Bartolomeu Dias rounds the Cape of Good Hope, establishing a sea route to the East.

1492 Around 60,000 Jews are expelled from Spain and take refuge in Portugal.

1494 Treaty of Tordesillas: Portugal and Spain divide the world.

1497–98 Explorer Vasco da Gama opens a sea route to India.

1500 Pedro Álvares Cabral discovers Brazil.

1502 Construction of Jerónimos monastery begins.

1510 Conquest of Goa establishes Asian empire.

1514–20 Torre de Belém constructed.

1519–22 Ferdinand Magellan circumnavigates the globe but dies before his mission is completed.

1536 Holy Inquisition is introduced.

1557 Trading post is established in Macaú (Macao).

1580 Portugal falls under Spanish rule. The third dynasty, the Habsburgs, commences.

WARS AND REVOLUTIONS

1640 The Spanish are overthrown; the Duke of Bragança becomes João IV, commencing the fourth dynasty, the House of Bragança.

1662 Catherine of Bragança marries England's King Charles II.

1668 Treaty of Lisbon, under which Spain recognises Portugal's independence.

1703 Methuen Treaty signed, giving England dominance in the wine industry.

Early 1700s Gold is discovered in Brazil and boosts the Portuguese economy.

1755 The Great Earthquake devastates Lisbon. Marquês de Pombal, granted emergency powers by the king, sets about rebuilding Lisbon.

1777 Maria I becomes queen; Pombal dismissed.

1807 Portugal invaded by the French; royal family leave for Brazil.

1808 The Peninsular War. Portugal invokes the British Alliance. Sir Arthur Wellesley (later Duke of Wellington) leads British forces.

1820 Liberal revolution.

1822 Liberal constitution lasts only two years, but ends Inquisition. Brazil proclaims independence.

1829–34 Miguelist Wars between factions led by the brothers Miguel and Pedro. The latter wins and becomes Pedro IV in 1834.

1834 Religious orders expelled from Portugal.

1834–1908 Rise of political parties, Septembrists (liberals) and Chartists (conservatives). Power alternates between them through the reigns of successive monarchs.

1901 Elevador da Santa Justa opens.

1908 King Carlos and the Crown Prince are shot dead in Lisbon. Manuel II ascends the throne.

1910 Portugal becomes a republic; Manuel II exiled.

1910–26 A period of political turmoil, military coups and assassination.

SALAZAR AND AFTERWARDS

1926 Military coup overthrows Democratic government and brings General Carmona to power.

1928 Carmona appoints Dr António de Oliveira Salazar finance minister.

1932 Salazar becomes prime minister and rules Portugal as a dictator until 1968.

1936–39 Salazar defies League of Nations and secretly aids Franco in the Spanish Civil War.

PRECEDING PAGES: an ancient map of Lisbon.
LEFT: statue of Dom Pedro II in Cascais.
RIGHT: the Vasco da Gama Centre in the Parque das Nações typifies the forward-looking city.

1939–45 World War II: Portugal remains neutral.

1955 Portugal joins the UN.

1961 Angolan uprising brutally crushed.

1960s Wars in Africa continue; at home, support for them dwindles.

1966 Suspension bridge over the Rio Tejo opens; originally called Ponte Salazar, now 25 de Abril.

1968 Salazar suffers a stroke.

1970 Death of Salazar. Marcelo Caetano becomes prime minister.

1974 "Carnation Revolution" restores democracy. Armed Forces Movement governs until 1976.

1976 Socialist leader Mario Soares becomes prime minister. Minimum salary instituted; new

constitution upholds socialism and democracy.

1979 Coalition of the right takes power.

1986 Portugal, together with Spain, becomes a member of the European Community (EC).

1987 Aníbal Cavaco Silva wins election.

1988 Fire destroys the Chiado district.

1992 Lisbon wins presidency of the EC. The Centro Cultural de Belém is built to house the presidency and thereafter used for cultural events.

1995 Socialist António Guterres becomes prime minister.

1998 Lisbon hosts Expo '98. The Expo site becomes the new Parque das Nações.

1999 Portugal joins the European Monetary Union.

2001 The Euro becomes the official currency. ❏

LEGENDS AND FACTS

The role of Ulysses in Lisbon's history is probably mythical, but the Romans and the Moors had a very real influence, the latter holding sway for 500 years

There is a legend that would have us believe that Ulysses, hero of Homer's *Odyssey*, founded the city of Lisbon at some point along his illustrious route. If he did, it was a job well done, for the city close to the sea on the River Tejo (Tagus) has been a centre of power for a series of invaders and settlers combined with safe anchorage and local metal deposits, afforded benefits for more advanced, trading cultures.

The earliest visitors to arrive at Lisbon via the sea were the Phoenicians, who founded a port there circa 1200 BC, calling it Alis Ubbo (Serene Harbour). They settled on the hill

throughout the centuries. The nation of Portugal grew steadily around the gracious natural harbour. It has been said that all roads lead to Rome; in Portugal all roads lead to Lisbon.

Another ancient chronicle sets the founding date of Lisbon as 3259 BC, claiming that the founder was Elishah, a grandson of Abraham. The area was, of course, inhabited long before this biblical founding father could have arrived.

Members of prehistoric *castro* cultures set up impermanent camps in the area and the natural geographic conditions – the hills providing defence, the seas plentiful fish, the river fresh water – made it relatively populous during the Neolithic ages. Later, these same blessings,

where the Castelo São Jorge now stands and the first true village was established on the site. The name Alis Ubbo apparently went through many derivations and has survived as modern Portugal's Lisboa.

Olisipo

By the time the Romans arrived, the settlement had become Olisipo. Their name for it, *Felicitas Iulia*, after Julius Caesar, didn't stick. In Visigothic times, it was Olissibona; in Moorish, Ulixbona or Al-Usbuna. With the Christian reconquest, more or less, came the modern spelling. The English name, as late as the 19th century, was Lisbona.

Under the Phoenicians, the Greeks and the Carthaginians, Lisbon served as a major port of call for ships travelling between northern Europe and the Mediterranean. However, little evidence of these early visitors remains, mostly because of continual rebuilding work by the civilisations that followed.

In 205 BC, as part of the Second Punic War, Rome absorbed Lisbon into the province called Lusitania, which roughly corresponds to southern Portugal. Northern Portugal (and northwest Spain) were then part of Galicia. By the time the war ended, four years later, Rome dominated the whole of the western Mediterranean.

Julius Caesar took over the governorship from 61 to 45 BC, exercising firm control and further raising the city's stature within the empire. Roman Lisbon was one of three major centres in the western part of the peninsula along with Emerita (modern Badajoz, in Spain) and Braccara (Braga, in northern Portugal). It was categorised as a *municipium*, the largest administrative division, and became a hub in the region's network of Roman roads. These important constructions led north, south and east to all the other major population centres. The lines they defined, and indeed some of the roads themselves, still exist.

Anti-Roman rebel

In the 2nd century BC, the Roman consul Decimus Junius Brutus administered the government of Lusitania from Lisbon and strengthened the Roman hold over Galicia. From 147 to 139 BC the Lusitanians rebelled, led by Viriathus, who would later be revered in history and literature as a national hero. His murder in 139 BC effectively quelled the revolt, though it was Pompey who finally put the Lusitanian uprisings to rest in 72 BC.

LEFT: the Temple of Diana in Évora.
ABOVE: a reclining sculpture from the Roman theatre.

But the Roman administration made little use of Lisbon's position as a maritime centre. Fish and salt were harvested from the sea and fruit from the surrounding countryside, but the harbour city's potential was never exploited.

Loss of power

The end of the *pax romana* and invasion of the barbarian hordes meant atrophy for Lisbon. Deprived of its administrative importance, the city once again became a mere fortification. It would remain so until resuscitated by the Moorish conquest. In AD 407, the Alani conquered the city. In 585, the Visigoths swept south and added it to their extensive territories, while the

Alani retreated from the peninsula altogether, crossing to North Africa. Little remains of either culture.

The arrival of the Moors

In 711, the Moors arrived in Spain and began a rapid conquest. The Visigoths were defeated at the Battle of Jerez, and Lisbon soon fell into the hands of Muslim Spain. While battles between Christians and Muslims continued to rage in the north for centuries, Moorish domination resuscitated the capital in the south. There were occasional raids on the city, notably by Alfonso II of León in 798, Ordoño III of

León in 955, and Alfonso VI of León and Castile in 1093, but it lay deep in Moorish territory, and on each occasion the Christian armies were forced to retreat behind established lines. The "Moorish" walls that can still be seen in parts of Lisbon were actually built earlier, most likely during the period of barbarian control, but they were probably expanded under the Muslims to fortify the city.

Muslim innovation

With relative peace came cultural and commercial advancement, as the new government took advantage of Lisbon's position for both

ROMAN REMAINS

A number of Roman remains have been uncovered in Lisbon, some during the expansion of the Metro system. Most of them can be visited only by special arrangement. Archaeologists believe that four inscribed stones located inside a building on the corner of Travessa do Almada near the cathedral were part of a temple devoted to Cybele, an ancient goddess of nature.

The most extraordinary find, the Teatro Romano near Rua de São Mamede, was discovered accidentally in 1798, but has only recently been properly catalogued. The orchestra and proscenium, dated 57, are dedicated to the Emperor Nero. The theatre's other remains include two re-

clining figures, columns and well-preserved inscriptions. Many of the relics are displayed in the City Museum.

There is also a grand spa, near the corner of Ruo da Prata and Rua da Conceição, that dates from Emperor Tiberius's rule in the 1st century. Still sturdy if a bit stuffy and wet, the spa is composed of arched vaults over a series of galleries and baths. The walls are lined with white stone. The spa was dedicated to Aesculapius, the Roman god of medicine and healing, and legend holds that its remarkably clear waters have wide-ranging curative powers. Local tradition also says there is a hidden treasure somewhere in the galleries.

trade and agriculture. The Muslims introduced many innovations, like a bucket wheel for drawing water from deep wells and a waterwheel for milling grain.

New species and crops were also incorporated into the economy: wheat, rice, oranges and saffron among them. Lisbon continued to be a producer of salt and fish. In addition, copper and silver mines in the surrounding countryside were now exploited, and there is evidence of a growing shipbuilding industry.

The Roman roads were maintained and expanded, while various crafts – pottery, masonry and tailoring – saw their beginnings. The housing. Some Moorish elements of decorative architecture were revived by later inhabitants, among them tiles *(azulejos)* and stucco.

The government was under the *valis*, whose authority stemmed from the Emir of Córdoba. However, this central power was often challenged. In fact, internal dissent would eventually contribute a great deal to territorial losses. Powerful landholders in the complex and shaky administration pressed their own interests forward, challenging the hierarchy. The rise of the *sufi*, a popular Muslim sect that revolted against the intellectualism and formality of the orthodoxy, added to the general unrest.

Muslims also imported paper and minted coins, both new to the area. Schools and the arts flourished. Religious tolerance was generally the rule, with Jews and Christians allowed to practise their own faiths openly – albeit in segregated ghettos – within the Muslim state.

Urban planning

Perhaps most important of all, Moorish rule brought urban planning to Lisbon, providing well-defined areas for markets, crafts and

LEFT: Moorish influence is apparent in a lot of Lisbon's architecture.
ABOVE: a portrayal of the Siege of Lisbon, 1147.

Christian weakness

The Christian forces raised for the *Reconquista*, the reconquest, also had their weaknesses. One of the reasons for Alfonso VI's failure to hold Lisbon in 1093 was simply that the soldiers looked on the attack as merely a raid and were more anxious to return to their farms for the harvest than to fight. Furthermore, a new group, the fanatical Al Moravid, had begun revitalising Muslim resistance.

Among Alfonso's successes was the liberation of the northern territory of Portucale, where he appointed Henry of Burgundy as governor in the county town of Coimbra. When Henry died his son, Afonso Henriques, declared independence for Portucale with himself as king, the first in the Burgundian line.

Crusade against Lisbon

In 1147 King Afonso Henriques persuaded some Crusaders passing through to help him conquer Lisbon in return for a share in the booty. Afonso had argued that fighting infidels in Portugal was morally equivalent to fighting them in the distant Holy Land. After the Pope had been won over to this idea, granting indulgences to martyrs of these battles, the "Western Crusade" began in earnest. Lisbon was already a port of call on the route from northern Europe

to Jerusalem, so it was often possible to convince these soldiers to stay and lend a hand before moving eastwards. They would join local military-religious organisations like the Knights Templar and the Hospitallers.

The Crusaders had sailed from Dartmouth, 164 ships full of French, Flemish, Germans and English. Some stayed in Portugal after the battle, including Gilbert of Hastings, who became Archbishop of Lisbon. This marked the beginning of a history of interchange and cooperation between England and Portugal.

The great hero of the battle that won Lisbon for good on 25 October 1147 was Martim Moniz. It is said that at the cost of his life he

kept one of the city gates open, allowing Afonso and the rest of the troops to enter. The scene is often depicted in Portuguese art, and there is a square in Lisbon named after the stalwart soldier.

At this time the capital of Portugal was Guimarães, the birthplace of Afonso. Lisbon, which had suffered with the decline of Muslim power, began to prosper again, though it was uncomfortably close to the military frontier. During this period Afonso I granted charters to many of the smaller surrounding towns: Cascais (1154), Almada (1179) and others. The capital was moved to the south, from Guimarães to Coimbra.

It was also around this time, according to tradition, that the body of St Vincent arrived in Lisbon. Legend says that the reliquary came to shore in an unmanned boat, accompanied only by two ravens. St Vincent became the patron saint of the city, and the small boat with a raven sitting on either end became its symbol, later appearing on the city's coat-of-arms. It can be seen today on top of the lamp posts along the Avenida da Liberdade.

Capital status

Lisbon was now beginning to prosper from international commerce. The growing importance of Italy and the Netherlands in world trade was a particular boon to the city, as it lay halfway between the two.

In 1255, with much more of the south secured under Portuguese rule, and Lisbon safe from Moorish raids, Afonso III moved the capital of the newly consolidated kingdom from Coimbra to Lisbon. Over the next half-century, kings Sancho II and Afonso III continued to expand their nation southwards and eastwards, taking Faro and the great fortress at Silves.

Recolonisation by the Christian Portuguese took time in the war-ravaged south, but slowly and surely went ahead. Under King Dinis (1279–1325) the nation's final boundaries were established. Neighbouring Spain was to coexist with the Muslims for almost two centuries more, while Lisbon had embarked on its long and continuing career as capital of one of Europe's oldest countries. ❑

LEFT: city charter granted by Afonso II in 1217.
RIGHT: King Dinis, depicted here in a 17th-century screen, established the nation's boundaries.

CRUSADE FOR A KINGDOM

After the Moors were driven out of Lisbon, there was an ongoing struggle to keep the city, and the country, free of Castilian control

When the Crusaders chased the Moors out of Lisbon in 1147, they found much to praise and admire in the city that was left behind. One contemporary chronicler described the *aere salubris* (healthy air) and noted that the architecture was *artissime conglobata* (most skilfully conglomerated). It was true that the sea breezes and sunshine of Lisbon made it far less polluted – and therefore more likely to be free of pestilence – than many medieval towns its size. Over the first century of Portuguese rule, as the Burgundian kings attempted to meld north and south into a coherent, defensible nation, Lisbon expanded dramatically, and for many reasons besides the quality of its air.

Geography, obviously, was the most important factor in Lisbon's growth, not only because of the welcoming anchorage, nearby mines and surrounding fertile farmland, but because the city lay between the country's two traditional territories. Throughout the history of Portugal, north and south, with their distinctly different geographical features, religious characters, traditions and economies, would continue to clash or to pull away from each another, and Lisbon would remain at the centre of it all.

With the Moors barely exiled (in 1179, in fact, an Arab fleet under the command of Camine I attacked Lisbon from the harbour), the control of the country was still very much in question. Afonso Henriques and his successors needed to be vigilant, and there could be no better watchtower than Lisbon.

Expansion and prosperity

By 1255, when Lisbon was made the capital of Portugal, it had long been the centre of the country's economic, social, cultural and political life. Though various members of royalty preferred to live elsewhere – Setúbal and Sintra,

for example – they could not stray far from Lisbon's political cross-currents. By 1400, it had four times more inhabitants and buildings than any other city.

Afonso III (1245–79) was much enamoured with his capital city and devoted a great deal of his royal resources to both acquiring and

D. AFFONSO III

improving it. While he attempted to better general living conditions, he also bought all the property he could, greatly increasing the monarch's share that had been established at the time of the city's conquest. However, his entrepreneurial efforts – which would be continued by King Dinis, Afonso III's son and successor – upset many of the townspeople of Lisbon, who complained of what they saw as his greed and abuses of authority.

Nonetheless, the royal house acquired a large part of the city and managed it to great advantage. Dinis, in particular, ruled over an era of expansion and prosperity. His agricultural reforms and bold suppression of the politically

---

LEFT: the 13th-century cross of Sancho I.
RIGHT: a tile panel depicting Afonso III, the king who completed the *Reconquista*.

dangerous Knights Templar further pacified and stabilised Portugal. The military-religious organisation of the Templars was converted into the Order of Christ. As such it remained powerful and wealthy, but under the king's authority rather than the Pope's.

Many of Portugal's great castles – 50 fortresses, it is said – were constructed during Dinis's reign, and the city of Lisbon benefited from his administrative wisdom. The inhabitants gradually overcame their resentment of royal acquisitions as they came to appreciate the protection that brought Lisbon both prestige and prosperity.

Outside interests

At the beginning of the 13th century, the commercial expansion of Europe gave the first indications of Lisbon's destiny – as the capital of an empire. Improvements in navigation had made shipping a lot safer. Even as Afonso III was conquering the last Moorish strongholds in the Algarve, European ships were making use of Lisbon's port.

Beginning around 1270, Italian merchants from Genoa settled in Lisbon. The city had become a regular stop along the shipping route to England and Flanders, and now these foreign businessmen established themselves as a controlling force.

They dominated Mediterranean exchanges, and even homed in on northern markets. It was an unfortunate precursor to Portugal's future, in which foreign interests would skim the profits from its empire. The skill and capital resources of the Genoese forced local merchants and government to set aside patriotism in exchange for a slice of the pie. To some degree these interlopers usurped the money-lending and political influence of Lisbon's Jewish community. More positively, they modernised the Portuguese fleet with innovations that set the country on its way to the Age of Discoveries *(see page 33)*.

Seat of parliament

Lisbon was also the centre for the *cortes*, the parliamentary group of representatives to the king. The first *cortes* had convened in 1211 (in Coimbra), and had consisted primarily of representatives of the church and nobility.

In 1261, the *cortes* obtained a promise from Afonso III that they would be consulted whenever new taxes were to be levied. Later, the representatives would include wealthy merchants and townsmen, a development that was forced upon the monarchy because of the frequent need to increase taxation.

Still later, the monarchy came to depend upon the support of the *cortes* in its disputes with the Church. During the reign of Fernando I (1367–83), the growing power of the nobles and the bourgeoisie would finally break out into social upheaval among the lower classes (although most labourers were completely unrepresented in this power play).

The great ships that now plied the international waterways brought wealth, culture and a cosmopolitan spirit to Lisbon. The city walls were expanded, increasing the enclosed area to five times its previous size, and rudimentary street lights were introduced.

The great plague

Unfortunately, these ships also brought a disastrous import: the plague. Although it is not certain where in Portugal the infamous Black Death began, it probably originated in Lisbon. The first major bout came in 1348. Initially, the population seemed to recover quickly, but new waves of the disease became a regular occurrence throughout the next 100 years. Whole generations were weakened and the population stagnated as the plague struck again and again between 1356 and 1458. Only the continual migration of rural workers into the city kept the population from declining further.

The urban decrepitude of the period was ushered in by the Black Death. Initially the city had beckoned workers with plentiful jobs, the excitement of the urban world, even the rare chance for social advancement into merchant classes. The ensuing countrywide economic depression led more and more migrants to the

LANGUAGE DIFFERENCES

In the 14th century the Portuguese and Castilian languages, previously fairly similar, diverged significantly, leading to the two quite distinct languages that exist today.

because there were many people in Portugal who strongly supported the idea of the further unification of the Iberian peninsula. This caused civil strife that kept Portugal in a state of political imbalance for many years. It was only the reign of Dom Dinis that brought relative stability to the land.

Under Pedro I (1357–67) turmoil stirred again and the conflict with Castile began to heat up. To many, unification seemed inevitable; the only question was, who would be the ruling monarch. When Fernando I took over

city, searching for those now-tattered promises. Crowding into whatever niches they could find, they created a typically restless urban proletariat.

Attempts at unification

In 1230, León and Castile, two great provinces of what eventually became a united Spain, had merged into a unified and powerful Castile. This was a problem for the Portuguese kings, partly because they owed ties of vassalage to the Castilian monarch, and more importantly

LEFT: Nuno Álvares Pereira, João I's young general, brandishes his sword.
ABOVE: the city's coat of arms, 1360.

the Portuguese throne in 1367, he set out to unify Portugal and Castile under his rule. However, there was a growing sense of national unity in Portugal, and no desire to become a part of Castile. Fernando's wars, three in all, were both unpopular and unsuccessful. France, on Castile's side, and England, on the side of Portugal, entered the fray during the first of the wars, making the peninsula another theatre of the Hundred Years' War.

During the second war (1373) Fernando signed an Anglo-Portuguese alliance with John of Gaunt, who had married a Spanish princess. In the same year, Enrique II of Castile sacked Lisbon, burning and pillaging the city to force

Fernando's army to surrender. After many changes of allegiance – made more complex by the Great Schism in 1378, which gave Catholic rulers a choice of popes – Fernando had to give up his grand scheme, and turn to matters at home.

In 1372 riots had broken out over his unpopular marriage to Leonor Teles. She was a Spanish princess, and therefore represented a Castilian union. When Fernando died in 1383, riots ensued once more, this time because Leonor was to rule as regent, with the help of her lover, the Galician count João Fernández Andeiro. When Leonor's only daughter married Juan I of Castile, the long-feared union was brought nearer to fruition.

Leonor, the Queen-Mother, had the support of the nobility and the clergy in her plans, but the middle class opposed her. Her lover, Andeiro, was assassinated by João, an illegitimate son of Pedro I and the Master of the Order of Avis. There was rioting in the streets, and the Bishop of Lisbon was murdered. Civil war ensued, with João riding the wave of nationalist feeling to victory over Leonor.

At the battle of Aljubarrota in 1385, João, aided by the great general Nuno Álvares Pereira and a troop of English archers, won a decisive

BRAIN DRAIN

The university, founded in Lisbon in 1290, was a benchmark of Portuguese culture, and tended to parallel the prevailing economic situation. Wealthy students preferred to go abroad, and generations of Portugal's leading theologians, doctors and lawyers all received their training in foreign universities. Afonso IV and Fernando I had both tried to resuscitate the fading institution, instigating various academic reforms. Under a variety of pretexts they transferred the university from Lisbon to Coimbra in 1308, back to Lisbon in 1338, to Coimbra again in 1354, then in 1377 back to Lisbon, where it would remain until 1537.

victory, despite being heavily outnumbered. He became João I, founder of the House of Avis, and signed the Treaty of Windsor, a mutual pledge of friendship with England, which was most recently invoked in World War II.

The rise of the House of Avis

The fall of the House of Burgundy and the ascendancy of the House of Avis meant little real change for the common people who had supported João's cause. Regular political representation was established for the mercantile class, but the real power was retained by the landed aristocracy. Rebellions continued, notably from 1438 to 41 and in 1449.

Some of these revolts were occasioned by grain shortages. These crises had multiplied as aftershocks of the outbreaks of plague, when harvests had declined as a result of the depleted rural population. Farmers found they could earn easier money devoting their efforts to export crops like wine and olive oil; vineyards demand less manpower than grain fields, and wine was already an important part of the Portuguese economy.

In Lisbon, in spite of the efforts of central government to regulate trade and to restrict the movement of farm labourers, urban demand continued to outpace the supply.

Economic muscle

If there was a single root to the general economic crisis of the 15th century, in Portugal as throughout Europe, it was the plague's effect on labour. Workers were suddenly a scarce commodity, and this gave peasants greater freedom and power. The government tried to constrain the new freedom, but without success. The law of 1375 bound workers to their traditional professions, kept wages low (and kept rural and urban rates equal) and penalised the idle, but it did little to slow the trend toward mobility. Within a century, the greater part of the labour force was free from vassalage.

During this period of economic distress, the Church increased its landholdings and its general influence. The plague had engendered apocalyptic thinking. Many landholders, certain that the Final Judgment was just around the corner, left their worldly goods to the various religious orders, hoping to buy a fragment of salvation. This only aggravated the agricultural crisis, because the Church, which did not discourage the practice, was not equipped to put the land to the most effective use.

LEFT: the 14th-century tomb of Lopo Fernandes Pacheco in the Cathedral.
ABOVE: Afonso de Albuquerque, by an unknown artist.

Even though serfdom was never reinstated, fluctuations in the economic situation meant that the improved strength of the workers' bargaining power would not be permanent. When the economy improved, the labourers would once again become expendable, and would have to accept lower rates if they wanted to continue working. Economic power would revert to the landholders.

And the upturn was not so far away. It could be seen glowing out beyond the cliffs of Sagres that had once been thought "the end of the earth". Portugal was only decades from discovering the rest of the world and, for a time at least, owning much of its riches. ❑

OCCEAN VN·MARE

THE AGE OF DISCOVERIES

*This important phase brought Lisbon to prominence as the wealthy
capital of an empire that covered huge areas of the globe*

The Portuguese Discoveries and the launching of the maritime trade empire brought Lisbon from the edge of the known world into the very centre of the newly expanded sphere. Suddenly, the city was a place to be reckoned with, and before long it became a true world capital, acquiring an empire that included Brazil, a country that covered nearly half of South America, and colonies around Africa, India, Indonesia and China.

The reign of Afonso V (1433–81) saw the first successful Portuguese efforts to create economic and political peace at home through overseas expansion. Afonso himself was not a great leader. He was a chivalrous romantic in an era when politics were growing increasingly complicated and ignoble. Fortunately, two of his most trusted advisors were his uncles Henriques (Henry the Navigator) and Pedro, the Duke of Bragança. Each helped make this age of exploration possible: Henriques used his resources as the Master of Avis to found a school of navigation at Sagres *(see page 42)*; the Duke of Bragança inspired the nobility to invest in these enterprises.

Ideal vessels

Preliminary to any exploration, of course, the sciences of navigation had to be discovered and mastered, and this is where Henry's school took a leading role. Lisbon's shipbuilding industry had quickly adopted the techniques of the Muslims and then of the Italians, refining their central-ruddered ships to develop the characteristically Portuguese wide-hulled *caravela*, an ideal cargo ship for crossing oceans. Lisbon became an international exchange centre not only for goods, but for geographical, navigational and technological information.

The overseas expansion began without systematic planning. The idea of empire grew slowly, being grasped most firmly, in fact, when

LEFT: a map by Sebastião Lopes, *circa* 1655.
RIGHT: Francisco d'Almeida was the first Portuguese viceroy to India.

it was already beginning to fade away. What little policy Portugal had was a strange mix of crusading ideals, romantic curiosity and the all-important profit motive. Charting the world was always a secondary matter. It was less important than fighting the infidels and less important, oddly enough, than the search for the strange mythical king-priest known as Prester John, who was supposed to have been the leader of a vast Christian empire in the heart of Africa, an earthly paradise peopled by mysterious characters. This legend was a powerful impetus.

Elusive gold

Gold, of course, was always a goal, but it seemed to slip away from Lisbon as easily as it arrived, even later on, when the Brazilian mines seemed inexhaustible. Gold did, however, buy prestige for the nation. One of the lasting accomplishments of Afonso's reign was the minting of the first *cruzado*, the renowned gold coin that became a symbol of Portuguese wealth. Meanwhile, more stable trade was found in African grain, sugar, dyes and slaves, and later in the spices and rare woods of India and the Orient.

An age of heroes

The great Age of Discoveries was tailor-made for heroes, as fearless mariners sailed off into the mysterious realms of sea monsters and cannibals. As well as Henry the Navigator, "the Father of the Discoveries", there were Gil Eanes, Pedro Cabral, Vasco da Gama and Ferdinand Magellan.

Pope settled the fierce competition between Spain and Portugal with the Treaty of Tordesillas, which divided the world between them at a line of demarcation 595 km (370 miles) west of the Azores. This put the then unknown Brazil (Pedro Álvares Cabral discovered it six years later) within Portugal's sphere. There are those who say that the discovery had already been made and Portugal was simply keeping it under wraps – and who could blame them?

In 1497, Vasco da Gama set sail from Lisbon and returned two years later having discovered the sea route to India, and lost many of his crew in the process. New voyages along this

Once Portugal's ships began to press back the known world, the new boundaries fell quickly. The litany of the discoveries is familiar, yet still impressive. Madeira and the Azores had both been claimed by 1427 *(see page 43)*. Then Gil Eanes, perhaps the first indisputable hero of the age, went beyond the promontory of Cape Bojador in Africa, finding not the edge of the world, as was widely believed, but more coastline and safe waters. Eanes led later voyages down the coast in search of the Rio do Ouro, the River of Gold.

By 1482, Portuguese ships had explored the mouth of the Congo. In 1487, Bartolomeu Dias rounded the Cape of Good Hope. In 1494, the

route were immediately planned, setting Portugal at odds with Muslim and Venetian spice traders who did not welcome the competition.

In 1519 Ferdinand Magellan, a Portuguese in the service of Spain, led the first voyage to circumnavigate the globe, although he died before his mission was completed.

Tipping the balance

The discoveries tipped the balance of trade away from the Mediterranean, away from Venice and Genoa and towards Lisbon. The city grew in bounds. The lower town was packed with merchants trading gold, silver, ivory, silk, spices and everything else under the sun.

The expeditions opened the seaways, but not without the occasional skirmish. Although the Portuguese initially had no intentions of political conquest, but were simply striving to establish and maintain a monopoly of the high seas, they were constantly at war in the Indies, mostly with the Arabs who were protecting their own trade interests, and later with Western European usurpers. The leader of these naval campaigns was Governor-General Afonso de Albuquerque, a brilliant strategist who made Goa

THE GROWTH OF GOA

Goa grew at an extraordinary rate. By 1540, 30 years after conquest, it was the seat of a bishopric and there were 100,000 households of European descent.

Fickle fortune

Overseas trade enlivened the economy and made Lisbon rich, although somehow it failed to enrich the rest of the country. Because of this core flaw in the economy, individuals eventually found it difficult to hold or build their fortunes, even in the capital. What happened is a matter of speculation, but certain contributing factors are clear.

The burgeoning Portuguese empire demanded little from its diminutive fatherland at first: a little manpower, some financial back-

his centre of operations and established ports and fortresses in key locations such as Hormuz in the Gulf, Sri Lanka and Macao in China. The policy in the Indies was colonisation rather than sheer exploitation. In contrast, the African, Brazilian and island territories were treated as simple trade stations until centuries later, when the idea of permanent colonies began to seem like a boon to the eternally anaemic home economy.

LEFT: a portrait in the Museu da Marinha shows the discoverers presenting their charts.
ABOVE: the cloister of the Mosteiro dos Jerónimos was financed by the wealth of the New World.

ing and political support. As in the other small trading empires of Italy and the Netherlands, organisation and central authority were more significant than mere size. Only later, when Portugal was forced to go to war to control the world shipping lines it had founded, did its small home population begin to tell.

Another explanation for Portugal's failure to grow naturally after its booming start as a world power was the crucial lack of a middle class – its beginnings having been quashed by royal and noble dominance of commerce – that might have provided qualified and educated planners, leaders and administrators. Others speculate that it was widespread corruption or foreign control of profits that prevented Portugal from laying a solid economic foundation.

Manuel I

This is not to say that Portugal did not enjoy its prosperity. For just under a century it flourished in an age ushered in by the diplomatic and forward-looking administration of Manuel I (1495–1521). Over this period the estates of the noble families – usurped by João I – were largely restored, although the nobility's political power was kept in restraint. Judicial and tax reforms brought regularity and authority to government at both national and local levels.

The increasing complexity of managing the nation's affairs was matched by much-needed increases in government bureaucracy. The postal system was instituted and public services such as hospitals were centralised.

Manuel's enlightened despotism also fostered contacts with the proponents of Renaissance humanism then spreading throughout Europe. In 1487, even before he came to the throne, a printing press had been established in Lisbon. Portugal entered the 16th century with a rush of new cultural currents, and more than ever, Lisbon eclipsed all other Portuguese cities as the focal community.

THE GROWTH OF LISBON

The city of Lisbon was the prime beneficiary of the country's new wealth and of Manuel's organisation. In 1492 the Hospital de Todos os Santos (All Saints' Hospital) was opened, and in 1498 the Confraria da Misericórdia was created in Lisbon Cathedral, later becoming the Misericórdia da Lisboa. The town spilled over beyond its walls, and great squares were built to accommodate the population, its numbers swelled by immigrants both from inland and from all over Europe, making Lisbon a continental melting pot. The new buildings were embellished in the Manueline style – with nautical images and exuberant decoration everywhere (see page 105).

Education

Under Manuel's rule, young men were encouraged to study abroad, at universities in France and Spain. New colleges and educational reforms within Portugal were a fundamental element of 16th-century progress, but these advances were not crisis-free. The University of Lisbon had become a source of cultural and political power that the crown found threatening. It was difficult to impinge upon the University's traditional autonomy, but Manuel, as part of his process of centralisation, tried to force change through economic and legal pressure, without success. His son, João III, continued these efforts and finally more or less quashed the

University in 1537, shifting it to Coimbra, and vitiating it in the process. Later in the 16th century this conflict culminated in João giving control of education to the Jesuits. It was a victory for the monarchy, but a great loss for Lisbon. The city would not have a university again until 1911.

Literary zenith

The century nonetheless inspired a broad-ranging intellectual vigour, a worthy parallel to the voyages of discovery. And like the voyages, it all began in Lisbon. Some of the works that were produced were directly attributable to the

to great acclaim in the city. Luís de Camões, by contrast *(see page 41)*, was little known at the time, but is today considered Portugal's greatest writer. *Os Lusíadas*, his masterpiece, is an epic poem that follows Vasco da Gama on his voyage to India.

Soon, however, a new turn in Portuguese culture would cast a pall over learning and creativity. The Inquisition was established in Portugal in 1536. Intended to be a tool of the monarchy, it quickly took on an authority all of its own. Portugal turned away from the humanist influences of Europe and toward Catholic fanaticism. The bureaucracy of the Inquisition

expeditions. Travel books, both scientific and cultural, were a rich vein of literature. Tomé Pires described his journeys to the East in his *Suma Oriental*. Perhaps the most renowned travel chronicler was Fernão Mendes Pinto, whose *Peregrinação (Pilgrimage)* told of his voyages to the Orient in a lively, popular style.

Out of the troubadour tradition, by way of Italian verse, came Gil Vicente, founder of the Portuguese theatre, who wrote scores of satirical and comic one-act plays that were staged

LEFT: the Torre de Belém stands guard over the Tejo.
ABOVE: under the 16th-century Inquisition, public confessions were followed by executions.

expanded quickly, its main target being the converted Jews known as New Christians.

The Inquisition takes hold

There had been earlier rumblings of resentment against the Jews and New Christians. In 1506, full-scale riots had broken out in Lisbon and 100 Jews were murdered by a mob. At that time the municipal council was run by the labour guilds, through a central committee called the House of 24. They were initially held responsible by Manuel I, but apparently the riots had been started by two Dominican monks, zealots who had run through the streets inciting the crowds. The Jews were persecuted as much for their role as middle-class merchants as for religious reasons. Manuel, like other kings, protected them primarily because their education and capital made them valuable citizens. The monks were put to death for their role in the rioting. From ancient times, Lisbon had been a city where tolerance was both a necessity and a blessing. This intolerant turn of events was something new.

The power of the Inquisition expanded throughout the 16th century. The Inquisitor-General carried the right of excommunication

> ### PUBLIC EXECUTIONS
>
> The Lisbon *autos-da-fé* – public torture and executions – were held in the central square known as the Rossio, a grisly thought as you walk through this busy place today.

Sebastian's shortcomings

The economic and political crumbling that led to Spanish domination was complex, but the final straw is easy to understand. It was King Sebastião's disastrous attack on Alcácer-Quibir in 1578.

When Sebastião came to the throne in 1568, the flaws of the maritime empire were already beginning to show. Looming above all the small signs of decrepitude was the 1560 bankruptcy of the Casa da India, the national trade corporation. Sebastião became

and took direct orders only from the Pope. Using the public and spectacular *autos-da-fé*, the Inquisition soon assumed power far beyond its legal authority. The first *auto-da-fé*, literally "act of the faith", in Lisbon was held in 1540. These "acts" were public confessions, accompanied by torture and followed by execution, generally by burning the victim at the stake.

The Inquisition's influence, with its rigid orthodoxy, vengeful judiciary and general religious fervour, was not only barbaric, but stultifying to both culture and commerce. After 1580, when Spain and Portugal were unified under Spanish domination, the Inquisition would virtually govern Portugal.

king at the age of 14, but it was not only his youth that made his rule a disaster. Unintelligent, arrogant and generally unstable, the idealistically chivalric boy took upon himself a crusade against the Moors of North Africa. A lack of funds prevented him from undertaking the task for many years, but in 1578, scraping together every *cruzado* he could, he left Lisbon with 18,000 soldiers and mercenaries.

He was no better a general than an administrator, madly dismissing stratagem and planning as signs of cowardice. Outnumbered and outmanoeuvred at the battle of Alcácer-Quibir, his army was destroyed. Some 8,000 men were killed, among them Sebastião.

Spanish rule

This debilitating and demoralising disaster left Portuguese leadership in chaos and the way clear for Spain to step in. Cardinal Henriques became king, but died in 1580, leaving no direct heir. In 1580, António, the Prior of Cato, entered Lisbon as claimant to the throne. The Duke of Alba, a Spanish general, then arrived and routed António's army at the bridge of Alcântara clearing the way for the rule of Felipe II of Spain.

The new king made Lisbon his residence and was acclaimed King Felipe I of Portugal in 1582. Under Spanish rule, Lisbon became the

Autonomy returns

In 1640, due largely to Spain's wars on other fronts, the Duke of Bragança rode the crest of a successful uprising in Lisbon, reasserting Portugal's autonomy. Bragança became King João IV. For the next 25 years there were sporadic wars between the two countries. Afonso VI, who succeeded João, suffered both physical and mental handicaps, and was eventually usurped by his brother, Pedro II.

In 1654, Britain was the first European country to sign a treaty of friendship with Portugal. While this seemed a good idea at the time, it was to make Portugal economically

point of departure for the Spanish Armada of 1588. The port was closed to British and Dutch traders the following year and throughout the years of Spanish domination, Portugal's overseas empire fell more and more into ruin.

Felipe I allowed Portugal to retain a large measure of autonomy, and his reign was an efficient one, but his successors (Felipe II and III) ruled less wisely, especially during the period (1618–48) when Spain was involved in the Thirty Years' War against France.

LEFT: a portrait of the unstable young Sebastião.
ABOVE: Caterina, sister of Afonso VI, sets off for her wedding to Charles II of England in 1661.

SEBASTIANISMO

The period of Spanish Habsburg rule was made more difficult by the fact that King Sebastião, although dead, refused to lie down. During the 1580s, when national pride was at a low ebb, there arose the phenomenon of "Sebastianismo", a popular messianic belief that the young king would return to lead Portugal again – presumably more ably than before.

Many false Sebastiãos appeared in Lisbon, attempting to rouse the rabble and seize the throne. A few of them found supporters, either true believers or other opportunists, but most simply made up a laughable and motley crew of pretenders.

subservient to Britain for centuries. The alliance was cemented by the marriage of the Portuguese Princess Catherine to Charles II of England. Tangiers and Bombay were part of her dowry. In 1668, under the Treaty of Lisbon, Spain recognised Portuguese independence.

In 1703, Portugal signed the Methuen Treaty with England, which gave the country economic stability but allowed British interests to dominate many of its industries, particularly wine exports and textile imports. Grain shortages throughout this period may have been due to the fact that more investment went into viticulture than into cereal growing.

The indulgences of João V

João V's ascension to the throne in 1706, along with the emergence of Brazil as both a figurative and literal gold mine, ushered in a period of delirious indulgence. The revenue from Brazilian gold – and from its other lucrative products, such as sugar, cotton and tobacco – was not invested in industry, but frittered away.

João, who was nicknamed "The Magnanimous", was a strange mixture of devotion and sensuality, avowing ardent faith in the Catholic Church, but taking the worldly French court of Louis XIV as his ideal. He had a great interest in the arts, and his passion for opera brought many operatic works to Lisbon. In 1720 he established the city's Academy of History. He built splendid palaces, churches and monasteries, yet converted convents around Lisbon into aristocratic brothels.

In fulfilment of a vow, João constructed a massive palace-convent at Mafra, to the northwest of Lisbon. The project, started in 1717, took 18 years to complete and rivals Spain's Escorial in size and splendour *(see page 205)*.

Continuing earlier demographic trends, Lisbon had grown too large to be supported by its country, a head too large for its body. But cloaked as it was in opulence, it was hard to see the problems in the city. And still João continued to build.

The great aqueduct

Although Mafra cost more, the crowning architectural achievement of João V's rule was the Aqueduto das Águas Livres (Aqueduct of Free Waters) which still brings fresh water into Lisbon. Running 19 km (12 miles) from Caneças to the distribution building in Amoreiras, the aqueduct's massive capacity supplied a series of underground branches that fed, among other outlets, the city's fountains.

Construction began in 1729 and ended in 1748, under the direction of architects Manuel da Maia and Custodio Vieira. Its strength and intelligent design – the arches, for example, were at one point spaced unevenly, a violation of aesthetic ideals, to take into account a fault in the earth – enabled it to survive the Great Earthquake of 1755, one of the few structures that did *(see page 45)*.

Almost a century later, in 1844, the promenade over the huge arches in Amoreiras would be closed because of a heinous thief called Diogo Alves, who accosted victims on the walk, robbed them and then threw them off the aqueduct to their deaths.

The aqueduct, completed just two years before the death of João V, stood out as a promise of things to come at a time when the country was still economically unstable and increasingly dependent on the profits pouring in from Brazil and on its trade relations with Britain. A new day was dawning for Lisbon. But it is always darkest just before dawn. ❏

LEFT: the Aqueduto das Águas Livres, an impressive feat of engineering, still carries fresh water into Lisbon.

Luís de Camões

Luís de Camões was an epic poet who dramatically exalted the voyages of exploration and the Portuguese people, the "sons of Lusus". His masterpiece, the 10 cantos of his poem *Os Lusíadas (The Lusiads)*, published in 1572, is the greatest work in Portuguese literature. He is a national symbol of Portugal's grandest era. He was also, in his lifetime (1524–80), a born loser.

From a poor but noble family, he studied the classics at Coimbra and fell in with a fast crowd in Lisbon. Youthful passion led him to an inauspicious love affair. Banished from court, he sailed for Ceuta and, during active service as a soldier, lost an eye. Back in Lisbon in 1549, he was soon in trouble. Imprisoned for nine months after a brawl, he gained his release and a pardon on condition that he sailed to India in the service of João III.

The long voyage was stormy and frightful (his father had died in a shipwreck). Of the fleet that left Lisbon for India, his ship, the *São Bento*, was the only one to survive. The storms, the suffering and the seamanship were experiences he would evoke in his poetry. He endured a hard soldier's life in India, and in 1556 was dispatched to Macao but found it oppressive and returned to Goa. Physically exhausted, yearning to see his poem published, in 1567 he set his hopes on Lisbon.

In 1569, another soldier-writer, royal chronicler Diogo do Couto came upon a penniless Camões in Mozambique and raised the funds to pay his passage home. He arrived, frail and unwell, in 1570. His epic was passed by Inquisition censors despite their concern over verses on fictitious gods. Two years later, hardly noticed, it was published.

King of Portugal now was the wilful young Sebastião, who acknowledged the merit of the poem and awarded Camões a small pension. But in 1578, Sebastião was killed in battle, aged only 24 *(see page 38)*. Camões lay ill in hospital, and Portugal was left without an heir. "And so I shall end my life," he wrote, "and all will see that I loved my country so that not only was I content to die on her soil, but die with her." He died in 1580, the year Spain's Felipe II usurped (as the Portuguese see it) the throne of Portugal. It was Felipe, full of admiration for the epic work, who brought it to public attention and ensured it was not forgotten.

RIGHT: Luís de Camões, the epic poet who exalted the Portuguese voyages of exploration.

Luís de Camões expressed the spirit of the times but he was far from being Portugal's only significant poet or writer. The voyages of discovery brought an outburst of intellectual excitement. Francisco Sá de Miranda (1481–1558) returned from Italy to his birthplace in the north of Portugal and his sonnets flourished. Between 1502 and 1536 Gil Vicente wrote scores of plays – farces, comedies, tragi-comedies – many still performed today.

The navigators and explorers themselves wrote treatises and reflections. One such was *Esmeraldo de Situ Orbis* by sea captain Duarte Pacheco Pereira. The much-travelled João de Barros (1494–1570) wrote a series of *Décadas* for a huge

work, *Ásia*. A Portuguese physician in India, Garcia da Orta, inspired by the plants he found there, wrote an illustrated botanical work, *Colóquios dos Simples e Drogas da India (A Dialogue on Indian Herbs and Drugs)* in 1563. It was promptly pirated and published in several languages.

There were also philosophical works like *Livro das Idades do Mundo (Book of the Ages of the World)* by Renaissance architect and humanist Francisco de Holanda (1517–84). But the colour and detail of the age of discovery appear most vividly in the prose of chroniclers like Gaspar Correa and the thrilling, if not always truthful, merchant-adventurer Fernão Mendes Pinto, author of *Peregrinação (Pilgrimage)*. ❏

HENRY THE NAVIGATOR

Henry may have been something of a 15th-century armchair sailor,
but it was his initiative that fuelled the Age of Discovery

Henrique, known to history as Henry the Navigator, was one of the five legitimate sons of João I, who ruled Portugal from 1385 to 1433. João installed all his sons in powerful positions as leaders of military-religious orders – Henry as head of the wealthy Order of Christ. After the death of Duarte, as eldest

sail into oceans that legend had filled with fearsome monsters. Navigators, familiar with the Pole Star, dead reckoning and the compass, began to establish their position with the quadrant, the astrolabe adapted for sea use, and a simple cross-staff from which they calculated latitude. Celestial tables and the so-called

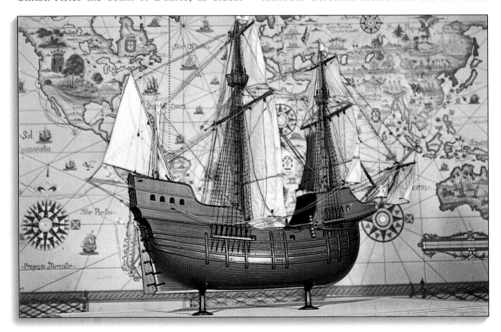

brother, Henrique became the trusted adviser of his young son, who would reign as Afonso V.

School for sailors

Henry has become known as the Father of the Discoveries although, in fact, he seldom sailed anywhere. His great contribution was the foundation of a school of navigation at Sagres (at Cabo de São Vicente in the Algarve). He realised that before any exploration could begin, the technical aspects of navigation had to be mastered and improved. Maps were accurate enough to suggest that there were islands in the unknown Sea of Darkness, and land beyond it, but it needed courage and determination to

portolano charts (basic maps), became ever more detailed. Ships, too, radically changed – neatest of all was the nimble caravel, derived from the heftier cargo-carrying *caravela* of the Rio Douro. Prince Henry, who was born in Porto, would have known it well.

He surrounded himself with highly skilled astronomers and shipbuilders. His financial sponsorship and enthusiasm made him a profound influence, and the research material he assembled was unrivalled at the time (much of it contributed by his brother, Pedro, a true wanderer who sent Henry every relevant map and book he could find). But discovering the world – the Portuguese were the first Europeans to find two-thirds of it – was beyond the scope of any one man, however energetic and farsighted, and there were other, unsung, heroes.

With many hands at the tillers, the enterprise was not always well-coordinated. The main goal of the time was a religious one – to press the Crusade forward and eventually to reconquer Jerusalem – all other ambitions had to play second fiddle to this great drive to get rid of the infidel.

Prince Henry's primary goal was the taming of the North African coast, which meant the banishment of the Moors. He never travelled further than Morocco himself, where he had

Living legend

It is easy to see why history might accord undue credit to someone like Henry. The Age of Discoveries was a time for heroes and adventurers, as well as a period for the rebirth of chivalric ideals. His legend lives on: his cenotaph (along with that of Vasco da Gama) is housed in the National Pantheon in Lisbon's Santa Engrácia church. And his is the figure that stands on the prow of the huge caravel-shaped Monument to the Discoveries on the Belém waterfront, commissioned and built in 1960 by the Salazar regime to mark the 500th anniversary of Henry's death. ❑

taken Ceuta in battle in 1415, and gained his lifelong interest in discovery and conquest.

The chronicles portray Henry devoting most of his time to squeezing profits out of his various tithes, monopolies and privileges. Only later in life, they suggest, with increasing reports of wondrous and far-off places to inspire him, did he give the discoveries his full attention. Yet this may be unfair: he ploughed much of his profits back into the costly enterprises, and died in debt.

LEFT: a model in the Museu da Marinha of the *Santo Gabriel*, one of the ships in Vasco da Gama's fleet.
ABOVE: an *azulejo* pattern of ships on the high seas.

A HAPPY ACCIDENT

It was expeditions initiated by Henry the Navigator that accidentally discovered Madeira and the Azores. In 1415, two ships were blown off course, and landed on the uninhabited island that sailors named Madeira (meaning "wood") because it was thickly forested. The first of the nine Azores (Açores) islands was discovered a dozen years later, the others over a period of 25 years. Henry proved to be an efficient and able coloniser, introducing wheat, vines and sugar cane to Madeira, and organising the settlement of the Azores, which later became recognised ports of call for sailors en route to and from the New World.

THE CITY THE MARQUÊS BUILT

The devastating earthquake of 1755 was regarded by some as divine retribution, but it proved a great opportunity for the Marquês de Pombal

On All Saints' Day, 1 November 1755, a massive earthquake jolted the city of Lisbon. The first thundering convulsions ripped through the earth in the morning, while many of the inhabitants were attending Sunday Mass. The churches' toppling candles started fires throughout the city and the panicked crowds fled toward the River Tejo. But a tidal wave, an after-effect of the seismic tremor, steamrollered the port and lower town with devastating force. As many as 5,000 people were killed in the initial impact and, with the flooding, burning and weeks of famine, untended wounds and epidemics, the total death count may have been 40,000.

Lisbon had known earthquakes before – some historians speculate that the one of 1531 may actually have been more powerful – but none had wrought so much havoc. And because the government took the opportunity to rebuild the city from scratch, no other historical moment made a greater change in the face and character of Lisbon.

Shaken convictions

The earthquake also set off ground swells of fear and pessimism. Was the city being punished by God for some indiscretion? Was there a God who would strike this Catholic country during the festival of All Saints, when the faithful were at High Mass?

Speculation about the disaster circulated throughout Europe, providing fodder for cynics and critics of the rationalist theology that all events are necessary parts of the grand scheme and therefore "good". The French writer Voltaire (1694–1778) composed *Poem upon the Lisbon Disaster* and included an account of the earthquake in *Candide (see page 51).*

The Jesuits, on the other hand, blamed the Marquês de Pombal, who was the power

behind the throne of King José I, the son of João V. They claimed that it was divine retribution for the Marquês's anti-clerical and anti-religious government.

But far from being Pombal's downfall, as his Jesuit enemies hoped, the earthquake sealed his dominance over the age.

The rise of Pombal

The Marquês de Pombal was born Sebastião José de Carvalho e Melo, a member of the minor aristocracy. He had risen through the ranks as a diplomat when José I (1750–77) chose him as prime minister.

José had inherited his father's profligacy and his love of opera, but had no interest in affairs of state or the day-to-day business of ruling a country. Consequently, he allowed Pombal to control the entire government.

Pombal responded to the opportunity eagerly. He became the classic enlightened despot, forcing economic, judicial and philosophical reform upon a sometimes unwilling populace, while at

LEFT: the Marquês de Pombal who masterminded the rebuilding of Lisbon after the earthquake.
RIGHT: the triumphal arch, Praça do Comércio, built on the site of the destroyed royal palace.

the same time pressing his absolutism so far that he paved the way for the liberal revolutions of the early 19th century.

Pombal's city

Pombal was the greatest of the *estrangeirados* (imitators of foreigners), a large group of leaders and intellectuals of the period who were derisively given that label. Educated abroad, they brought Enlightenment ideals to Portugal, where they were not always welcome. Pombal alienated the nobility and the church – the interests of the former were ignored, those of the latter were actively attacked – with his crusade

winding paths and tortuously criss-crossing streets were done away with.

The great architects of the day were set the task of creating a rational, aesthetic plan for the rebuilding. Out of the many drawings submitted, that of Manuel da Maia, one of the principal architects of the magnificent aqueduct, was chosen. Incorporating a few Gothic and Manueline remains, the plan, revolutionary for its time, set out straight, wide avenues with plainly stylised houses. It was rigidly and neatly geometrical, with balance not only in the grid, but in the buildings, towers and monuments. Streets were designed to be functional in merchants'

to modernise. He expanded, systematised and secularised the state's bureaucracy. He reformed policy on international trade and abolished slavery. He rebuilt the decrepit educational system – and instilled the new schools with rationalist philosophy. But his most lasting accomplishment was the reconstruction of Lisbon out of the rubble. While many panicked, Pombal looked to the future. "Bury the dead and feed the living" was his credo.

The earthquake had not destroyed all of central Lisbon, but Pombal, with his idealism backed by authoritarian powers, saw an opportunity to begin at the foundation. The standing buildings were torn down and the haphazardly

districts, and were named after the trades and crafts that would inhabit them. This is the Baixa section of the modern city.

Ruling with a heavy hand

Pombal's mastery of Lisbon's phoenix-like rebirth established his power, but he continued to press his dominance ruthlessly. A purported assassination attempt on the king (some say it was staged by Pombal) gave the government a pretext for destroying its enemies. A speedy trial led to the brutal public execution of half a dozen members of the nobility. Many more were banished, along with the entire Jesuit organisation, one of the first major blows in an attack all over Europe that eventually led to the order's dissolution by the Pope. The Inquisition, long since faded in power, was extinguished during Pombal's reign. The last public *auto-da-fé* in Lisbon took place in 1767.

When José I died in 1777, the Marquês unsuccessfully schemed to stay in power by pressing for Maria to cede her right to the throne to her son José, one of his protégés. Instead, Maria I, as the new queen, tried Pombal for crimes against the state and banished him, though his sentence

DESTABLISING NEWS

The mental and physical health of Maria I was always poor, and news of the French Revolution dealt a blow to her stability from which she never recovered.

Economic failure

However, despite the urban planning that had made Lisbon the very model of an enlightened city, not all was well. Throughout the 18th century, Lisbon's population grew comparatively slowly. At the time of the earthquake there were 150,000 residents. By 1820 there were only 200,000. Compared to the rapid growth shown by other European cities, Lisbon was stagnating.

While other cities expanded with a growing middle-class economy that was enriched by

was stayed because of his old age. Maria brought religion back within the fold of the state, but the rest of Pombal's changes remained in place.

"Mad Maria", always eccentric, more or less lost her mind in 1791. Under the regency of her son, João, progress continued in Lisbon, building on Pombal's foundation. In 1796, João created the National Library and the Royal Academy of Science. He became João VI while in exile, on his mother's death in 1816.

LEFT: an 18th-century engraving of Lisbon's harbour during the great earthquake.
ABOVE: a tile panel depicting the Praça do Comércio.

technological and agricultural advances, Lisbon found itself still yoked to a backward economy which made it entirely dependent upon the whim of international trade.

At the same time – and perhaps this was a form of decentralisation that would be for the long-term good – many smaller towns in Portugal were prospering, growing to compete with Lisbon for inhabitants and trade. Oporto and Viana do Castelo to the north, and Faro in the far south, came to relative prominence during this period. All in all, just as Portugal found itself losing its influential role in world affairs, so Lisbon was slipping to second rank among European cities.

Napoleonic wars

As though to confirm these economic and demographic trends, the events of the early 19th century stripped Lisbon of its title as capital. The Napoleonic wars in Europe eventually reached Portugal in 1807, when Napoleon's diplomats in Lisbon delivered an ultimatum demanding that Portugal declare war on England. The demand was refused and General Junot marched on the city unopposed. The royal family fled to Brazil aboard a British warship *(see panel below)*.

Portugal became a battlefield between British and French forces and in September 1808 the

Peacetime plots

The years of war had taken their toll on Lisbon by the time the English had cleared the way for the Portuguese dynasty to take the throne once again. Looting and vandalism had destroyed museums, monuments, archives and other national treasures. And the British liberators, under Marshal Beresford, were not entirely prepared to leave the country over which they had battled. In 1817 a plot to overthrow Beresford was thwarted, and a dozen ranking members of the Portuguese military – who came to be known as the "Martyrs of Liberty" – were executed at Campo de Santana.

Duke of Wellington (then Sir Arthur Wellesley) led British and Portuguese forces to victories that forced the French to accept a truce and retreat. When the French returned in 1810 under Masséna, they found that Wellington had prepared for them, with the Lines of Torres Vedras protecting Lisbon.

These "lines" were essentially a brilliant series of defensive features – fortifications, trenches, etc. – conceived by Wellington. They stretched from Torres Vedras 19 miles (30 km) north of Lisbon to the Tejo in the east. Masséna tested the system, saw its power and, after a long stand-off, turned north for what would be the final retreat.

FLIGHT TO BRAZIL

When Napoleonic forces threatened Lisbon and the royal family fled to Brazil, Rio de Janeiro became the capital of the Portuguese empire – an unprecedented situation for a colonial city. João VI arrived with an entourage of 15,000 noblemen, thrusting Rio into a world of courtly manners and elegance that hardly fitted its backwoods character. Determined to make the best of the situation, João set about upgrading his new capital. This was advantageous for Rio which, under João and then his son, Pedro, became more Europeanised than any other New World capital, and its trade relations, previously conducted only with Portugal, were opened up.

The repressive measure only served to foment revolutionary action. In 1820, rebellion broke out in Oporto, and then in Lisbon. A junta seized power and before long the *cortes* was summoned. It demanded João VI's return from Brazil. He arrived in July 1821, promising to uphold the pending constitution. Lisbon was again the capital of the empire.

Family feuds

In 1822, however, Brazil declared its independence – a severe blow to the prestige of the *cortes*, which had tried to keep the empire united. Lisbon consequently became the centre

João VI died in 1826, leaving the throne to his oldest son, Pedro. Pedro IV attempted to reunite Portugal and Brazil, but failing to do so, he chose to remain in Rio de Janeiro where he reigned as Pedro I. He abdicated the Portuguese throne in favour of his seven-year-old daughter, Maria, with his brother Miguel serving as regent. His hope was that the two would marry when Maria was of age. But Miguel was not satisfied with this arrangement, and had himself elected king by a newly invoked *cortes* in 1828.

During this period, the essential division was between the constitutionalist liberals and the

of political turmoil, which continued for decades to come. One of the first revolts, however, happened not in the capital but in the small town of Vila Franca de Xira 20 km (12 miles) up the Tejo River.

Counter-revolutionary forces, known as the *Vilafrancada* movement, proclaimed the restoration of the monarchy with Miguel, João VI's younger son, as king. Aboard a British ship, João forced Miguel into submission and returned to Lisbon triumphant in 1823.

counter-revolutionary monarchists. Military uprisings and guerrilla warfare were kindled. British troops returned to be garrisoned in Lisbon, in the hope of containing the violence. Nonetheless, from 1832 to 1834, the Miguelist Wars – also known as the War of the Two Brothers – raged, with the reactionary King Miguel I leading the absolutist forces and receiving a certain amount of popular support.

The death blow to Miguel's hopes came with the return of Pedro and his liberal followers in 1834, aided by British forces. Miguel was forced to capitulate; Pedro took control, briefly, but he died the same year and his 15-year-old daughter was crowned Maria II.

LEFT: Portugal became a battlefield for Napoleon and Sir Arthur Wellesley (later the Duke of Wellington).
ABOVE: Maria I ("Mad Maria"); the scheming Miguel I.

Social revolution

An exhausted nation now had a constitutional monarchy with a liberal government led nominally by a teenaged queen but in fact by her firebrand reforming ministers. Her chief minister, Mouzinho da Silveira, swept away ancient systems of tax and feudal privilege, reorganised courts and laws, separated judicial from administrative duties.

At the same time, his fiercely anti-clerical minister of justice abolished the religious orders and all monasteries and convents were seized. The sale of properties to pay war debts and the social revolution – for such it was – did more

for the already rich than it did for the poor. Yet balances were gradually shifting.

Alternating power

Queen Maria II – Maria da Glória, daughter of the liberal Pedro – had grown up amid storms of constitutional crisis. She reigned from 1834 to 1853, her governments led by old and clever dukes who skilfully juggled surging political ambitions. The conservative Chartists from her father's era were reborn as Regenerators and the so-called Septembrists – liberals, who gained their name after staging a revolt against the government in September 1836 – became the Historicals.

The Chartists took control for a few years, following a coup led by António da Costa Cabral in 1839, but they were swept from power by a popular uprising in 1846.

In 1836 Maria had married Ferdinand of Saxe-Coburg-Gotha, a cultivated man mainly remembered for building the exotic Pena palace in Sintra but who was also responsible for rescuing national treasures from anti-clerical disfavour. Maria, a dutiful wife and mother, gave birth to 11 children and died in childbirth in 1853. She was 34 years old.

The Regenerators

Her oldest son, aged 16, became Pedro V. In a brief reign – he died of typhoid fever in 1861 – a remarkable transformation of Portugal's moribund society was taking place. The Regenerators, led by a determined engineer, António Fontes Pereira de Melo, introduced telegraph lines and constructed a section of railway between Lisbon and Oporto.

From his energetic efforts sprang a new word: *fontismo*. But still many were concerned that Portugal's entry to the industrial age was slow and late – England's railway lines had been laid 31 years earlier. The heavy public debt, a heritage of war, remained a painful burden and poverty was widespread.

For many Portuguese people there was only one solution: emigration. There had always been a flow of emigrants – in the era of exploration, as hopeful adventurers to the colonies, to mine gold. After 1870, the standard problems – lack of work, oppressive landlords, wretched conditions – became worse when phylloxera, a plant disease striking at the roots of vines, afflicted the land. Between 1886 and 1926, desperation and hunger spurred 1.3 million people to leave.

Despite this national outflow, there was, paradoxically, a leap in Lisbon's population during the second half of the 19th century. In 1860 the city had 200,000 inhabitants, but 30 years later there were 300,000.

For some, the closing decades of the 19th century, under the benign and somewhat *laissez-faire* rule of Luís I, who succeeded his brother in 1861, were good years, as we shall see in the next chapter. ❑

LEFT: Pedro II, who was obliged to return to Lisbon from Brazil in 1834.

Voltaire's Candide

The rational theology of the Enlightenment, influenced by foreign ideas and practised by intellectuals and politicians including the Marquês de Pombal, interpreted Lisbon's earthquake as part of life's grand scheme, and therefore for the general good. In response, the French philosopher Voltaire dipped his sharp pen in blackest satire and wrote the story of *Candide* in which "all is for the best in this best of all possible worlds".

Voltaire (1694–1778) had been moved by the earthquake and he returned to the subject on a number of occasions. In *Candide*, his characters land in Lisbon just in time to witness the disaster: "Scarcely had they set foot in town... when they felt the earth quake underfoot; the sea was lashed to a froth, burst into the port, and smashed all the vessels lying at anchor there. Whirlwinds of fire and ash swirled through the streets and public squares; houses crumbled, roofs came crashing down on foundations, foundations split; thirty thousand inhabitants of every age and either sex were crushed in the ruins.

"The sailor whistled through his teeth, and said with an oath: 'There'll be something to pick up here.'

'What can be the sufficient reason for this phenomenon?' asked Pangloss.

'The Last Judgement is here,' cried Candide.

"But the sailor ran directly into the middle of the ruins, heedless of danger in his eagerness for gain; he found some money, laid violent hands on it, got drunk, and, having slept off his wine, bought the favours of the first streetwalker he could find amid the ruins of smashed houses, amid corpses and suffering victims on every hand. Pangloss however tugged at his sleeve.

"'My friend,' said he, 'this is not good form at all; your behaviour falls short of that required by the universal reason; it's untimely, to say the least.'"

In the next chapter of *Candide*, Voltaire, who devoted himself to tolerance and justice, satirised another Lisbon tradition: "After the earthquake had wiped out three-quarters of Lisbon, the learned men of the land could find no more effective way of averting total destruction than to give the people a fine *auto-da-fé*; the University of Coimbra had established that the spectacle of several persons being roasted over a slow fire with full ceremonial rites is an infallible specific against earthquakes."

Voltaire also composed *Poem upon the Lisbon Earthquake,* subtitled *An Inquiry into the Maxim 'Whatever is, is right'.* `It reads in part:
*Approach in crowds, and meditate awhile
Yon shattered walls, and view each ruined pile,
Women and children heaped up mountains high,
Limbs crushed which under ponderous marble lie;
Wretches unnumbered in the pangs of death,
Who mangled, torn and panting for their breath,
Buried beneath their sinking roofs expire,
And end their wretched lives in torments dire.*

*Say when you hear their piteous, half-formed cries,
Or from their ashes see the smoke arise,
Say will you then eternal laws maintain,
Which God to cruelties like this constrain?
Whilst you these facts replete with horror view,
Will you maintain death to their crimes was due?
And can you then impute a sinful deed
To babes who on their mothers' bosoms bleed?
Was then more vice in Lisbon found, than Paris, where voluptuous joys abound?
Was less debauchery, to London known,
Where opulence holds her throne?
Earth Lisbon swallows; the light sons of France
Protract the feast, or lead the sprightly dance.* ❑

RIGHT: Voltaire wrote about Lisbon's earthquake in his biting satire, *Candide.*

MONARCHY TO MILLENNIUM

Rebellion, regicide and dictatorship all played a part in Lisbon's history but the new millennium has seen it take its place as capital of a thriving, modern democracy

With siege towers and catapults and rowdy crusaders, Portugal's first king, Afonso Henriques, forced the ruling Moors from their hilltop citadel and won the prize he had hungered for – the São Jorge castle and all of Lisbon. The fall of Lisbon in 1147 and the subsequent conquest of Moorish strongholds to the south ended five centuries of the Moors' civilising presence in Portugal. Afonso Henriques I lived until 1185, and his House of Burgundy was the first of four dynasties of kings and queens who reigned over a unified nation almost without interruption until the monarchy ended in 1910.

An overview of history

Within the citadel, sword in hand, the king's statue stands today, and from the castle walls all Lisbon's history seems encapsulated. From the ramparts views reach across the centuries – down to the tangled Moorish quarter of Alfama, westwards across to the 17th-century warren of the Bairro Alto and the ruined Igreja do Carmo, an eloquent memorial to the Great Earthquake of 1755. Below is the tidy grid of the 18th-century Baixa streets built to the command of the Marquês de Pombal. An odd structure catches the eye – the French-designed Santa Justa elevator, inaugurated in 1901, the year electric trams began a still-popular transport service on the hilly, winding city streets.

East is the waterfront zone, spectacularly redeveloped since the Expo '98 world fair. You can see down to the Tejo and across the river to the outstretched arms of the monumental Cristo-Rei, a 1959 colossus from the grim decades of Salazar's dictatorship.

Downriver, beyond an expanse of modern buildings, the exquisite Torre de Belém, a 16th-century masterpiece, celebrates Portugal's great explorers and grandest era, a time – from the mid-15th century to the late 16th century –

LEFT: the Cristo Rei statue, built in 1959 under the Salazar regime.
RIGHT: military pomp celebrates the 1974 Revolution.

when Portugal's King Manuel I was the richest monarch on earth and Lisbon was the world's wealthiest capital.

Never again would the city experience the dazzling fortunes that flowed on the tides of Portugal's maritime achievements. Ships sank, fleets vanished, powerful opponents (mainly

the Dutch and the English) encroached on Portugal's unmanageably vast domains.

The reign of Dom João V (1689–1750) was illuminated by the shine of gold from Brazil, the brightest flower in Portugal's sprawling empire. The king was generous and spent lavishly – though at least one enduring reminder of his reign, the great Aqueduct of Free Waters, its 109 arches striding across Lisbon, was largely paid for by the *povo*, the ordinary folk, through a tax on meat, olive oil and wine. The aqueduct survived the 1755 earthquake. Most grand structures did not.

The urban renewal programme conceived by the Marquês de Pombal, all-powerful premier to the weak King José I, brought Lisbon a lasting lustre. As well as the neoclassical architecture of the Baixa – a style rapidly dubbed *pombalina* (after the Marquês de Pombal) – the rebuilt lower city acquired handsome arches and a large, well-proportioned square, the Praça do Comércio, with an imposing statue of King José mounted on his favourite horse, Gentil.

For Lisboetas the square has always been known as the Terreiro do Paço, the Place of the Palace. The English, whose alliance with Portugal is long and close, often refer to it as Black Horse Square (although the horse is not and never was black).

entered its closing decades, satirical poetry and drama reflected the political situation.

Government during these years was a matter of Regenerators rotating with Historicals – who, allied with Reformists, became Progressists. The Civil Code introduced in 1867 was markedly progressive. It allowed civil marriage and abolished primogeniture (though an unfortunate effect of this was fragmented properties with cloudy titles).

A wife now shared parental control of their children with her husband – and if he died they were no longer held to be orphans. The code also abolished the death penalty for civil crimes

The 19th century draws to a close

In 1861, King Pedro V was succeeded by his brother, Luís. Luís was 26, blue-eyed, fair-haired and popular. He had planned a career at sea and was the only king in Portugal's centuries of seafaring to command a ship. His interest in naval affairs led him to found Lisbon's Museu da Marinha.

His reign, which lasted until 1889, was productive. A cultured man, who translated Shakespeare into Portuguese and sensibly left politics to the politicians. Literature flourished during his reign. Alexandre Herculano (1810–77) wrote a magisterial history of Portugal and, as the century

– an enlightened commitment from which the Portuguese have never retreated.

The Pink Map

Industry grew, trade expanded, notably in textiles, cork and canning. The British were prominent, with the old alliance dating back to a 1386 treaty seemingly still going strong. Yet British imperialism, arising from the ambitions of Cecil Rhodes in Africa, was about to heap humiliation on Portugal.

Indignant that Germany's Bismarck and Belgium's King Leopold had their African claims accepted in the 1885 Berlin Conference ruling on the "scramble for Africa", the Portuguese cartographers drew up a map from the maps and historical records of their own explorers, in which Portuguese territory stretched across the continent from Mozambique in the east to Angola in the west.

King Luís died in 1889. The impact of the *Mapa Cor-de-Rosa* (the Pink Map) fell thunderously upon his son, Carlos, king at 26 and already encountering militant republicanism and a host of economic challenges. In 1890 Britain's Lord Salisbury issued an ultimatum: Portugal was to renounce and withdraw from the vast territory (including today's Zambia and Zimbabwe). There would be no compromise.

Elections to the Chamber of Deputies were rigged, the House of Peers had no validity. Crisis followed crisis. Intellectuals committed suicide. Emigrants left in waves. Republicans planned. Conspiracies multiplied.

In 1906, in an attempt to contain the charged situation, King Carlos appointed as premier a determined reformer, João Franco. Failing to make headway, Franco dismissed the *cortes* – the Peers and Deputies – jailed his opponents and governed by decree, a virtual dictatorship that was deeply unpopular.

On 1 February 1908, as Carlos, his wife and two sons were driving in an open landau

The old alliance was at stake. A profoundly mortified Portugal was forced to concede.

Political chaos

Bitterness and anger surged across Lisbon. The Progressive government fell; its successor, the government of the Regenerators, also fell. A coalition foundered. King Carlos was blamed for his failure to uphold the interests of the nation. In 1892 the government was bankrupt. The rotating system of government collapsed.

LEFT: the Praça do Comercio has always been known as the Terreiro do Paço, the Place of the Palace.
ABOVE: an allegory of the 1908 elections.

through the Terreiro do Paço, two shots were fired, instantly killing the king. A third shot fatally wounded his eldest son, Luís Filipe. Later, it was said the assassins were seeking João Franco and it was chance that the king's carriage drove by. The first regicide in centuries of monarchy forced Carlos's unprepared younger son, Manuel, to the throne. He would be Portugal's last king.

The last monarch

Manuel II was sympathetically received. But governments continued to change rapidly – there were six in the young king's 20-month reign. Yet Republican fever was white-hot and there was a profound sense of the inevitable. On 4 October 1910 a republican revolution, backed by elements within the army and navy, won the day. As the republic was formally declared from Lisbon's city hall on 5 October, the king, his mother and grandmother sailed from the little port of Ericeira for Gibraltar and then England.

The monarchy, constitutional since 1834, was abolished by Republicans who desired "an era of peace, of prosperity and of justice", as a Republican paper put it. Yet reality did not match aspiration. The republic proclaimed in 1910 was ended by a military coup in 1926. In

of war on Portugal, more than 100,000 reluctant Portuguese fought in the Great War, suffering heavy losses. Political plots arose on all sides. There were strikes and protests. One president, Sidónio Pais, who was elected by so-called universal suffrage (although it was still men only) in April 1918 as the man of the hour, was assassinated in December in Lisbon's Rossio railway station.

More positively, António José de Almeida, who became president on 5 October 1919, achieved a record by completing a full four years in office. In 1922, thrilling all Portugal, two daring pilots, Sacadura Cabral and Gago

16 years the long-suffering Portuguese people had experienced 45 governments.

From idealism to disillusion

Honourable academics like Dr Teófilo Braga and Dr Manuel de Arriaga headed the first, idealistic governments but fierce divisions of opinion, even violence, caused one government after another to fall.

The outbreak of World War I brought a "sacred union", but it was shattered before the war was over. The British inveigled Portugal into the war in 1916, promising defence if the country requisitioned German ships sheltering in Portuguese ports. After Germany's declaration

Coutinho, made the first crossing of the southern Atlantic in a tiny seaplane (Charles Lindbergh's transatlantic flight was in 1927). Yet inflation and instability still ruled. Dilemmas seemed insoluble.

On 28 May 1926, in a military coup, the Democratic government was overthrown, the National Assembly dissolved, and the 75-year-old President Bernardino Machado dismissed from office. Military dictatorship, headed by General Óscar Carmona, lasted until 1933 when the Estado Novo, the New State, was established. Carmona was elected president in 1928, and three times after that for seven-year terms. Still in office, he died in 1951. Under the 1933 constitution, he had the authority to name his premier. His choice was Dr António de Oliveira Salazar.

The Salazar dictatorship

Salazar was an economics professor at the University of Coimbra. In 1928, demanding total financial control, he achieved the astonishing feat of a budget without deficits and even, from 1929 on, surpluses. Influenced by the spreading fascism of the 1930s, his restrictive policies began to echo those of Hitler, Mussolini and Franco. He established a rigid system of censorship. A special "Social Vigilance" police

Major events in those bleak decades included the Concordat of 1940 which restored the legitimacy of the Catholic church. Dams and bridges were constructed – the suspension bridge over the Tejo, inaugurated in 1966, was, for a time, the longest in the world. Roads were laid and airports built. Never resolved, however, were agricultural and land issues, neither in the fragmented north nor the vast feudal estates of the south.

A treaty of friendship with General Franco of Spain enabled both countries to remain nominally neutral in World War II. The British gained access to the Atlantic staging post of the

force, which later become the infamous PIDE, was trained by the Gestapo. A youth group, Mocidade Portuguesa, was modelled on the Hitler Youth and was compulsory for children from 11 to 14.

Salazar built a network of informers. The effects of these restraints and a rigidly authoritarian government were to lock the Portuguese into an unprogressive and widely despised police state from which they were released only by the revolution of 1974.

Azores. Lisbon buzzed with spies and filled with refugees (notably oil millionaire and art collector Calouste Gulbenkian whose fortune, willed to Portugal, funded an immensely beneficial cultural and social foundation). The Portuguese colonies became provinces from which only a few monopolies (the so-called 20 families) benefited from Salazar favouritism.

Resistance to Salazar's repression was sporadic and futile. A noble effort came from respected General Humberto Delgado. Defeated by Admiral Américo Tomás, an inflexible reactionary, in patently fraudulent presidential elections in 1958, he was murdered in 1965 by PIDE agents near Badajoz in Spain.

LEFT: the declaration of the republic was made from the city hall in October 1910.
ABOVE: Salazar, the Portuguese dictator.

Looking to the future

In August 1968, Salazar fell from his chair, banging his head on the tiled floor. In September, a haematoma was diagnosed and on 7 September doctors operated. Ten days later a heavy haemorrhage struck the opposite side of the brain. The last rites were given. President Tomás invited Marcelo Caetano, an expert in constitutional law, to act as premier. Salazar did not die until 27 July 1970. His conversation with visitors was normal. He was never told Caetano had replaced him.

Caetano, trying to please both diehard and democratic views, made cautious changes. The African territories, he said in 1972, were a problem constantly in his mind. Early in 1974 he read a pre-publication copy of a book called *Portugal e o Futuro, Portugal and the Future*, by 64-year-old General António de Spínola. The general, who had been governor-general in Guinea-Bissau, believed Portugal could never win its war in Africa. New policies were now needed.

On 25 April 1974, in a smooth military coup, joyfully received by Lisboetas, 48 years of Salazarist repression came to an end. Alerted by a song entitled *Grândola, Vila Morena,* broadcast at midnight by folk hero José (Zeca)

THE COLONIAL WARS

In 1961 a rebellion of freedom fighters in Angola exploded into war across Portugal's African territories – Guinea-Bissau, Mozambique, the Cape Verde islands and tiny São Tomé e Principe, as well as the huge, resources-rich Angola itself. By the late 1960s the attempt to suppress them absorbed half Portugal's budget.

Not only was there international pressure on Portugal to get out of Africa, but the Colonial Wars were deeply unpopular with the Portuguese themselves. In 13 years of fighting, more than 100,000 young men were conscripted (thousands more emigrated to avoid the draft); 8,290 died and 26,200 were maimed or injured.

Afonso, some 200 junior officers and troops occupied Lisbon without a shot being fired (except by a few PIDE agents).

The group of "Young Captains" who headed the bloodless revolution – red carnations became its enduring symbol – had formed an Armed Forces Movement (MFA) and promptly announced a programme in which decolonisation and the restoration of democracy were the prime points.

General Spínola, briefly president and involved in forming initial provisional governments, was soon forced aside. Of the coup leaders Major Otelo Saraivo de Carvalho became the best known, a charismatic man who for years afterwards was involved in radical left-wing politics.

Clamorous graffiti covered Lisbon. Months of turbulence included the manoeuvres of communists whose revolt against Salazar had been long and persistent. In March 1975, banks and insurance companies were nationalised, monopolies taken over by their employees. Vast Alentejo estates were occupied by peasant farmers who formed cooperatives – although few proved successful.

On 25 November there arose a confrontation, a revolutionary razor's edge, between conservative northerners and fiery radicals. The fraught

economy was in chaos. Some 700,000 Portuguese settlers in Africa fled to Portugal – *retornados* needing help to begin again. Industrial workers waited months to be paid.

Mário Soares, back from a Salazar-imposed exile, quickly built a Socialist Party that took first place in elections but never, in a 250-seat parliament, with an overall majority. Sixteen governments were elected between 1974 and 1987. Until July 1987 no single party achieved an overall majority and when at last this happened, the patient Portuguese, tired of austerity and political juggling, voted for the Social Democrats, who were led by a young free-market

showdown was ended by commandos led by António Ramalho Eanes. An austere officer, soon general, then commander-in-chief, Eanes was persuaded to stand as candidate in the July 1976 presidential elections and won by a landslide. Re-elected in 1981 he was a trusted and pragmatic president until 1986.

Mário Soares takes over

These were particularly hard years, made worse by the world oil-price crisis and recession. The

LEFT: banners are held high in the 25 April anniversary parades.
ABOVE: Mario Soares signs Portugal into the EC, 1988.

economist, Aníbal Cavaco Silva. Balancing this right-of-centre government was the shrewd and eloquent Mário Soares, who was elected president in 1986.

The tide turns

The tide began to turn. In 1986, together with neighbouring Spain, Portugal joined the European Community, now the European Union. Inflation and unemployment fell. From 13.4 per cent in 1990, inflation was just over 3 per cent by 1996. Empowered by a new, less revolutionary constitution, Cavaco Silva's government privatised rapidly and returned 750,000 hectares of land to its owners.

An unblocked, liberal economy opened up banking and the financial markets and investment (tourism and service industries made rapid advances). Though heavily dependent on oil imports, Portugal in 1997 was receiving natural gas through a pipeline from North Africa. A huge Ford/VW investment was the largest private investment in 10 years.

Structural funds, pouring in from the EU (by 1996 amounting to more than $23 billion), went into new roads and railways, ports and airports, dams and irrigation, telecommunications, agriculture (always problematical), and job training. Stability and the buoyant econ-

omy won Prime Minister Cavaco a second four-year term in October 1991.

Democracy alive and well

In the 1995 elections, the hope of broader social reforms brought to power the Socialist Party (PSP) led by António Guterres. In January of the following year, when Mário Soares had served as a popular president for the maximum period of 10 years, Jorge Sampaio, another well-liked Socialist, was elected – and then re-elected in 2001.

Political debate in Portugal in the new millennium, in a 230-seat parliament, is lively, sustaining a healthy democracy.

In 1999, with the passing of Macao to China and a frail East Timor under United Nations administration, Portugal made a dignified exit from empire. The former African colonies and Brazil had, three years earlier, joined their former rulers on equal terms in a Portuguese-speaking community.

In 1999, as a longstanding member of NATO, Portugal was one of 11 EU nations qualified to enter the European Monetary Union (EMU) – and in March 2002, having phased out the escudo, will use the Euro as currency. Although real wages remained below most European countries, so did inflation, and per capita GDP in 2000 was above $14,000.

There are still complaints about bureaucracy, an old bugbear, and about the slow-moving judicial system. Despite this, Portugal's economic performance has been highly praised by the Organisation for Economic Cooperation and Development (OECD) and, based on its good record, the country won from the EU a vast new package of structural funds for the years 2000 to 2006.

A thoroughly modern city

The new millennium shows an altered, enlarged and vibrant Lisbon. Historic neighbourhoods and venerable buildings retain their grace and charm, while modern suburbs, shiny shopping malls and broad highways add a new dimension. People are well dressed, many with mobile phones constantly at the ready – Portugal has more mobile phones per capita than almost anywhere in Europe.

Expo '98, the world fair held on the 500th anniversary of Vasco da Gama's epic voyage to India, brought Lisbon benefits far larger and more lasting than a simple facelift.

In what were once run-down, shabby docks there is now a cheerful waterfront residential and leisure area and an entertainment park – the Parque das Nações – with a splendid new mainline station, the Gare do Oriente, linked to Lisbon's expanded metro. Across the River Tejo stretches the gleaming 18-km (11-mile) Vasco da Gama bridge. A third Tejo bridge was in the planning stage when this book went to press in 2001.   ❏

LEFT: fire ravaged the Chiado district in 1988.
RIGHT: there is some stunning architecture in the Parque das Nações, where Expo '98 was held.

A CITY FIT FOR CADS AND KINGS

Lisbon has always been a cosmopolitan place, praised by poets, favoured

by monarchs and hospitable to those with nowhere else to go

Europe's most westerly capital occupies a special place on the Continent. Tucked away far beyond the Pyrenees and only reached by those specifically aiming to go there, it has been both a haven from Old-World troubles and a springboard for adventures in the New. All history's conquering and itinerant hordes have found their way here – Phoenicians, Romans, Visigoths, Moors, not to mention Spaniards and French – while its colonies have brought settlers from Africa, South America, South East Asia and China.

Down through the centuries this cosmopolitan city has offered shelter to Europe's outcasts, hope to its invalids, pleasure to its tourists and a last refuge to kings who have been kicked off their thrones.

Foreign friends

Of all Portugal's friends and allies, none have endured as the English. It was a largely English contingent on the way to the Crusades in 1147 that Afonso I managed to divert to help him take Lisbon from the Moors. The two countries have been bound by friendship and treaties ever since.

As a result of the incursion, a priest in the crusading party, Gilbert of Hastings, was appointed first Bishop of Lisbon, while a chronicler called Osbern embellished his version of the events. Admiring the Tejo as the Phoenicians had done before him, he wrote: "This noble river was most abundantly fishy and there was gold on its banks."

Of the numerous English connections with Lisbon, the most illustrious was Philippa of Lancaster, daughter of John of Gaunt, who married King João I in 1387, the year after he signed the Treaty of Windsor with her father. Philippa, who was much admired by the Portuguese, was the mother of Henry the Navigator.

In 1661, there was another Anglo-Portuguese marriage, this one between the English Charles II and Catherine of Bragança. Subsequently, Anglo-Portuguese armies were not unusual. The most notable, perhaps – certainly the best recorded – was the contingent commanded by Sir Arthur Wellesley, later Duke of Wellington,

which built the defensive lines known as the Torres Vedras and helped Portugal win the war against Napoleon.

Nuns in peril

When the Great Earthquake struck Lisbon in 1755, all Europe waited for news of survivors. There was a sizeable contingent of English nuns in the city, as there had been for centuries. One of the sisters in the English Bridgetine nunnery later wrote: "I was washing up the tea things when the Dreadfull affair happened. It began like the rattling of Coaches and the things before me danst up and down on the table, I look about me and see the Walls a

---

PRECEDING PAGES: sharing a joke in the spring sunshine; schoolchildren in the Parque Eduardo VII.
LEFT: King Carlos with the English Queen Alexandra.
RIGHT: Henry Fielding, who died in Lisbon.

shakeing and falling down then I up and took to my heels, with Jesus in my mouth…"

The nuns all survived, but the convent did not. It had been a popular institution with visiting sailors, and it was afterwards rebuilt.

Writers' trail

Lisbon has attracted foreign writers for several centuries. In 1754, Henry Fielding, author of *Tom Jones*, came here for his health. This proved to be a bad move. He lasted two months and is buried in the city's English cemetery, though the slab that marks the spot is something of a guess as to the precise site of his grave.

The reputation preceded him to Lisbon where he was at first shunned by the British community. Although he managed to impress the aristocratic Marialvas family with the great fanfare of his life, surrounded by his own court of musicians and dwarfs to fight off incipient *ennui*, he was unable to achieve his ambition of becoming a British envoy in the city. "The dirty fag-end of Europe," he called it, when in his cups, although when he later moved into a house he had built in the city, he wrote: "St Anthony conducted my furniture safe, and inspires me with a supernatural affection for this moonish, silly country."

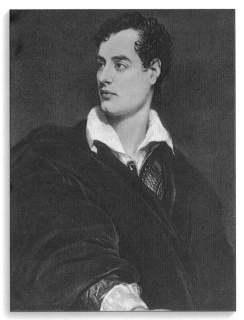

By the end of the 18th century grand tours were beginning to attract romantic imaginations. Lisbon's more famous visitors included William Beckford, George Borrow *(see box)* and such poets as Lord Byron, Robert Southey and John Keats, who were all much taken with the palace at Sintra.

One of the first to arrive, and set up house near Sintra in 1787, was William Beckford, who is closely associated with Lisbon. In fact, it is possible that this wealthy writer and collector from Fonthill in Wiltshire may be better known in Portugal than in England, as he spent much of his life escaping rumours in his own country of his homosexual behaviour.

BORROW'S LANGUAGE COURSE

George Borrow, who travelled to Portugal in 1835 as an emissary of the Bible Society, has left to posterity some wonderfully descriptive accounts of his journeys. He also offered advice to travellers on how to speak to the natives: "Those who wish to make themselves understood by a foreigner in his own language should speak with much noise and vociferation, opening their mouths wide." Some people today seem to have taken this advice to heart. Borrow was convinced that he could speak Portuguese fluently after just two weeks in the country and refused to accept that it was his fault if people could not understand what he was saying.

Lord Byron's bad humour

Inspired by Beckford, Byron came to Sintra in 1809 and appears to have enjoyed himself. "I am very happy here," he wrote, "because I loves oranges, and talks bad Latin to the monks who understand it, and I goes into society (with my pocket pistols) and I swims in the Tagus all across at once, and I rides on an ass or a mule, and swears Portuguese, and have got a diarrhoea and bites from the mosquitoes. But what of that? Comfort must not be expected by folks that go a-pleasuring."

However, this is by far the most complimentary thing Byron ever said about Portugal. He and now lay in the English cemetery). "The gay and glittering city proves to be a painted sepulchre," he wrote. "Filth and beastliness assault you at every turn, in their most loathsome and disgusting shapes."

Of all the city's sights, however, one in particular continued to impress everyone who saw it: the Águas Livres aqueduct. Completed in 1748 it survived the earthquake and is still carrying water today. J.B.F. Carrere, a French visitor, said it was the only edifice in Lisbon worth seeing. "It is a superb aqueduct," he wrote in 1809. "It unites beauty and magnificence with boldness and solidity of execution."

was not enamoured of the country in general or Lisbon in particular. In his epic poem, *Childe Harold*, the Portuguese – described as "Lusian brutes" – are picked out for special attack.

Fans of the aqueduct

Travellers were not infrequently rude about the post-earthquake city. Henry Mathews, an English consumptive in search of a healthy climate, arrived in Lisbon in 1817 (perhaps he hadn't heard that Fielding had done the same thing

Far Left: William Beckford set up home near Sintra.
Left: Lord Byron was not very kind to the Portuguese.
Above: exiled King Umberto of Italy and his daughters.

George Borrow, the intrepid 19th-century author and Bible salesman, was more extravagant in his praise: "I boldly say that there is no monument of man's labour and skill, pertaining to either ancient or modern Rome, for whatever purpose designed, which can rival the waterworks of Lisbon; I mean the stupendous aqueduct whose principal arches cross the valley to the northeast of Lisbon, and which discharges its little runnel of cool and delicious water into the rocky cistern within that beautiful edifice called the Mother of Waters..." Borrow also waxed lyrical about Lisbon in general, which he thought "as much deserving the attention of the artist as even Rome itself".

Turkeys, cows and goats

Early in the 20th century a Captain Granville Baker found the Jerónimos monastery the most impressive sight. He also noted the number of turkeys for sale in "Turkey Square", which is the name that had been given to the Rossio because the animals in it were so plentiful. "Another sight peculiar to the city is that of cows, mostly black-and-white, also being taken from house and milked on the doorstep while a poor little muzzled calf looks on unhappily. Goats, too, perambulate the streets in the same line of business. Their progress is more eventful, but often wanting in dignity."

The animals may have gone now, but some aspects of the city, including the character of its inhabitants, have not changed all that much. Captain Baker's description of a street labourer could have been written not too long ago by someone watching the *calceteiros*, the men who make the geometrically patterned paths found in the Parque Eduardo VII and elsewhere throughout Lisbon: "The value of time can be measured by watching the repairing process of a piece of side walk. The workman – and perhaps a companion or two – squats on the ground, mallet in hand, a pile of stones beside him. From these he selects now a black, now a grey stone with deliberation."

Royal visitors

The Lisbon that Captain Baker wrote about was the Lisbon Edward VII visited when he reaffirmed the Treaty of Windsor in 1902 – the park was named after him, and this event. The English king was a frequent visitor, staying at Belém Palace, and he and King Carlos seemed close.

Carlos and his son Luís were assassinated in 1908, and first the Republic, then the dictatorship of Salazar, dominated this century. But the kings came back. Here, in Lisbon and in its resorts of Estoril and Cascais ("The Coast of Kings"), is where Europe's cast-off monarchs came to the end of the line. Among them were Umberto of Italy, Carlos of Romania and Horthy, regent of Hungary.

Generous patron

Of all the foreign visitors to Lisbon during the 20th century, one undoubtedly did more for the city than any other. Calouste Gulbenkian, the oil millionaire "Mr Five Percent", gave Lisbon the kind of patronage it needed. His foundation, art gallery, orchestra, ballet, bursaries, grants and aids are a rich and continuing part of Lisbon fabric.

Gulbenkian was an Armenian, born in 1869. In 1888 he joined his father's oil business and he soon became a successful financier, industrialist and diplomat. In 1902 he took up British citizenship. During World War II the British authorities confiscated his petroleum interests in Vichy France and, in what has been subsequently described as "a clerical error", declared him an "Enemy under the Act". Outcast, Gulbenkian chose exile in Lisbon, the wartime city of intrigue where British intelligence officers such as the writers Malcolm Muggeridge, Graham Greene and Ian Fleming pitted their wits against their opposite numbers in the city.

Under Salazar's dictatorship, the rich were allowed to become very rich. When he died in 1955, Gulbenkian left his considerable personal art collection to the city that had provided him with a refuge. Along with it he bequeathed a great chunk of his $70 million fortune to run the Foundation which continues to give the city its cultural drive. ❑

Left: Graham Greene served in British Intelligence in Lisbon during World War II.
Right: Gulbenkian was given refuge in the city.

EVERYDAY LIFE

The traffic is chaotic, the cafés and bars always humming. For a family-oriented society, Lisboetas spend a lot of time on the streets of their city

As the cocks crow and the first trams clang their bells, Lisbon once more becomes the last city in continental Europe to be touched by the sun's morning rays. The light is somewhere between the watery opacity of the North Atlantic and the deep glow of the Mediterranean. It catches the castle of São Jorge, warming the old yellow walls, then creeps down the hills piled up beside the Tejo, wiping mist from the river and gilding the sleek Vasco da Gama bridge at the start of its gentle curve across the broad estuary. In this grassy, airy east Lisbon neighbourhood keep-fit enthusiasts are already jogging on the riverside boardwalk.

Breakfast in Lisbon means wholesome bread with coffee or tea, which is called *chá*, as it is in Chinese and in British slang, a reminder that the Portuguese explorers were involved in introducing the West to many new and life-enhancing delights.

Learning for life

Children are usually the first out of the house, leaving for school by 8am. Or most of them. The hard-pressed education system in the city means that some classes rotate, having morning and afternoon sittings.

Most children go to state schools, but private schools are neither elitist nor unusual: a lack of places in a local school may leave no choice. Books are almost invariably bought by the parents. The country had one of the highest illiteracy rates in Europe in the immediate post-Salazar days. Old people never learned to read or write and children dropped out of school early. Now illiteracy has fallen to below 12 percent of the population. But new businesses are experiencing a shortage of skilled labour and a range of intensive training courses has been set up. In the evenings classes are open for adults, the schools' third shift of the day.

LEFT: boys cool off in an explosive water fountain at the Parque das Nações.
RIGHT: off to work they go.

Commuter crush

The rush-hour builds up around 8.30–9am. Everyone who can, drives, it seems, and the traffic crawls and hoots towards the town centre, where even the new car parks may not be enough. Commuters come in from the suburbs on new ring roads around Lisbon, the smarter

ones from Estoril and Cascais where a motorway runs inland. Statistically, the Portuguese are among the world's most dangerous drivers. Until a concrete barrier separated the lanes the hair-raising coast road, the Marginal, was the most accident-prone in the country.

During the 1990s, European Union structural funds helped build a national network of "expressways" and highways. The country's first major motorway linked Lisbon with Oporto, reducing the journey time between the country's two most important cities to under three hours. The opportunity to break records has been hard to resist, however, and pile-ups have been frequent.

Where old warehouses, refineries and dock-yards in eastern Lisbon a few years ago were a riverside eyesore there is now a cheerful residential, entertainment and leisure zone, the happy consequence of a major clearance for the world fair, Expo '98. Here and everywhere, the day's work gets busily under way. The traditional bright orange ferries, a catamaran and speedy blue-and-white river craft bring people and cars from the south bank of the Tejo. Suspension bridge tolls are gathered from traffic going both ways, coming into the city or heading south, perhaps to the expanding manufacturing and industrial region of Setúbal.

The main market is beside Cais de Sodré station where the Atlantic catch, from swordfish to sardines and edible barnacles, sparkles on iced slabs. Fishwives *(varinas)*, some from Cape Verde, buy the fishermen's catch. In the past, they carried their baskets in the same way as other women in the city carried large bundles: squarely and comfortably on their heads.

In the Metro subways, clothes vendors tape their wares to the walls. Trinkets and gimmicks are laid out on portable tables. News-stands do a brisk trade. In the Rossio, flower sellers bunch fresh blooms and fan out artificially bright sprays of dried flowers. Café counters

Trains are crowded – arriving at Rossio from Sintra, at Cais do Sodré from the Cascais direction, at Santa Apolónia and the vast eyecatching Gare do Oriente as well as at Terreiro do Paço by the rail line recently built under the bridge. The buses are a squash, the funiculars full and the colourful trams rattle along their imperturbable lines.

Colourful produce

Fruit and vegetables are laid out on stalls. There are exotic loquats and guavas, coconuts, persimmons, yams and paw-paws, as well as locally produced staples, irregularly shaped and looking unashamedly straight from the earth.

crash with cups and saucers as people stop for a *bica*, the first small, strong coffee of the day. Already beggars are on the streets, old and young. Lottery ticket sellers take up their pitches. In the streets of the Baixa, gypsy fortune tellers pester passersby.

A courteous people

At bus stops people stand in queues. Lisboetas are courteous citizens – never mind the older people's habit of spitting. They are the least Latin of the Latin nations; they can speak without using their hands. They like animals and are kind to pets. Though poorly paid by most economic standards, they are industrious but not, research says, particularly competitive. Looking around, it is clear that, demographically, this is a young nation. Many people are smartly dressed, mobile phones at hand or clamped to an ear. And an exceptionally high percentage of men have moustaches.

Of more than a million Portuguese who went to France, Germany, Luxembourg and other countries to find work, many thousands have returned in recent years. Their numbers were supplemented as professionals, such as doctors and lawyers, arrived from Brazil and elsewhere to ride on the boom created by the injection of European Union capital. They all brought their

leading up from the old town to the Praça Marquês de Pombal. It has been called the Champs Elysées of Lisbon, although it doesn't have quite the style of the Paris original.

Above Liberdade is the Edward VII park discreetly enclosing a beautiful greenhouse garden, the Estufa Fria, near graceless pillars, a legacy of the unappealing Mussolini-style architecture of Salazar's New State. When the regime fell, the whole city became a gallery of graffiti art. Another legacy from Salazar is a bureaucratic attitude, a love of forms and documentation. You are nobody without passport or identity card.

taste, their styles and their habits and even introduced a few new words into the Portuguese language. Beer competes with wine as the city's favourite drink.

Most businesses in the city, and the country, are small, employing only a handful of people. Finance houses and large technologically advanced companies are where the bright young graduates head to find their fortunes. Many modern offices are located around the Avenida da Liberdade, the mile-long avenue

LEFT: traditional bright orange ferries carry commuters across the river.
RIGHT: Lisbon girls in a Bairro Alto bar.

HARMONIOUS MIX

The Portuguese like to think of themselves as the least racist nation in Europe, and this may well be true. During the colonial period, racial mixing and intermarriage in the overseas colonies were the norm, not the exception as they were in the British empire. In the city you will see the faces of the former far-flung empire: Chinese, Indian, African and Latin American.

The 700,000 people who fled the turmoil of the post-revolution and independence period of the African provinces in the mid-1970s have adjusted to a new life and new enterprises in Portugal or else joined different migration routes.

Life in old Lisbon

For a feel of the city's timeless qualities, it is necessary to go to the old riverside districts of the Bairro Alto, Lapa, Madragoa and Alfama. Here, life is lived on the streets, in the small squares and in the bars. A front door leading straight into a tiny living-room may remain closed but framed in its little open window there is likely to be an old woman, standing on her doormat, looking out, talking to neighbours, watching the world go by. Around her geranium pots bloom and caged birds sing. Pan pipes herald the knife grinder. *Varinas* wash their fish baskets. Old men sit in the shade of trees in the

Eating habits

Lunch is eaten between 1pm and 3pm, but from midday onwards business is brisk in the city's myriad restaurants and cafés. People eat two-and three-course meals, often standing shoulder to shoulder at the counters. A bowl of nourishing soup and a roll can be had at very little cost. Set menus might be supplemented by white, red or the piquant *vinho verde* "green" wines. Business lunches take place in the more formal surroundings of uptown restaurants like Faz Figura or A Travessa.

Lisbon is a place to eat out: at *cervejarias* and *tascas*, at Chinese or Brazilian or African

squares and on the *miradouros* overlooking the city and the river. Children, who sometimes roam in small gangs, are tolerated almost beyond reason.

In summer tourists stand out above the Lisboetas. They, too, are tolerated and treated with courtesy. They are part of the human tide on which the city has always thrived.

A surprising number of Lisboetas speak English and the special relationship, the old alliance between the two countries, remains strong. For Britons there are incongruous familiarities, such as old-style trams built in Sheffield and a few round, red letter boxes made by A. Handyside of Derby & London.

restaurants, or at fish specialists where the windows look like aquariums. Americans sometimes complain they have difficulty buying iced beer in shops. To the Portuguese this is a curious cause for complaint: beer is drunk in bars.

In the late afternoon, the counters fill up again: at the Pastelaria Nacional in the Baixa, women stand like men propping up a pub bar, nibbling tarts and cakes and quaffing tea, chocolate and coffee. Cafés and tea rooms chatter into life. By 7pm, office workers are pouring on to the streets, meeting up at the Nicola on Rossio or having waffles in Praça da Figueira. In the Chiado, shoppers are settling themselves at pavement tables outside the Café

A Brasileira beside a lifelike sculpture of the poet Fernando Pessoa. In the phone booths on Rossio and Restauradores, immigrants queue to make phone calls home.

Family life

Home for Lisboetas is a family affair, though it is often economics as much as filial devotion that keeps families together. Only about a third of the city's homes are owner occupied. Although it has become less expensive to buy, with a bank loan, than to rent, property is not particularly cheap or readily available and many adult children live at home until they are

The traditional large families, of perhaps 10 children or more, nearly all with their roots in the conservative Catholic north, are now less common, but they have built vast dynasties and their family nets are wide. Many who live in Lisbon don't claim to be Lisboetas, but tell you the name of the town or village where they were born or where the family originates from. They are proud of their rural heritage. Portugal has the lowest urban-rural population ratio of any country in Europe. Only a third of the people live in cities or towns.

Although eating out is a way of life in the city, there is also a great pride in cooking at

married, sometimes even afterwards. Perhaps that is why there is a great deal of kissing in the parks. About 30 percent of babies are born out of wedlock; living together is no sin in the city and partners have equal legal rights. But most still opt for a full white wedding, blessed by the Catholic church. This may take place in the family's home village, or perhaps in one of the city's favourite churches, such as São Roque in the Bairro Alto or the church at the Jerónimos monastery in Belém.

LEFT: women still sell fish in the streets of Alfama.
ABOVE: a traditional shoeshine and a shiny, modern bank represent old and new in Rossio Square.

TELEMANIA

Television has greatly intruded in the home and, indeed, in many bars and restaurants. Even before two private channels began operation in 1992, satellite channels flourished and the two state channels attracted more viewers than in any other European country.

There is the usual mix of chat shows and game shows, some of them Portuguese versions of those that flourish in the rest of Europe, but the big attraction is *telenovelas*, the dramatic soap operas made by the great TV studios of Brazil. A third private television station is backed by the Roman Catholic church and shows no sex or violence.

home, where dishes of the family's region of origin can be prepared to perfection.

Life in the streets

Those eating out will often head for the *tascas* of the Bairro Alto, while the tiny streets of the Alfama sizzle with smoky barbecues, infusing the air with the smell of grilled sardines to whet the appetite. This is a safe town to walk around, even at night. Increased wealth, or rather increased disparity in wealth, is pushing up crime figures and Lisboetas and visitors alike will be asked for money and hissed at by sellers of marijuana, and now and again find their

pockets picked. Yet Lisbon remains one of the least threatening cities in Europe.

In summer everyone is out on the streets and the old town bustles with music and life. Just as there are no particular racial ghettos in the city, so there are no apparent divisions between rich and poor: poor people live in old houses originally built by the rich: rich people eat in the districts where the poor live. In the Bairro Alto, in a small *tasca*, in a disco, or even in an unmarked *fado* house where the waitresses or kitchen staff will suddenly feel moved to sing, tourists can rub shoulders with youthful politicians, yuppies, actresses and ordinary working men and women.

Younger people may head for the brighter, more modern lights of one of the large shopping malls like Colombo or Amoreiras, or the Vasco da Gama commercial centre in Parque das Nações, or maybe just to the inevitable McDonald's.

On Friday or Saturday, people will be out late. There are *fados* to be heard in the Alfama and Lapa as well as the Bairro Alto. There are discos to be danced in and bars to be seen in and new movies to catch. There is African and Latin American music, and there is pop and *fado*-pop. Those who last till dawn go to the market for breakfast.

Sometimes there is opera at the São Carlos, or a concert at the Gulbenkian Foundation or the Grande Auditorio of the huge Caixa Geral bank building, or in the cultural centre in Belém. Or there might be a play at the national theatre, or a review at one of the play houses off the Avenida da Liberdade.

The arts

The Portuguese artistic tradition is narrative: the nation most admires its playwrights, poets and authors, but the other arts do get a look in.

The city's architects are among its celebrities: José Quintela da Fonseca, who designed the Colombo mall; Tomás Taveira, creator of the postmodern shopping complex at Amoreiras; Arsénio Cordeiro for his starkly elegant Torre do Tombo national archives building which guards millions of documents, including nearly 40,000 Inquisition cases, in the heart of Lisbon's University City; Alvaro Siza Vieira, team leader of the project that resurrected the fire-damaged Chiado, is a name that extends far beyond Portugal. In fine art Paula Rego, who has been in residence at the National Gallery in London, is an internationally admired painter, as is Maria Helena Vieira da Silva, who died in Paris in 1992. Then again, there is remarkable art in all the *azulejos*, the glazed tiles that adorn so many buildings and the newer metro stations.

But it is literature that continues to attract most awe and praise. Its practitioners have streets in the city named after them: the 20th century's most respected poet, Fernando Pessoa, the 19th-century historian Alexandre Herculano, and great novelist Eça de Queiroz; Gil Vicente, the 16th-century dramatist, and Luís de Camões, whose epic poem *Os Lusíadas* is a national classic, though he rates only a modest street near the suspension bridge, abutting the Rua dos Lusíadas.

Sport and leisure

When it comes to spectator sports, Lisbon is little different from other European cities in being football crazy. Most people in Portugal support one of the country's three leading teams: F. C. Porto in Oporto and Sporting and Benfica, both in Lisbon. In athletics they like to watch world-class track races in which, again and again, Portuguese distance runners win gold. The Formula 1 motor racing at Estoril

Many Lisboetas still prefer the Feira Popular, the amusement park up at Entrecampos. There is a big wheel and Dodgem cars, merry-go-rounds and the usual sideshows and games. Grilled fish and piles of chips are the popular snack, and there are dishes of snails to pick at. The fun goes on until 1am.

Taking time out

Few Lisboetas go abroad for their holidays. Many visit relatives in the country at Christmas and during the hot summer months of July and August. For weekends and days out, the sea is close by: the *linha* beaches on the Cascais

attracts people to every radio and television set all over the city and is impossible to miss. On Thursdays and Sundays in season the bullfight, the *corrida* or *tourada*, is a popular event. Youngsters, for their part, are out and about at the riverside, on bikes, roller skates and whizzing skateboards.

On summer evenings families often make their way to the Parque das Nações with its riverside attractions including the impressive and immense aquarium built for Expo '98.

LEFT: Lisbon's teenagers know how to have fun.
ABOVE: on weekends, Lisboetas flock to the beaches near Cascais.

commuter line, and the Costa da Caparica beaches on the far side of the Tejo are popular spots. People also go to Cascais to shop at its supermarkets and boutiques and visit its markets. Cascais lies at the mouth of the River Tejo, on the Atlantic coast where the water, along with the waters off a few nearby cleaned-up beaches, is finally safe to bathe in.

One of the most memorable sights in the city of Lisbon is the round, red westering sun slipping behind the suspension bridge over the river, silhouetting the homeward-bound traffic at the day's end. Slowly it gives itself up to the darkening Atlantic, the ocean from which the whole city draws breath. ❑

FOOTBALL CRAZY

Lisboetas are divided between those who support Benfica and

those who support Sporting, but are united in their passion for the game

To the Portuguese, football is religion and politics rolled into one. Where else would you get three national, daily papers dedicated solely to sport (and by 'sport' read effectively 90 percent football)? But here, fans can buy *A Bola, O Record* and *O Jogo*. If you superimpose on to this national passion the

Where it all began

Both clubs had their origins in the early years of the 20th century. Benfica was formed by a group of football enthusiast families living above a chemist's shop in Belém. At first called the Clube Sport Lisboa, it played its first game on New Year's Day in 1905. After a difficult

local rivalry existing between the two main Lisbon clubs, Benfica and Sporting, you have a recipe for endless conversations and debates in cafés and restaurants. (Porto is the only team outside Lisbon with such a strong following.)

There is hardly a *Lisboeta* who is not a supporter of one of the two clubs. As your flight approaches Lisbon airport you will fly first over a large stadium with red seats, Benfica's Estádio de Luz (Stadium of Light). A few moments later you will see below you the green-seated stadium of Sporting, the Estádio de Alvalade. When you leave the airport by taxi, almost certainly the driver will have the red or green colours of his club showing somewhere.

start, and having no ground of its own, the club merged with the nearby Sport Clube de Benfica. Thus was born Sport Lisboa e Benfica (SLB). The club flourished from the start, and was always in the forefront of Portuguese football. In 1954 the current Estádio de Luz was opened, the largest football stadium in Portugal with a capacity for about 75,000 people.

The golden age – and beyond

The 1960s saw what was for many the golden era for Benfica. A young player from Mozambique was hidden away in the team's luggage on their return from an African tour. In this highly inauspicious way the most famous star in Portuguese football – Eusébio – entered the game. During the course of the decade he and several other brilliant players became household names throughout Europe. Benfica played in no fewer than five Champions League Finals and Eusébio scored a total of 791 goals in his time with the club.

More recent years have been less auspicious for Benfica. The big wins haven't been there, and the club has suffered from considerable instability both in management and in its choice of trainers. The end of the 20th century saw the club in considerable financial difficulty but such is the passion of the Benficistas and such

The father of one of the young members was the Viscount of Alvalade, who was elected Honorary President. The club grew rapidly and became a social as well as a sporting institution until a few years later when the footballing activities separated to form the Sporting Clube de Portugal, moving to its present location, named after its first president.

Although never having quite the equivalent of a Eusébio to grace its history, Sporting has, nevertheless, an impressive record both nationally and on a wider European field.

The rivalry between these two clubs, both almost a century old, is real, exuberant and

is the depth of support for the club that no one seems to doubt that the glory days will return.

The rivals

The Sporting team has no less a colourful history. It claims over 3 million paid-up supporters and is the only Portuguese club to have won the European Cup Winners' Cup – although that was back in 1964. The club had its beginnings in 1907, when a group of young enthusiasts formed the Campo Grande Football Club.

LEFT: Benfica supporters celebrate a victory at the Estádio de Luz.
ABOVE: Sporting fans also know how to celebrate.

healthy. It is not difficult to get tickets to see a match, but it's even easier to watch it on television in a bar, as so many fans do. The atmosphere can get pretty lively.

Who are the champions?

The awarding of the 2004 European Championship to Portugal is regarded by the Portuguese as fitting recognition of the importance of football to their nation. Sporting will have a brand new stadium ready for the competition, and Benfica's should be completely refurbished. The rivalry will intensify as the great date draws closer. Who will put on the better show for Europe? ❏

FADO

It is nothing less than the soul of Portugal, an ancient, haunting music that has survived the centuries and is still revered today

As *flamenco* is to Spain, *fado* is to Portugal... but whereas *flamenco*'s vibrant dance, guitar music and haunting lament are familiar to almost any visitor to Spain – even if they only hear the made-for-tourists version – many people will come to Portugal and never come across the word *fado*, let alone hear the music played and sung.

The soul of Portugal

Literally translated, *fado* means fate, but it carries a much broader significance. It is a deep expression of the Portuguese soul, of the self-perception and character of the nation. As any traveller will concede, it is extremely difficult truly to understand someone from a culture widely different from one's own, but sometimes this gap can be narrowed by a comprehension of one another's musical idiom. Music has a way of cutting through superficial and linguistic barriers. In this regard, *fado* is a very clear and definitive vehicle; anyone succeeding in plumbing its melodic and poetic depths is one important step closer to understanding just who the Portuguese people are.

Fado is not for all ears. Even within Portugal there are many who will readily admit that they neither like its melody nor appreciate its poetry. But whether they like it or not almost everyone will provide a strong argument either for or against. It is not something about which the Portuguese feel apathetic.

A song with a long tradition

In terms of Portuguese culture, and the intricate business of getting to know the Portuguese, two things really jump at the outsider. One is the gigantic literary presence of Luís de Camões, both his own extraordinary rough-and-tumble life, and his masterly epic poem, *Os Lusíadas (The Lusiads)*, which recounts the

LEFT: *O Fado*, a soulful depiction of the music, painted by José Malhoa.
RIGHT: a poster advertising *fado* in one of Bairro Alto's many bars.

story of Portugal's early navigators and their discovery of the New World *(see page 41)*.

The other is *fado*, the musical expression of that part of the Portuguese soul that seeks release. It came into being largely because of the traditions that arose in following the 15th- and 16th-century Discoveries that Camões describes so lucidly. Through different forms of artistic expression – the one literary, the other musical – and separated in time by some 200 years, there is a direct line between Camões, who published his epic verse in 1572, and *fado*, which was unknown before the late 1700s.

The Discoveries heralded the end of medieval Europe. It could be said, perhaps, that Prince Henry the Navigator, who initiated the voyages of discovery *(see page 42)*, was the first great Renaissance thinker. Portugal fairly burst out of the Dark Ages on to a world stage that she was to dominate for the next 150 years. The era was to give the Portuguese a vitality and zeal that manifested itself in many ways, both good and bad. Portuguese merchants grew wealthy on the trading of spices and exotic products from far corners – silks from the east, gold from Brazil, slaves sent into bondage in all corners of a huge domain. As fervent missionaries, they carried the Christian faith everywhere. As imperialists, they were to hold reins of power in Africa, Asia and the Americas – a desperate grip they released completely only in 1974 with the Revolution.

Homesick souls

Such deeds required that Portugal assemble a large navy. In the long months away from their

"*Saudade* is Portuguese," *fadista* Amália Rodrigues believed. "It is very much us, the way we are. To us it is instinctive, something we learned through the hardships of our history."

Fado's queen

Amália Rodrigues, who died in October 1999 at the age of 78, was acknowledged during her lifetime as the greatest *fadista* of all time, and a lady who, almost single-handedly, made *fado* a well-known phenomenon. She carried the spirit of this Portuguese expression to audiences everywhere, singing in concert halls in almost every major city in the world.

native shores, on voyages that were far less certain than travel today, these simple sailors met all kinds of strange and wonderful landscapes and peoples. They learned new ways, new languages, new customs. One can easily imagine how, in their hearts, when they were away on these voyages they longed for hearth and home; or how, once home, they would long to return to the exotic places and people they had met far away. This complexity of feelings is summed up in a single word in Portuguese: *saudade*. There is no accurate translation for it into any other language: longing, perhaps; homesickness; the feeling of missing something, someone. An ache in one's soul.

"There are two schools of thought about the origin of *fado*," she explained, a few years before her death. "One is that it comes to us from Brazil; the other is that it originated on the ships. As to what my opinion is – well, I prefer to think that it must have come from the sailors who spent such long months away from home. It makes more sense to me. But *fado* is so many things – the feelings of so many people suffering such terrible hardships. *Fado* grew from the people… but we will maybe never know for certain."

Lisbon *fado,* as it is known today, can be traced to the dock and cabaret areas of the city shortly before the turn of the 19th century. It first appeared as a form of dance very similar to the African *lundum* – a type of belly dance known throughout northwest Africa, and transported, presumably, through the slave trade with Brazil. Even today, *fado* is remarkably similar in many respects to the *morna* music of Cabo Verde.

Early roots

As you might guess from its roots, early *fado* was not quite acceptable to polite society because of its earthiness and unapologetic emotion – elements that still suffuse true *fado*. Over the years, the dance was supplanted by the hooding of eyes, or the opening of a hand. The tautness is important because it seems to convey – and quite forcefully – the tension of the soul crying out.

When it is well sung and with good accompaniment, *fado* is exquisite, having the capacity to hold listeners spellbound and – like it or not – to engender in them the wrenching ache of something deep inside that is not really there. *Saudade*, in fact. It is nearly always sung in a minor key, a musical way to express the melancholy contained in the song.

When it is not well sung, *fado* can be awful, inducing in a captive audience little more than

melody, the instrumentation and the poetry. Early *fadistas* included the Brazilian mulatto Caldas Barbosar, José Dias and, a little later, Maria Severa.

Today Lisbon *fado* is strictly voice and instrumental accompaniment. Indeed, one of the first things that will strike the viewer is the formal, somewhat wooden stance of the singer who, despite the most versatile vocal gymnastics, will seldom elaborate with more body movement than the lifting of the chin, the

LEFT: there are cafés, bars and clubs all over Lisbon where you can hear *fado* played and sung.
ABOVE: a performance in the Casa do Fado.

a feeling of the most acute embarrassment. But even in such extreme cases, the fair-minded Portuguese audience will allow the singer to labour on to the bitter end. Even if the resultant suffering is due to the singing rather than a consequence of any falteringly expressed *saudade*, respect is nonetheless accorded to the singer who tried, and he or she will be given a resounding hand.

End of an era

The applause for Amália, as all Portugal called her, was never less than wholehearted. Born in 1921, she became a legend, and her passing was the end of an era. Well into old age, although she did not appear in public very often, she continued to sing and did not officially retire. And the truth is that, as the years went by, her voice became better and better. Nobody who has ever heard Amália sing could possibly forget the haunting sound of her voice.

Her *fado* was strictly Lisbon *fado*. "It comes from the people who live in these streets, you know," she once said. "It's from the suffering in their hearts. Coimbra *fado* – that's a different tradition. The people who sing Coimbra *fado* are different from the poor people of Lisbon. There they are students – troubadours. They can afford to languish with a love song without

knowing the pain of love. They come from the tradition of the *fidalgo*. Their songs are beautiful – but they are not the same songs we sing here in Lisbon…"

International influences

Traditionally, the *fado* accompaniment consists of two *guitarras* – Portuguese guitars that originated in England centuries ago, and provide the intricate melodies – and two Spanish guitars (which the Portuguese call *violas*) providing rhythm. The *guitarra*, unique to Portugal, is a pear-shaped, flat-backed 12-stringed instrument. Its silvery, shimmering tones contrast with the soft, warm tones of the *violas*.

Although Lisbon *fado*'s major influence appears to have come from the sea and from the slave music of Brazil, there is also a distinct Moorish quality to it – and one will also find musical similarities between it and *flamenco*, particularly in the use of the *galleo*. This is a deep wail or cry, a call to the timbre of the song that somehow connects the music indelibly with the meaning of the poem. In *flamenco*, the *galleo* is given at the beginning of the piece; in *fado* it comes at the end, signalling the end of the song and the moment when an appreciative audience will burst with applause, loud hurrahs and cries of "*Fadista!*"

Tourist traps

There is a list of *fado* houses in the *Yellow Pages* of the Lisbon telephone directory – under the headings of *Casas do Fado* and *Restaurantes Típicos*. This is a good place to start but it requires a word of warning: Lisbon is full of tourist traps – among them a selection of *fado* houses that supply dinner, drinks and floor show all inclusive, and very often hang a neon sign outside along with photographs of the artists performing inside. The floor show might or might not include *fado*, and sometimes an ensemble of dancers perform some regional folk fare. Some are good. Some are frightful.

Fado at its purest is something rather low-key. Often the best places to hear it are little bars and restaurants tucked away in the back streets. These places change – sometimes as frequently as every week or so. If you are anxious to hear the real thing, take a walk through the narrow streets of Bairro Alto. Here, through low little doors, in poky places, is where you are apt to discover true Portuguese music.

But the Portuguese are friendly people. Try dinner in a little *tasca* and see if you can strike up an acquaintance with some local residents. Many Portuguese speak English, so meeting people is really not hard. They may well know where you can hear some really fine *fado*.

You could also visit the House of Fado (*see page 143*) to find out more about the music, and take some of their recommendations on reliable places to hear it at its best. ❏

LEFT: Amália, the queen of *fado*.
RIGHT: small, smoky bars are often the best venues for authentic renditions of the music.

FEASTS OF THE SAINTS

Portugal has scores of festivals throughout the year. In Lisbon,
by far the most important are those that celebrate "the people's saints"

The city of Lisbon bursts into summer aban-
don in June when Christian legend and
pagan celebrations merge during the *Festas dos Santos Populares*, which celebrate the
feast days of Santo António, São João and São
Pedro (Anthony, John and Peter). The festivities, almost a month long, range from sporting
events to dancing in the streets, from religious
rituals to bacchanalia. As the celebrations
begin, thousands of people cram into Lisbon's
cobble-stoned alleyways and squares in the
warm evenings to join the noisy, light-hearted
neighbourhood parties that precede the solemn
Catholic ceremonies of the saints' days on 13,
24 and 28 June.

Popular favourite

The liveliest night is 12 June, eve of the feast of
Santo António, the unofficial patron saint of
Lisbon. São Vicente is the official patron, but
he has never been as popular as Anthony, who,
more than 750 years after his death, is still
loved and remembered as a miracle-worker and
matchmaker. Many of the faithful attend mass
in the Igreja de Santo António, which stands on
the site where he was born, in the shadow of
the more imposing cathedral. This modest
church was first built by King João II and
reconstructed after the 1755 earthquake.

Born Fernando de Bulhões on 15 August
1195, he took the name of Anthony when he
became a Franciscan monk. He left for Africa
and then Italy where he became known as St
Anthony of Padua. But the people of Lisbon
consider him "theirs". Many still pray to him,
touching his painting in the church, and each
year dozens of brides, having asked for his in-
tercession, are married there on 13 June.

The *sardinhada*

Lisbon's oldest neighbourhoods, Castelo,
Mouraria, Graça and Alfama, lead the festivities

on 12 June, although some lesser-known areas
also join in, sharing the huge crowds that con-
verge on the city for the traditional *sardinhada*,
a meal of grilled sardines, washed down with
plenty of wine and followed by folk dancing
and singing and, these days, rock and pop
bands, which play well into the night.

A TASTE OF GINGINHA

At the feast of St Anthony, before the *sardinhada* begins,
people tend to kick off the night with a small glass of
ginginha, the potent cherry liqueur for which Lisbon is
famous. It can be drunk *com elas* or *sem elas*, that is,
with or without the cherries.

The most famous gathering place is a tiny bar on
the edge of Rossio Square, aptly called A Ginginha. The
blue-and-white tiles that line the walls are the originals,
and the sticky red liquid is tapped out of one of the
large wooden barrels stacked along the back wall.
There are other *ginginha* bars in the nearby Rua das
Portas de Santo António and elsewhere in the city.

LEFT: a neighbourhood feast to celebrate Santo
António's day.
RIGHT: girls dance in the Praça do Comércio.

These parties are truly a community effort, organised weeks in advance by local families. They buy streamers and paper lanterns to decorate every street corner, and at night they pick up their modest wooden kitchen tables and chairs and carry them out on to the street to seat the hundreds that arrive. Everyone chips in with cutlery, plates and glasses, and helps clear the spaces for the late-evening musicians.

During the day, the local women clean and decorate, while the men trudge up the hill with hundreds of crates of fresh sardines covered in rock salt, 5-litre carafes of red and white wine, crates of beer and soft drinks, and the inevitable

bagaço – a clear, unaged brandy served in tiny shot glasses and guaranteed to have you under the table before you know it.

Everyone is welcome to these celebrations and the parades, barbecues and dancing that go with them. By late evening the once-aristocratic Alfama suburb, still graceful in spite of its decay, has set up its charcoal broilers, with huge brown paper bags filled with freshly baked bread nearby, and the smell of grilled sardines and excited shouts soon fill the air.

The great parade

The traditional parade, or *marchas populares,* is held in Praça do Comércio overlooking the

Tejo. The *marchas* used to be held along the Avenida da Liberdade, with hundreds of participants representing Lisbon's 14 original parishes – each with its own history, customs, costumes and songs. Campo de Ourique, for example, used to be the home of the millers and bakers, while 16th-century Madragoa is where the fishwives lived. The parade has shrunk over the years because of harder economic times and the increasing homogeneity of the areas, which has eroded old customs. Lisbon City Hall, however, is making efforts to revive the parade to its former glory.

Those who prefer (and can afford) to splash out on a more private and organised celebration, can charter an orange-and-white ferry boat for a floating party, complete with band. The best part of this is watching the firework display spilling over the river, with Castelo de São Jorge, the cathedral and the church of São Vicente stunningly floodlit behind.

Nothing can dampen the festive mood. Even if it rains, people will say it is a sign that God is blessing and baptising the revellers.

Sweet basil

Around St Anthony's Day you will see women all over the city selling small earthenware pots of fresh basil festooned with a paper carnation and a romantic poem. The belief is that as the basil grows, so will the buyer's love. However, as it's an annual plant it will die at the end of the year, so its seeds must be gathered and re-planted to ensure eternal love.

More sober celebrations

The next day's religious processions tend to be more sombre. The devout will gather to carry the statue of St Anthony, covered with flowers, either on their shoulders or on a car supplied by local firemen. The procession winds through the tortuous streets of the Alfama, singing the *Te Deum.* Many in the crowd bless themselves or kneel as the saint passes, while others toss down flowers, petals or coins from their windows above the street.

Other centuries-old traditions include the selling of *paezinhos de Santo António*, little bread rolls to collect money for the poor, and the building of the *tronos de Santo António*, small votive thrones. Street urchins used to make these out of matches, matchboxes or any other cheap material, competing with each other for the tallest or most elaborate model, which would win the most money from passers-by. Today, the thrones are made by rival neighbourhoods and are on view at the Feira Popular funfair at Entrecampos.

Galician feast

Other areas of Lisbon have their own particular celebrations. One is the festival of Santo Amaro de Alcântara, known as the Feast of the Galicians, held around a small 16th-century chapel in the neighbourhood of Alcântara near the Ponte 25 de Abril. Legend has it that the chapel was built by sailors from Galicia in the north of

Parque Eduardo VII for their own celebration. They bring hundreds of kilos of pork and goat kid to roast over open charcoal fires during this day-long festival. It winds up in an evening of *flamenco* dancing, singing and guitar music. The women dress in all their finery, with their hair falling loose to their waists, and with huge, gold earrings and flowing dresses of purple velvet, black ruffled satin or white embroidered silk. Many of the men wear black suits and black felt hats, others are more relaxed, their jackets tossed bullfighter-style over their shoulders. The arrival of the *flamenco* guitarist kicks off the dancing.

Spain in thanks for surviving a shipwreck off this coast in 1549. The ubiquitous grilled sardines and thin pork steaks are eaten to the sound of Spanish castanets and harmonicas and the celebration ends late at night with *fado*.

The gypsies come to town

The feast of São João (St John) on 24 June is far more popular in the northern city of Oporto, but in Lisbon it is the day when gypsies come from all over the country to gather in the central

São Pedro

The last religious occasion of the month, the feast of St Peter, on 29 June, is celebrated the night before in much the same way as the others, with outdoor parties called *arraials*. In older neighbourhoods and in the outskirts of Lisbon, the tradition is to build a good-sized bonfire, sometimes sprinkled with herbs, in the middle of the street. Following this old fertility rite, couples jump over the fires holding hands. On the south bank of the Tejo a ceremony is held to bless the fishing boats.

There are many other festivals in Lisbon (*see Travel Tips*), but the *Festas dos Santos Populares* are undoubtedly the main events. ❏

LEFT: traditional costumes topped off with intricate flower arrangements, balanced with great care.
ABOVE: *Marchas Populares* celebrate the saints.

BULLFIGHTING

*Bullfighting is a hotly debated subject but it remains an intrinsic part of
Portuguese culture – even if the younger generation prefers football*

The impressively named Dom Pedro de Alcântara e Meneses, IV Marquês de Marialva (1713–99) was one of the greatest bullfighters – *cavaleiros* – in Portugal's history. He was Master of the Horse to King José I, author of a classic treatise on horsemanship and the best bullfighter of his day at a time when the

The *tourada*

The Portuguese *tourada* differs from the Spanish in several significant ways. At its heart is the artistry of the bullfighter on horseback. He dresses in an ornately embroidered costume, the style of which had its origin in the 17th century, and always rides a highly trained stallion.

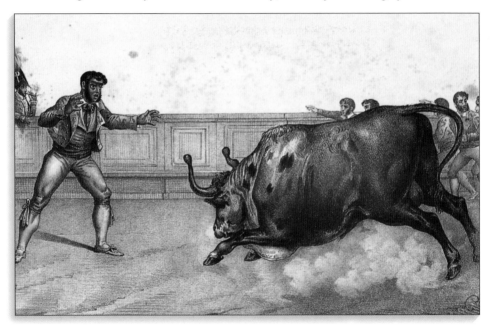

sport (or art, as many Portuguese regard it) was very popular among aristocrats.

Nearly 200 years later the individuals and families involved in bullfighting and the breeding of horses and bulls are still referred to as *Marialvas*, and there is a well-known *fado* song called the *Fado Marialva*.

The *cavaleiro* way of life passes from one generation to another. Most of the families live in the Ribatejo and Alentejo regions, the broad stretch of land from the Lisbon coast to the Spanish border cut by the River Tejo. It is here that the majority of the country's *corridas* (bullrings) are found, the most famous being Campo Pequeno in Lisbon itself.

There are no *picadors*, as there are in Spain, riders who weaken the bull by cutting its neck muscles before the fight begins. The bull is not killed in the ring, although most people who know anything about it agree that it would be a lot less cruel to kill the bull on the spot rather than finishing him off several hours later *(see box, page 93)*.

During a bullfight the *cavaleiro* and his horse perform many special *sortes*, or manoeuvres, at the end of which (if successful) he plunges a dart, either the *farpa* or the shorter *ferro* – which is more difficult to place – into the bull's neck. Compared with the Spanish darts, these wound the bull only superficially. The quality of the *sortes* is generally well understood by a Portuguese audience, who will cheer or jeer as occasion demands. In Portugal the tips of the bull's horns are cut and sheathed in leather; in Spain they are left untouched.

The bull-catchers

Six bulls are used in a Portuguese bullfight, and each performance has two sections, that of the *cavaleiro* and that of the *forcados* (bull-catchers), a team of eight men who stand in a line before the bull and then, as the beast charges them, actually grab and wrestle him to

centage of Arab blood. These animals are brave and extremely adept at rapidly changing manoeuvres. Their temperament is ideal for the job, though they are more difficult to train than those crossbred with English thoroughbreds, which have more strength for racing.

The training of the horse involves the use of the *tourinha*, which is a pair of bull's horns on a bicycle frame; the *cavaleiro* teaches the horse how to move as an assistant pushes the *tourinha* in realistic charges. It takes four or five years to train a horse properly because a rider and horse must be very used to each other before they can face a bull.

a halt. This is the *pega* (bull-catching), and it's an unforgettable sight. The *forcados* are amateurs; they wrestle bulls – and break bones – for the fun of it. *Cavaleiros* are the professionals, and the better ones; they are household names in both Portugal and Spain, and command high prices for performances.

The horses

Only stallions are used, usually the big Peninsula horses, many of which have a large per-

LEFT: a 19th-century lithograph shows a bull-catcher *(forcado)* facing a raging bull.
ABOVE: young bulls in Ribatejo.

A BLOODY DEBATE

The killing of bulls in the ring was stopped in 1933, but many *cavaleiros* would like to finish by killing the bull, as they do in Spain. This may well be because it would make a more dramatic end to the performance, but it is also true that, although the animal is "humanely" killed later on, it suffers added stress in the waiting hours.

Some years ago, Manuel dos Santas finished a sensational performance in Lisbon's Campo Pequeno by killing the bull. The crowd was delighted. Dos Santas was arrested and hauled off to prison, accompanied by most of the audience. Only after a trial and payment of a large fine was he freed, to great rejoicing.

Delicate manoeuvres

The *tourada* starts with opening fanfares by a bugler. Two *peões*, or cape men, stand on either side of the *cavaleiro*, to distract the bull if things go wrong. After the bull has run around the *corrida* a few times, giving the *cavaleiro* an idea of his form, the first task is to place the *farpa*, the long dart. *Farpas* and *ferros* should never be placed unless the animal is charging.

The passes *(sortes)* are split-second manoeuvres in which the bull and horse should have no actual contact – the safety of the *cavaleiro*'s mount is vital. The bull's attacks are *sortes de frente, de dianteira, ao estribo* or *acilhas pas-*

Some *sortes* will involve the *cavaleiro* riding between the bull and barrier, which is highly dangerous and much appreciated by the crowd. If anything goes wrong, the only salvation for horse and rider is the rapid appearance of the *peões*.

The umpire at a bullfight is known as *o inteligente*, "the clever one". During the *tourada* he stands beside the bugler and decides whether more *farpas* or *ferros* should be placed and whether, when the public call for it, music should be played by the bugler. Also, he decides when the *cavaleiro* should finish his performance and the *pega* begin.

sadas, depending on direction. The *poder-a-poder* begins with horse and bull at opposite sides of the ring. They begin to move at the same instant, meeting in the centre. A *recebendo* is where the *cavaleiro* waits as the bull charges and then, at the last instant, moves to the left as he places the *ferro*.

In the *sorte de gaiola* the bull charges as the rider moves across his path; the *cavaleiro* places the dart as the bull nears the horse's flanks. The *sorte de garupa* is where the bull chases the horse around the ring and then the rider turns to place the dart: this move is only favoured by audiences when the bull follows very closely.

Sizing up the bull

Like the *cavaleiro*, the *forcados* also study the form of the bull intently. They need to know the way he attacks the horse and the spot he likes to stay in; whether he keeps his head high or low during the charge; and the distance between him and the horse when he starts to charge. So-called long bulls, those with long necks, are not as strong as short bulls.

When all is ready the bugle is sounded again and the *forcados* enter the arena. The *peões* hold the bull's attention while the eight *forcados* form their line. Then the leading *forcado* claps his hands or shouts or whistles to the bull, which turns and charges. The men stand there as the bull charges. The first one remains motionless until the last moment, when he steps backwards a few paces to reduce the impact.

The instant of impact

In a split second the leading *forcado* throws himself between the bull's horns and clasps his hands together under the animal's neck. His body is thrown feet-first into the air. An instant later the second man in the line clasps the bull's head, then the third, and the next, like a row of falling dominoes, slowing the bull and holding his shoulders and body, with the last man holding the tail. When the bull has been stopped,

Sometimes, if the bull has *farpas* and *ferros* protruding between the horns, the usual *pega* is impossible. Then oxen are let into the arena, and as they and the bull run around, two *forcados* enter. They run beside the bull and one will hold its shoulders and the other its tail. By this method just two men can stop a bull. After the *pega,* the oxen are let in and the bull then follows them out, although sometimes he must be coerced by the *peões* and ropes.

After inspection, the bull is then killed humanely, either straight after the event or the following day, and the meat is sold by a butcher. A bull is allowed to fight only once,

there is a signal from the leader and all let go except the man on the tail.

Although this is the ideal sequence of events, much else can happen in the *pega*. The bull may suddenly twist to one side as it reaches the first man, knocking him down and causing chaos. The bull will then charge anyone in sight until distracted by the capes. There have been fatal accidents – during the 19th century the sport was banned after the deaths of two *forcados*, but it was soon reinstated.

LEFT: a *forcado* is pinned to the ground while his colleagues try to distract the bull.
ABOVE: acknowledging applause from the crowd.

although a few are preserved for breeding or for practice in the riding schools.

When the *tourada* is over, it is time for the public to go to the cafés to discuss the performances, while the *cavaleiros, forcados* and their friends and families go to their *festa,* to relive the day's excitement, drink wine, eat good food and sing the *fados* that celebrate another day in the history of the *tourada.*

Bullfighting provokes strong feelings in Britain and elsewhere, but it is very much part of the Portuguese way of life. If you want to see what all the fuss is about, visit the flamboyant, Moorish-style Campo Pequeno, where the ring seats 8,000 people *(see page 184).* ❑

THE ART OF AZULEJOS

Azulejos, or painted tiles, are the Moors' most lasting legacy. Adapted to suit changing times and fashions, they are still evolving today

Anyone visiting Lisbon, or indeed Portugal, for the first time will be amazed at the abundance and variety of that singular Portuguese art form – the *azulejo*, or painted tile. Lining church walls, embellishing palaces and manorial residences, and gracing gardens and fonts, these ceramic tiles are a delight.

By the 15th century there were various *azulejo*-producing centres in Spain, most notably in Seville. It was not till the middle of the next century that Portugal produced its own. In the 15th and early 16th centuries, *azulejos* from Seville were most lavishly used to line the walls of the Old Cathedral in Coimbra.

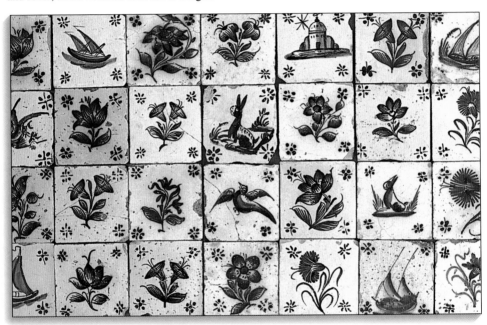

Legacy of the Moors

The *azulejo* was introduced to the Iberian peninsula by the Moors in the 14th century. The word *azulejo*, which was adopted in Portugal from the Spanish, is likewise of Islamic origin. It derives from the Persian word *azul* meaning lapis lazuli – that extraordinary semi-precious blue stone. (The Portuguese and Spanish word for blue – *azul* – obviously derives from the same root.) The Persian *azul* gave rise to *zulej,* meaning polished to a smooth, shiny finish. The term *azulejo* thus has connotations of preciousness, blueness and smoothness, all characteristics that would later come to dominate Portuguese ceramic tiles.

There are relatively few surviving archaic *azulejos* in Portugal. The floor in the chapel at the Royal Palace in Sintra (now the Palácio Nacional, *see page 202*) is the most complete example of the oldest type of *azulejo* technique, where small multicoloured mosaic-like pieces are combined to form complex, interlaced, geometric patterns of Islamic derivation. Unfortunately, the jewel-like effect this achieved has been diminished, as much of the original glaze has been worn away by years of wear and tear.

In the Spanish workshops, this complicated and costly technique was simplified into one where furrows incised in the unbaked clay held the glazes, thus preventing them from running into one another, as in the *azulejos* in the chamber of Afonso VI in the Royal Palace at Sintra. Later the glazes were poured into a relief pattern produced by the impression of a mold on to the damp clay; there are *azulejos* of this type also in the Sintra palace, in the floor of the Arab Room. The patterns remain essentially Islamic in inspiration – usually interlaced or star-like geometric forms.

The majolica technique

The first *azulejo* workshops in Portugal were established around 1550. By then, a major innovation had occurred that was to allow the Por-

Some of the earliest and loveliest of these *majolica azulejos* are the allegorical panels at the Quinta da Bacalhoa in Azeitão, some 40 km (25 miles) south of Lisbon. The finest tiles of this period in Lisbon itself are the Renaissance panels in the Chapel of São Roque in the magnificent church of the same name in Bairro Alto. The foliage, urns and cornucopia are gracefully drawn. The predominant blue, white and yellow subtly set off a central medallion representing one of the miracles performed by São Roque. This panel is signed and dated "Francisco de Matos, 1584". Unfortunately, no other work by de Matos is known.

tuguese *azulejo* to become the rich, varied and original means of expression we know today. This innovation, known as the *majolica* technique, reached Portugal from Italy, by way of Flanders and Spain. The unbaked clay tile is covered in a white glaze that easily accepts brush strokes in other glazes; it is not necessary to separate the colours by molds or grooves. The geometric forms gave way to expansive, organic drawing.

PRECEDING PAGES: section of a tiled Lisbon scene from a wall in the Museu Nacional do Azulejo.
LEFT: blue and white *azulejos* were very popular.
ABOVE: 17th-century *azulejos*.

A LIVING ART

An early example of the painterly freedom achieved by the *majolica* technique is the panel of *Nossa Senhora da Vida* dating from around 1580, which is now in the Museu Nacional do Azulejo, housed in the Convento da Madre de Deus. The composition is in the shape of an altarpiece, with the luminous, coloured glazes used literally to make a painting on tiles, depicting with great refinement the Adoration of the Shepherds in the centre and the Annunciation at the top.

This is just one of many reasons to visit this stunning museum, which traces the development of *azulejos* right up to the present day *(see page 144)*.

In addition to these sophisticated *azulejos* produced by masters and their schools of apprentices, a simpler type of *azulejo* also became popular – single-coloured tiles applied on to the wall in chequered patterns (usually blue and white or green and white) of great simplicity and decorative strength. Here again, there's a handsome example to be found in the Palácio Nacional in Sintra, in the Sala dos Cisnes (Swan Room).

Cultural isolation

In the 17th century, Portugal's loss of independence to Spain and the subsequent economic

along with so much else, in the devastating earthquake of 1755, but one very fine example survived in the chapel of São Sebastião in Paço de Lumiar, a suburb to the north of Lisbon, where the carpet pattern is punctuated at intervals by the symbolic motif of St Sebastian – a crown pierced by three arrows.

Any visitor who is really interested in the art and development of *azulejos* will find a trip to Évora, 150 km (95 miles) inland, well worthwhile *(see page 220)*. In this lovely city a number of the churches, such as Igreja de Espírito Santo, Santa Antão and São João Evangelista, all have their superb "carpet-lined" walls.

crisis led to greater cultural isolation. Artisans' workshops replaced the work of masters and apprentices. The flamboyant painted panels gave way to more austere decoration, usually in the form of the so-called ceramic "carpets" *(tapetes)* which were vast expanses of polychrome *azulejos* lining entire walls and vaults.

A pattern formed on a square of four, 16 or 36 tiles was repeated many times over, and enclosed in a decorative border. These carpet panels were especially used in churches, often in conjunction with carved and gilded woodwork and paintings.

There are not many of these to be seen in Lisbon today, as the majority were destroyed,

Influences from the New World

Altar frontals dating from the 17th century – such as that at Nossa Senhora da Graça in Lisbon, with its rich, warm tones – commonly reproduce the effects of sumptuously brocaded textiles. Most of these *azulejo* frontals include exotic elements – peacocks proudly disporting themselves on delicately wrought boughs, for example. This exoticism reflected the influences of Indian fabric designs, which had been brought back to Portugal by mariners on their voyages of discovery.

The end of the 17th century was a period of great change. The economic recuperation led once again to a period of artistic expansion. The severe tile-carpets gave way to a new surge in figurative *azulejos* of great variety and imagination. In the church of Santo Amaro to the west of Lisbon, the scrolls and foliage and charming *putti* derive from ceiling painting of the same period.

Often, in secular settings, playful and ironic elements make a naughty appearance: for example, monkeys and other animals whose frolics mask a biting social criticism. In one particularly fine panel at the Museu Nacional do Azulejo *(see page 144)*, a leopard is looking at itself in a mirror with a mixture of surprise and vanity.

Portuguese ceramics were strongly influenced by Chinese blue-and-white porcelain of the Ming Dynasty, so that by the end of the 17th century, blue and white was synonymous with quality.

Domestic Dutch tiles

More typically Dutch than the large panels are the single tiles with graciously drawn animals, flowers, chimerical allegories, boats, landscapes and horsemen – joyful images made mostly for domestic use. These were also imported to Portugal and the idea was adopted by national workshops. One pleasing example is in the kitchen of the palace that now houses

Narratives from the Netherlands

The appearance of Dutch tiles on the Portuguese market, due to the strong trading links between these two countries, had a marked influence on the national style. The monumental Dutch narrative tile panels in blue and white, produced, curiously enough, principally for the large Portuguese market, stimulated the Portuguese to produce their own narrative panels enclosed within foliate borders or above decorative horizontal panels. Both Dutch and

LEFT: detailed scenes of daily life were depicted in tiles in the 19th century.
ABOVE: other pictures were allegorical.

the Museu da Cidade – Lisbon's City Museum *(see page 181)* – where individual tiles representing animals and plants surround a delightful, naïve representation of a slave woman cleaning fish. These popular tiles continue to be copied by artisans and manufacturers today for use in private homes, often in kitchens.

Portuguese production

By the first decade of the 18th century, Portuguese production of blue-and-white *azulejos* was flourishing and Dutch importation had ceased. Superb early examples of Portuguese *azulejos* are to be found in the splendid Palácio dos Marquéses de Fronteira *(see page 180)* –

in the Battle Room with its *azulejos* depicting various scenes from the War of Restoration which led to the Portuguese independence in 1640; on the patio panels representing the liberal arts; or in the breathtaking Kings' Gallery which overlooks the garden.

The gold and diamonds that reached Portugal from Brazil made the reign of João V a period of great opulence. It was João who commissioned the most grandiose projects in Lisbon and its surroundings – from the vast convent and palace at Mafra to the city's famous aqueduct. The king is portrayed in an *azulejo* portrait (c. 1710) in the majestic church of

São Vicente de Fora to the east of the Alfama – a repository of magnificent blue-and-white *azulejos* of this period.

Secular decorations

The social and political upheavals in the early 19th century resulted in a drastic decrease in the production of *azulejos*. With the dissolution of the monastic orders in 1834, a large part of the incentive for and funding of ambitious *azulejo* projects fell away. But even the most casual stroll around Lisbon will show that the *azulejo* continued to have a secular use, most notably in façades.

THE ROYAL WORKSHOP

The earthquake of 1755 was followed by the Pombaline reconstruction of the capital, and rapid production of *azulejos* was necessitated by the repair work being done on many old buildings and the construction of new ones. At the Royal Workshop of Rato (Real Fábrica do Rato), established in 1767 to keep up with these needs, high-quality *azulejos* were produced with speed and efficiency. Many tiles from the end of José I's reign and that of Maria I were manufactured there.

During the reign of José I (1750–77), *azulejos*, like other art forms, were marked by the rococo taste for fanciful flourishes, a lightness of touch and an abundance of

curling, curving forms. Colour was reintroduced, sometimes delicately offsetting the predominant blue and white as in the *Dance of Salomé* (*circa* 1755) on the southern wall of the garden at the Quinta dos Azulejos in Paço de Lumiar. This mansion (now a nursery school) has an extraordinary garden with pillars, benches and walls all lined in *azulejos* showing mythological scenes, plants and animals.

During the reign of Maria I (1777–92), the style of *azulejos*, ever adaptable, complied with the general neoclassical taste of the time. Typical were bouquets, and garlands, ribbons and plumes were all arrayed with great symmetry and sobriety, on pale backgrounds.

In the second half of the century, there was a resurgence of the tradition. All over the city, 19th-century *azulejos* in a variety of motifs and colours grace the façades of little shops and private residences. The tiled façade incorporating the allegorical figures of Commerce and Industry at the Lamego Workshop, Cerâmica Viúva Lamego, in Largo do Intendente Pina Manique, is justly famous. This was only one of the numerous *azulejo* workshops that opened after the Rato Workshop *(see box)* closed down in 1835. There's a good showroom there today (take the metro to the Intendente stop) and they will make tiles to order.

Campo Grande is dedicated to his work) was the central figure of this movement. He founded the ceramic workshop of Caldas de Rainha about 80 km (50 miles) from Lisbon. In addition to his extraordinary jugs, plates and vases with their caricatured human and animal figures, he was responsible for relief-surfaced *azulejos* of the highest quality and great originality. Some are inspired by Moorish and Manueline *azulejos*, others are graceful Art Nouveau floral and bird motifs – such as the façade of a bakery in Campo Ourique.

By the early 20th century, the manufacture of *azulejos* had passed its heyday, although

The fashion for decorating private houses with *azulejos* produced semi-industrially, with the motif stencilled rather than hand-painted, was introduced at this time by Portuguese who had emigrated to Brazil then returned to Portugal. It is still a widespread custom today.

Romantic revival

The romantic movement, which expressed a nostalgia for the past, had its effect on *azulejos,* too. Rafael Bordalo Pinheiro (a museum in

artists were commissioned to design *azulejo* panels for public places during the second half of the century. The styles are as numerous and varied as the artists themselves. The future of the *azulejo* in Portugal, however, now remains uncertain, as there has been a drastic decrease in large-scale public commissions. But there are contemporary artists creating fresh and innovative designs.

The falling away of this tradition would be a great loss. At their best, in their richness and variety, in the colourful note they introduce to outdoor settings, and their enhancement of religious and secular spaces alike, *azulejos* are an unsurpassable means of decoration. ❏

LEFT: a modern *azulejo* panel in Lisbon's Belém Metro station.
ABOVE: a modern tile picture with a sardonic twist.

ART AND ARCHITECTURE

*From ancient, sacred paintings and religious monuments to the gleaming new
Expo pavilions and Metro art, Lisbon has a rich artistic heritage*

The 15th century was the first great age of Portuguese painting. By far the most brilliant contribution was the introduction of Flemish-influenced, painted altarpieces called retables (*retábulos* in Portuguese). In 1428, the Flemish master Jan van Eyck was invited to the court of João I to paint a portrait of the Infanta Dona Isabel, future wife of Philip the Good (1396–1467), Duke of Burgundy.

During the reign of João II (1481–95), when voyages of discovery occupied the energies of the nation, there was a lull in artistic activity. But with the discovery of the sea route to India and consequent prosperity, painted *retábulos* again became a dominant form of expression. Many of the altarpieces in Portuguese churches were Flemish, and some can still be seen today.

The polyptych of St Vincent

The most outstanding *retábulo* of the 15th-century Portuguese School is the polyptych of São Vicente (St Vincent) attributed to Nuno Gonçalves, in the Museu Nacional de Arte Antiga *(see page 146)*. The mystery that enshrouds this work has increased its aura. The panels were lost for centuries, and there are conflicting accounts of their reappearance at the end of the 19th century. No sooner were they cleaned and hung than controversy arose as to the identity of their author. A touch of drama was added when one eminent scholar committed suicide after a dispute concerning two documents that radically altered the direction of the research. The documents were later proved false.

The theme of the polyptych has also given rise to dispute. Some see in it the veneration of the Infante Santo Fernando, the uncle of Afonso V, who died at the hands of the Moors in 1481. But it is generally thought to represent the adoration of St Vincent, the patron saint of the kingdom and of Lisbon. The important point

---

LEFT: the polyptych of São Vicente by Nuno Gonçalves.
RIGHT: Henry the Navigator, from the polyptych.

of departure for scholars was the identification of the Infante Henrique (Prince Henry the Navigator) to the left of the saint in the third panel from the left.

The panels, working from left to right, are known as the Panel of the Monks (of the Cistercian Order), the Fishermen, the Infante,

the Archbishop, the Calvary and finally, the Relic Panel. The work's real genius and originality lie in the exquisite portraiture and its masterful attention to realistic detail.

Manueline style

The local features that Portuguese painting maintained during João II's reign gave rise to what is known as the "Luso-Flemish" style. Manueline painting evolved during the next king's reign, that of Manuel I (1495–1521), although this style is really more closely associated with architecture *(see page 109)*. It is characterised by a fine sense of portraiture, brilliant, gem-like colours, a growing interest in the naturalistic depiction of architecture and landscapes, and, increasingly, with expressive detail.

During this period, painting was often the collaborative effort of a master and his assistants, which makes attribution extremely difficult. Often paintings are known as the products of particular workshops. The two principal workshops were those of Jorge Afonso in Lisbon, and of Vasco Fernandes in Viseu. Afonso was appointed royal painter in 1508: documents identify various projects with which he and his workshop were involved, but none shows his direct responsibility.

Grão Vasco

Vasco Fernandes, better known as Grão (the "Great"), was the most celebrated of the Manueline painters. His works are noteworthy for their emotional strength and drama, and are characterised by a denser application of paint than that used by the Flemish masters. The faces in his works tend to be less stylised and more expressive, and were probably drawn from local models. However, so many paintings, of so many styles, are attributed to the master of Manueline painting that he would have had to have lived more than one very productive lifetime in order to have completed them all.

The 16th and 17th centuries

The Renaissance was resisted by Portuguese artists and is mainly represented by those from abroad. Mannerism employed many elements of Renaissance classicism but the sense of an ordered, harmonious whole gives way to an exaggeration of those defining elements.

The 17th century saw portrait painting flourishing in Portugal as elsewhere in Europe. The most celebrated portraitist of the period was Domingos Vieira (1600–78), known as "the Dark" to distinguish him from his contemporary, Domingos Vieira Serrão.

His nickname stemmed from his predilection, in works such as the portrait of Isabel de

Moura (in the Museu de Arte Antiga in Lisbon), to make dramatic contrasts between deep, velvety backgrounds and rich, creamy whites of ruffs and headgear.

Neoclassicism

Two outstanding painters emerged during the 18th century: Domingos António Sequeira (1768–1837) and Francisco Vieira, known as Vieira Portuense (1765–1805). The two met in Rome, the essential venue for any serious artist. Vieira Portuense also spent some time in London, where the Roman influence was tempered by that of Sir Joshua Reynolds (1723–92).

stylistically freer and more individualistic, with Goyaesque contrasts of dark and light, rapid brushstrokes and sudden bursts of luminous white. The final phase of Sequeira's work corresponds to his visits to Paris and Rome. These late works show great painterliness and luminosity. The four cartoons for paintings in the Palmela collections, now in the Museu Nacional de Arte Antiga, are some of his most inspired, mystical works.

Romanticism and Naturalism

Romanticism was a form of escapism into medieval, oriental and mystical realms. Heroic,

The work of Sequeira is a study in the transition from neoclassicism to Romanticism. He was nominated court painter in 1802 by João VI, and commissioned to provide paintings for the rebuilt Palácio Ajuda. Political turbulence forced Sequeira to emigrate to France, and then to Italy, where he died.

His work can be divided into three stages: the first, largely academic and neoclassical in inspiration, corresponds to the first period he spent in Rome. The second stage (1807–23) is

religious and ceremonial works gave way to more intimate and personal pieces. The mid-19th century also corresponded to the rise of the middle class. Courtly art, it seemed, had breathed its last. Similarly, the idea that art expresses timelessly valid principles gradually gave way to the subjectivist and individualist notions that continue to hold sway today.

With the death of Sequeira, the Romantic movement in Portugal underwent a change: nature became the new religion. Tomás da Anunciação became the foremost romantic landscapist of his generation.

Portraiture became the art form of the bourgeoisie *par excellence*, and also gave increasing

LEFT: *O Inferno*, by an anonymous artist, in the Museu Nacional de Arte Antiga.
ABOVE: a noble family portrayed by Sequeira.

emphasis to the sitter's inner life. In Miguel Luipi's *Sousa Martins' Mother* (in the Museu do Chiado) the illumination of the hands and face, the most expressive parts of the body, conveys a sense of pensive dignity.

At the end of the 19th century, Romanticism gave way to Naturalism. Silva Porto, José Malhoa and Henrique Posão were the foremost Naturalist painters. But in stark contrast to their luminous outdoor scenes, Columbano Bordalo Pinheiro (1857–1929), considered the Grand Master of Portuguese 19th-century art, continued in the tradition of studio painting.

His brother, Rafael Bordalo Pinheiro, was

perhaps even more popular in his day. A celebrated ceramicist, he was also known for his biting political caricatures. There is a small museum dedicated to his work in Campo Grande *(see page 182)*.

Modernism

The artistic ferment that gripped Europe and America in the first decades of the 20th century arrived late, or in diluted form, in Portugal. The political turmoil that ended the monarchy in 1910 did not provide a propitious context for an artistic revolution, and there was then a window of only some 15 years before Salazar's authoritarian regime closed the door to external cultural influences.

But some ideas took root. In 1911, the Museu Nacional de Arte Contemporãnea was founded in Lisbon (it is now part of the Museu do Chiado, *see page 145*); and the first Salon of Humorists represented a move away from conventional salon painting.

One of the most daring and interesting of this generation of painters was the Cubist Amadeo Souza-Cardoso, whose premature death in 1918 was a great loss. Many of his works are now in the Centro de Arte Moderno at the Fundação Calouste Gulbenkian *(see page 178)*.

The military regime, initiated in 1926 and led by António de Oliveira Salazar from 1933 to 1974, actively prevented contact with any outside stimulus, so all the artistic and intellectual exchange necessary to keep the arts alive during these years had to be clandestine.

The return to democracy in 1974, however, breathed new energy into the arts and an outburst of fervent activity echoed the sense of exhilaration felt throughout the country after long years of repression and censorship.

Portugal's artists now have free access to external ideas, and the age-old conflict between the imported and the indigenous still provokes lively debate. Among contemporary artists, Paula Rego is one of the brightest stars, although she no longer lives in her home country. A collection of her powerful work can be seen at the Centro de Arte Moderna, part of the Fundação Calouste Gulbenkian and in the commercial Galeria III in Campo Grande.

Some of the most innovative work today, sometimes by young unknowns but mostly by recognised artists, can be seen decorating Lisbon's Metro stations *(see page 179)*.

THE VOICE OF A GENERATION

One of the brightest lights among the generation represented in the 1911 Salon of Humorists was José Almada Negreiros (1893–1970), one of the most charismatic and energetic cultural figures in Portugal. His early caricatures drew the attention of the poet Fernando Pessoa who became his friend, and whose posthumously painted portrait now hangs in the poet's old home, with a replica in the Gulbenkian Foundation. One of Negreiros's most important commissions was for the frescoes at the port of Lisbon, painted from 1943 to 1948 *(see page 147)*. His last major project was the mural for the lobby of the Gulbenkian Foundation.

ARCHITECTURE

Portugal's unusual geographical position, cut off from Europe by Spain on one side, facing the New World on the other, is reflected in its architecture. Its architects have always looked outside for influence and affirmation, and local traditions have blended harmoniously with imported ideas.

Romanesque

The story of Portuguese architecture begins in the Romanesque period of the 12th century, when nearly all important buildings were religious. This was when Portugal was (largely) reconquered from the Moors, and Christianity was strongly felt. The construction of cathedrals followed the path of reconquest from Braga to Porto, and south to Coimbra, Lamego, Lisbon and Evora.

Portuguese Romanesque is one of simple, dramatically stark forms, whose sturdiness is frequently explained by the need for fortification against the continued threat of Moorish or Castilian invasion. This is enhanced in Lisbon's cathedral by the crenellated façade towers.

The construction of Romanesque churches is based on semi-circular arches and barrel vaults, a cruciform plan and a solid, almost sculptural sense of form which allows for a play of light and shade. This sobriety is accentuated by the paucity of decoration, which is frequently reduced to the capitals of columns and the archivolts surrounding the portals.

Gothic

In France, new methods of construction involving pointed arches and ribbed vaults allowed for lighter, taller architectural forms. As the main weight of the building was now borne outside at fixed points by flying buttresses, the walls could be pierced at frequent intervals. The light filtering into these gothic interiors became a metaphor for Divine Light, replacing the Romanesque emphasis on Mystery.

The first building in Portugal to use these new construction methods was the majestic church of the abbey of Alcobaça, commissioned by Afonso Henriques. With its great height and elegant, unadorned white interior

LEFT: Fernando Pessoa by Almada Negreiros.
RIGHT: an ornate neo-Manueline window at the Palácio da Pena, Sintra.

bathed in a milky light, Alcobaça is one of the most serene and beautiful churches in Portugal. Begun in 1178 and consecrated in 1222, its plan echoes that of Clairvaux, the seat of the Cistercian Order in Burgundy.

The apogee of the national gothic style came after the Portuguese armies defeated the invading Castilians at the Battle of Aljubarrota. In fulfilment of a religious vow, King João I commissioned the construction in 1388 of the Monastery of Santa Maria da Vitória, better known as Batalha, which simply means battle.

The stylistic influence of Batalha is seen in various churches throughout the country, such

as the now ruined Convento do Carmo in Lisbon, begun at the end of the 14th century.

The Manueline style

The exhilaration of Portugal's overseas discoveries had a marked effect on art, architecture and literature. The term "Manueline" was first used in the 19th century to refer to the reign of Manuel I (1495–1521), during which Vasco da Gama reached the coast of India (1498), and Afonso de Albuquerque conquered the Indian city of Goa (1510). The name is now used more often to refer to certain stylistic features predominant during the Avis dynasty (1383–1580), especially in architecture.

Manueline architecture does not have major innovative structural features: its real strength lies in its decoration, the exuberance of which reflects the optimism and wealth of the period. Inspired by the voyages to the New World, it unites naturalistic maritime themes with Moorish elements and heraldic motifs.

The Monastery of Santa Maria de Belém, better known as Jerónimos *(see page 148)*, is one of the great *hallenkirchen* of the period – that is, a church whose aisles are as high as its nave. Perhaps the most notable feature of Manueline architecture is the copious carving that surrounds portals and semi-circular

Baroque and rococo

The baroque style uses a basic classical vocabulary, but strives for dissolution of form rather than definition. This obliteration of clear contours – by brushstrokes in painting and optical illusion in architecture – is enhanced by a preference for depth over plane. These features all stress the grand, the dynamic and the dramatic.

The first truly baroque Portuguese church is Santa Engrácia in Lisbon, with its dome and undulating interior walls. Begun in 1682, it was not completed until 1966. The richness of the coloured marble lining the walls and floor, the dynamic interior space and the sumptuousness

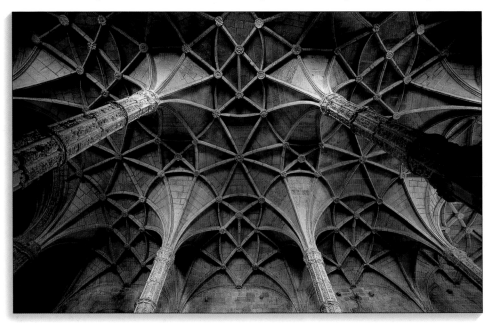

windows. The imposing southern portal of Jerónimos, together with the glorious interior, deserve the acclaim the building receives.

Renaissance and mannerism

The Renaissance in Portugal, in architecture as in art, was best represented by outsiders. Foreign sculptors were invited to decorate the portals and façades of Manueline buildings, introducing elements of Renaissance harmony and order within the general flamboyance of the decorative scheme. The coincidence of Manueline and Renaissance influences, and the later addition of mannerist forms, explains the hybrid style prevalent during this period.

of the edifice are typical of construction during the reign of João V (1706–50).

The wealth from Brazil and the extravagance of João V made this a period of great opulence. João commissioned the Chapel of St John in the church of São Roque. It was built in Rome, blessed by the Pope, shipped to Lisbon and reassembled in the church, where it shines with bronzes, mosaics, marble and precious stones.

Lisbon's Basilica da Estrêla, dating from the 1780s and commissioned by Maria I, was the last church to be built in the baroque style. Architectural styles had moved on and, with the dissolution of the monasteries in 1834, religious architecture lost its privileged position.

In the rococo style, drama was replaced by fantasy, and an emphasis on flourish and ornament. After the 1755 earthquake, Carlos Mardel designed many of the city's public fountains in a toned-down version of rococo. Mardel was also responsible for part of the Aqueduto das Águas Livres, which withstood the earthquake and is still a familiar landmark *(see page 175)*.

Pombal and neoclassicism

Although it took place at much the same time, the Pombaline style of the reconstruction of Lisbon – named after the Marquês de Pombal – is closer to classical than rococo. Pombaline at

After the Palácio do Ajuda the only other notable public building constructed in Lisbon in the first half of the 19th century was the Teatro Dona Maria II (1843), with its white, Greco-Roman façade.

Modern styles

The best-known and most typical examples of architecture under Salazar (1932–68) are the Monument to the Discoveries in Belém, the statue of Cristo Rei on the south bank of the river, and the Ponte 25 de Abril. The Museu Calouste Gulbenkian, opened in 1969, was also a product of this time. During the 1980s, the

its most typical can be seen in the arcades and great arch of the Praça Comercio.

The neoclassical style, with its emphasis on Greco-Roman colonnades and porticoes, was introduced to Lisbon at the same time. The first neoclassical building was the Teatro Nacional de São Carlos (1792). The style received court approval when used for the Palácio do Ajuda (begun in 1802) after a fire destroyed the wooden building that had been the temporary royal residence since the earthquake.

LEFT: the ceiling of the Mosteiro dos Jerónimos.
ABOVE: station architecture: the 19th-century Estação do Rossio and the ultra-modern Estação do Oriente.

post-modernist work of Tomás Taveira made an impact, particularly his striking pink towers at the Amoreiras Centre.

The Centro Cultural de Belém, designed in the early 1990s for the Portuguese presidency of the EU, was controversial at first, but is now accepted and appreciated. Expo '98 (now the Parque das Nações) produced some stunning modern pavilions. The architect responsible for the Oceanário was an American, Peter Chermayeff, while the striking Pavilhão de Portugal was the work of Álvaro de Siza Vieira, Portugal's current architectural star, who was largely responsible for the rebuilding of the Chiado district after the terrible 1988 fire. ❏

PLACES

A detailed guide to the city and outlying areas, with principal sites clearly cross-referenced by number to the maps

L isbon is an extremely satisfying city to visit. It is sufficiently off the beaten track to offer the visitor a pleasant feeling of discovery, yet accessible enough to make it a short-break destination – although such a break leaves most people wanting to come back for more.

The chapters that follow will guide you around the unmissable sights, taking you on the trams, funiculars and lifts for which the city is famous, and to the *miradouros* (belvederes or viewpoints) that give stunning views across the town and the River Tejo. We shall explore the shopping streets of the Baixa, laid out by the Marquês de Pombal after the Great Earthquake of 1755, and visit the churches, cafés and squares of the Bairro Alto.

Another suggested route will take the visitor to the imposing Castelo de São Jorge, and back through the narrow, winding streets of the picturesque neighbourhood of Alfama. A whole chapter is devoted to the Tejo riverside, which alone could keep a visitor occupied for several days, from the spanking new Parque das Nações in the east to the stunning Mosteiro dos Jerónimos to the west.

The northern part of the city is not so well known to visitors, but it contains some attractive parks and gardens and a number of interesting museums, including the Museu Calouste Gulbenkian, home of the Armenian oil magnate's vast art collection.

The remaining chapters suggest excursions to the resort of Estoril, the palaces at Sintra and Queluz, the beaches of the Arrábida Peninsula, the ancient city of Évora, and the great monasteries of Alcobaça and Batalha to the north, all within easy reach of the city and well worth seeing for any visitor with a few days to spare.

En route you will make your own discoveries, sample the local food, listen to the soulful strains of *fado*, talk to the local people, and begin to realise why travellers have been falling under Lisbon's spell for centuries.   ❏

PRECEDING PAGES: the cathedral towers above the rooftops; a quiet moment in the Praça dos Restauradores; the glorious façade of Mosteiro dos Jerónimos.
LEFT: feeding the pigeons in Praça do Comércio.

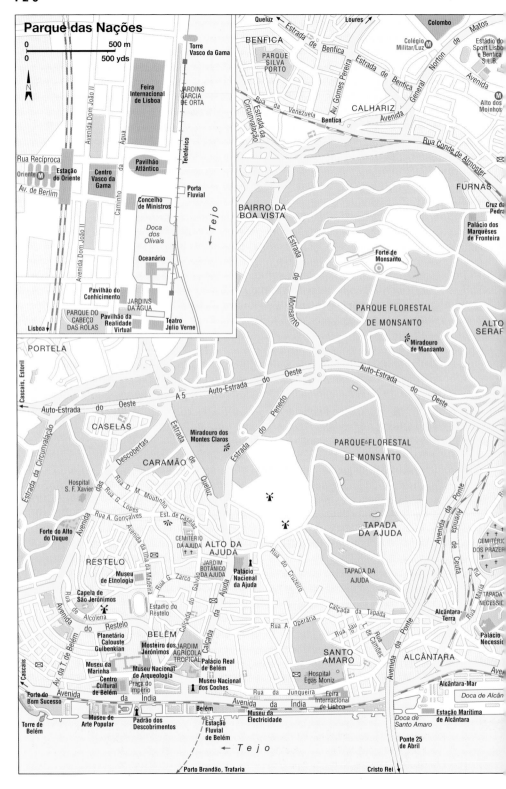

Parque das Nações

0 — 500 m
0 — 500 yds

N

Torre Vasco da Gama

Feira Internacional de Lisboa

JARDINS GARCIA DE ORTA

Avenida Dom João II

Água

Teleférico

Rua Recíproca

Oriente M
Estação do Oriente
Av. de Berlim

Centro Vasco da Gama

Pavilhão Atlântico

Caminho da

Porta Fluvial

Concelho de Ministros

Doca dos Olivais

Tejo →

Avenida Dom João II

Oceanário

Pavilhão do Conhecimento

JARDINS DA ÁGUA

PARQUE DO CABEÇO DAS ROLAS
Pavilhão da Realidade Virtual

Teatro Júlio Verne

Lisboa ↓

PORTELA

Cascais, Estoril

Auto-Estrada do Oeste

Estrada da Circunvalação

CASELAS

Descobertas

CARAMÃO

Hospital S. F. Xavier

Rua D. M. Moutinho
Rua G. Lopes
Rua A. Gonçalves

Est. de Caselas

Forte do Alto do Duque

Avenida da Ilha da Madeira

CEMITÉRIO DA AJUDA
ALTO DA AJUDA

RESTELO

Museu de Etnologia

JARDIM BOTÂNICO DA AJUDA
Palácio Nacional da Ajuda

Rua G. Zarco

Rua do Cruzeiro

Capela de São Jerónimos

Avenida do Restelo

Estádio do Restelo

Calçada da Ajuda

BELÉM

Planetário Calouste Gulbenkian

Mosteiro dos Jerónimos
JARDIM AGRICOLA TROPICAL

Museu da Marinha

Museu Nacional de Arqueologia

Centro Cultural de Belém

Praça do Império

Palácio Real de Belém

Museu Nacional dos Coches

Forte do Bom Sucesso

Avenida da Índia

Belém

Rua da Junqueira

Torre de Belém

Museu de Arte Popular

Padrão dos Descobrimentos

Estação Fluvial de Belém

Avenida da Índia

Museu da Electricidade

Tejo →

Porto Brandão, Trafaria

Queluz
Loures
Colombo
Matos

BENFICA

Estrada de Benfica

Colégio Militar/Luz M

Estádio do Sport Lisboa e Benfica S.L.B.

PARQUE SILVA PORTO

Estrada de Benfica

Norton

Avenida

Rua da Venezuela

Av. Gomes Pereira

General

CALHARIZ

Alto dos Moinhos M

Estrada da Circunvalação

Benfica

Avenida

Rua Conde de Almoster

FURNAS

Cruz da Pedra

BAIRRO DA BOA VISTA

Estrada de

Palácio dos Marquêses de Fronteira

Forte de Monsanto

PARQUE FLORESTAL DE MONSANTO

ALTO SERAF

Miradouro de Monsanto

Estrada de Monsanto

Auto-Estrada do Oeste

A 5
Auto-Estrada do Oeste

Estrada do Penedo

Miradouro dos Montes Claros

Estrada de

Queluz

PARQUE FLORESTAL DE MONSANTO

TAPADA DA AJUDA

TAPADA DA AJUDA

Avenida da Ponte

CEMITÉRIO DOS PRAZER

TAPADA NECESSI

Calçada da Tapada

Rua A. Operária

SANTO AMARO

Hospital Egas Moniz

Alcântara-Terra

Palácio Necessi

ALCÂNTARA

Avenida da Ponte

Alcântara-Mar

Doca de Alcân

Estação Marítima de Alcântara

Doca de Santo Amaro

Ponte 25 de Abril

Cristo Rei ↓

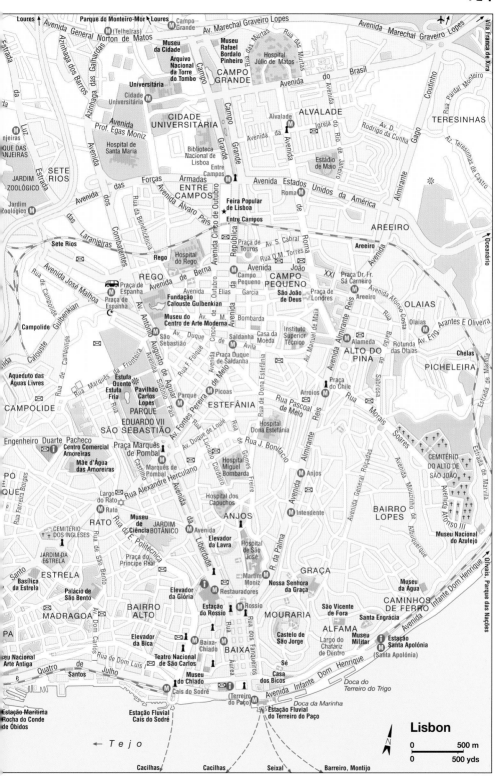

Lisbon

| 0 | 500 m |
| 0 | 500 yds |

BAIXA AND BAIRRO ALTO

A gentle wander through the streets of the lower town, then up an ornate elevator to visit a ruined convent and a stunning church, stopping for coffee at two of Lisbon's most atmospheric cafés

Map on page 124

T he city of Lisbon is an extraordinary sight. On a clear evening with the strong late sun reflecting off the tiled roofs, it looks just as it must have looked 200 years ago. Seven hills make up the old town, although they are difficult to count, as they have long since been blanketed with buildings and because many other hills surround them. On the heights of these hills are a number of belvederes, or *miradouros*, that offer good overviews of Lisbon, its gracious squares, its narrow streets and hidden delights.

Lisbon sites fall rather neatly into four geographical sections. There's the Baixa, the low-lying land running back from the Praço do Comércio and the western hill of the Bairro Alto; the main part of the old town, taking in the delightful neighbourhood of the Alfama; the riverside, which borders these two districts; and the city's northern heights.

Welcome to Lisbon

Before starting any tour of Lisbon it is worth going to the state-of-the-art **Lisboa Welcome Centre ❶** (open 9am–9pm), a tourist office enterprise located in a tastefully refurbished classical building on the corner of Praça do Comércio and Rua do Arsenal. Here, visitors can find out everything they want to know about the Portuguese capital, from the information post "Ask Me Lisboa". You can also buy the Lisboa tourist card – which offers substantial discounts on transport, museums and other venues – a shopping card and a restaurant card, all designed to help you enjoy your visit.

The Welcome Centre also houses a café, a tobacconist/newsagent and cigar shop; a store offering traditional Portuguese products from the regions, including wines, cheeses, olive oil and sausages; a shop dedicated to Portuguese fashion and accessories; a spacious exhibition gallery and a restaurant.

Praça do Comércio

This chapter encompasses the Baixa and Bairro Alto areas, for which the logical starting point for a tour is the lovely **Praça do Comércio ❷**. This large, gracious square lies directly on the harbour. It is known locally as **Terreiro do Paço**, Palace Terrace, in memory of the 16th-century royal palace that stood to one side of it until the earthquake of 1755. The neoclassical pink arcades that line three sides are the epitome of Pombaline Lisbon, the city that was rebuilt under the Marquês de Pombal, prime minister at the time of the great earthquake.

In the centre of the square stands a bronze equestrian statue of José I, who ruled Portugal during and after the earthquake. It was created by Machado de

LEFT: the Convento do Carmo.
BELOW: Pombal's great archway.

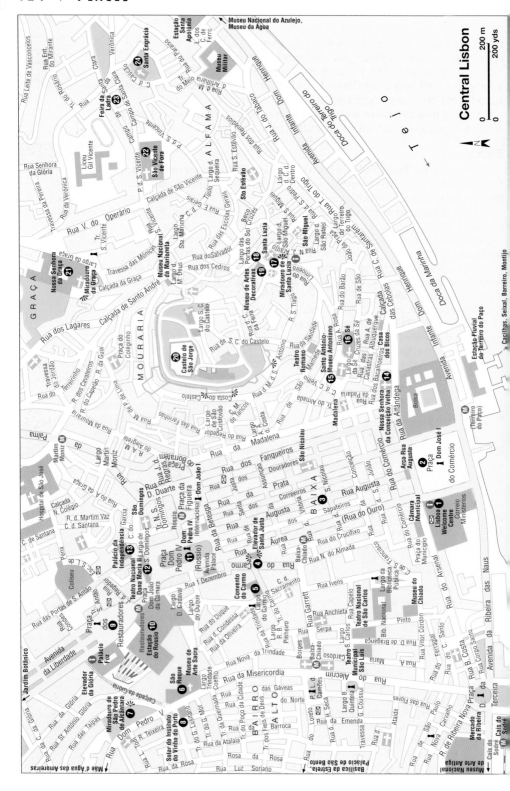

Central Lisbon

Castro, Portugal's best-known sculptor. The plaque you see of Pombal on the statue was removed for many years following the prime minister's exile, and was only replaced in 1833. It was in the northwest corner of this square, on 1 February 1908, that King Carlos I and his heir, Luís Felipe, were assassinated as they drove in an open landau.

For a long time the square was used as a car park but now it is once again a delightful open space, as well as the starting point for many tram routes.

Map on page 124

Baixa

To the north of the Praça do Comércio is the **Baixa ❸**, the lower town, which forms a perfect grid around three main streets, all built by Pombal. Its central avenue is **Rua Augusta**, which leads from the huge triumphal arch in the square – built to commemorate the reconstruction of the city after the earthquake – to the Praça do Rossio.

To the west of Rua Augusta is **Rua do Ouro** (Gold Street); to the east is **Rua da Prata** (Silver Street). The names refer to the goods that were traditionally sold here and although the area is still filled with jewellers, the original divisions have faded. The parallel Rua dos Sapateiros (Shoe Street – although there are not many shoe shops here today) is linked to Rossio Square by the **Arco do Bandeira**, an arch that is considered to be one of the finest examples of Pombaline architecture. This grid of traffic-free streets with their shops and pavement cafés is an enjoyable place to stroll. While you are here, you may choose to get one of the pavement shoe cleaners to give your shoes the shine of their life or, in winter and spring, sample some roasted chestnuts, served in small paper cones.

Bairro Alto

The neighbourhood of Bairro Alto, or "upper quarter" of Lisbon and one of its oldest sections, rises just to the west of the Baixa. Here there are several interesting sights close to one another. By far the best way to get up the hill is by riding the vertical, 45-metre (150-ft) **Elevador de Santa Justa ❹**. This whimsical iron structure with its ornate, wood-panelled lift cars, was designed by the French engineer Raoul Mesnier de Ponsard, a disciple of Gustave Eiffel, in 1899.

At the top of the lift a spiral stairase takes you further up to a viewing platform and a small café/restaurant with fantastic views over the city and the Tejo.

A walkway connects the lift with the Largo do Carmo; it looks down on the rebuilt Chiado district and, to the right, runs under a flying buttress of the church of the **Convento do Carmo ❺** (open Apr–Sept 10am–6pm, Oct–Mar 10am–1pm, 2–5pm; admission charge). It used to be possible to cross this walkway, but now the entrance is barred because it is unsafe. The remarkable ruin of the church has recently been extensively restored and reopened to the public.

It is surely one of Lisbon's most striking sights. It was built by Nuno Álvares Pereira, João I's stalwart young general who aided him in 1385 in the Battle of Aljubarrota in 1385; he spent the last eight years of his life in the monastery. When it was built, this was

TIP

The Elevador is part of Lisbon's public transport system, so you can use an all-day bus ticket and go up and down at will. See page 136 for details of best-value bus and Metro tickets.

BELOW: restaurants line the streets of Baixa.

A bronze statue of the poet Fernando Pessoa sits outside the café A Brasileira.

the largest church in Lisbon. The earthquake caused the nave to collapse but the remains give the most eloquent reminder of that event, with the roofless Gothic arches silhouetted against Lisbon's often intensely blue sky. An eclectic **Museu Arqueológico** is housed in the chancel. Exhibits range from the sword of Álvares Pereira to a Roman tomb, ceramics and some mummified remains from Latin America.

Access to the church is via the front entrance in the attractive **Largo do Carmo** which can be reached on foot, passing some interesting places en route. From the bottom of the lift continue up the steps and turn left for a short way to Rua Garrett, on the right. To your left is the Armazens do Chiado, the Chiado shopping centre with 40 shops, restaurants, a four-star hotel and megastores. The complex, rebuilt after the devastating fire in 1988, was reconstructed based on a project designed by the Portuguese architect Álvaro de Siza Vieira and involving Souto de Moura and the Catalan architect Joan Busquets.

Continue up Rua Garrett to the Largo do Chiado (Baixada Chiado metro) and have a coffee at **A Brasileira**, a traditional, mirrored and panelled café where Fernando Pessoa (1888–1935) and many other poets, artists and writers used to rendezvous. A much photographed bronze statue of Pessoa sits outside.

Just below the café, turn left into Rua Serpa Pinto and then right to reach the Largo do Carmo with the imposing edifice of the convent, a central fountain and the Carmo Barracks which played a major part in the Carnation Revolution in 1974. At No. 21 is **O Chá Carmo** tearoom (open daily except Sunday) where you can refresh yourself from a choice of 50 different flavoured teas in delightful surroundings, and choose from a wide selection of homemade cakes and snacks.

São Roque

A short walk to the northwest up Rua Nova da Trindade brings you to the **Igreja São Roque ❻** (open daily 8am–5pm). The architect was the 16th-century Felipe Terzi, although the result is very different from São Vicente, another of his Lisbon churches. This small building presents a flat, largely undecorated façade to the small square (Largo Trindade Coelho) on which it sits; the original façade collapsed in the 1755 earthquake. It is said that St Roque preserved the church from further damage during the disaster.

Inside there is little of this gem-like place that is undecorated. The ceiling is a beautiful *trompe l'oeil*. There are eight chapels, four on each side. Each is a work of art in itself: the Chapel of São Roque, third on the right, has beautiful tiles by Francisco de Matos, and an excellent canvas, *Vision of St Roque*, painted by Gaspar Dias around 1584; the first chapel on the left, the Chapel of the Holy Family, has some wonderfully exuberant wood carving.

The most famous chapel is that of St John the Baptist, said to be the costliest chapel in the world. It was commissioned in 1742 by João V, perhaps Portugal's most extravagant king. Luigi Vanvitelli and Niccolo Salvi designed and constructed the building in Rome, where it was blessed by Pope Benedict XIV before being dismantled and carried in three ships to Lisbon, where it was permanently installed in 1747.

The actual value of even the chapel's components is inestimable: the columns are made of lapis lazuli; the altar front of amethyst; the carved angels of Carrara marble and ivory; and the pilasters of alabaster. Above, everything is highlighted with gold, silver and bronze. Equally impressive are the remarkable "oil paintings" in the chapel, depicting scenes from St John's life: they are not paintings at all but finely finished mosaics.

Adjoining the church is the **Museu de Arte Sacra** (open 10am–5pm; closed Mon and public holidays; admission charge) containing a small but impressive collection of vestments and ecclesiastical furnishings in rich baroque designs.

View from the top

After leaving the church and museum continue on upwards until you reach the viewpoint called the **Miradouro de São Pedro de Alcântara ❼**, just at the top of the Calçada da Glória, a steep incline beside Rossio Station that is serviced by a delightful old funicular. This belvedere affords a perfect view of the Castelo de São Jorge. The cathedral, lower on the slope and close to the harbour, can be recognised by its two fortress-like towers. Far to the left, parts of new Lisbon stretch into the distance. To discover more of what is before you as you stand in this pleasant green space, consult the large pictorial tile table where all the distinctive buildings are marked.

Opposite the Calçada da Glória is the **Solar do Instituto do Vinho do Porto ❽** (open Mon–Sat 2pm–midnight). Housed in an 18th-century mansion, built around a courtyard, the Port Wine Institute has a selection of more than 200 different ports, including some of the rarer vintages, which you can sample in a peaceful, relaxed atmosphere.

Map on page 124

BELOW: the stunning chapel of St John the Baptist in the Igreja São Roque.

TIP

The splendid
18th-century Palácio
Foz, on Praça dos
Restauradores, houses
the main tourist
information office.

BELOW: preparing
for customers at
Café Nícola.
RIGHT: the Elevador
de Santa Justa.

Restauradores and Rossio

After visiting the Solar take the Glória funicular back down to the broad square called **Praça dos Restauradores 9**, named after the "Restorers" who helped Portugal regain its independence from the Spanish in 1640. An obelisk towering in the centre commemorates this important fact. Avenida da Liberdade begins here, running for about a mile, broad and green, and ending at Praça Marquês de Pombal, a space ringed by large hotels, and Parque Eduardo VII (see *Northern Heights chapter, page 173*).

At the bottom of the square is the 19th-century **Estação do Rossio ⑩** (Rossio Station), a magnificent neo-Manueline building with horseshoe arched doorways. Trains run from here to Benfica and Sintra.

Southeast of the station is the **Praça do Rossio ⑪**, officially known as Praça Dom Pedro IV. The Rossio is the true centre of Lisbon, a large, busy square, lined with cafés and shops. The story goes that the bronze statue in the centre of the square, ostensibly that of Pedro IV, is in fact Emperor Maximilian of Mexico. It is said that the statue was en route from France when word of Maximilian's assassination arrived, and when the boat put in at Lisbon, a deal was made and the statue erected.

The great open space of the square was, in the past, the site of most of the city's public events, including bullfights, carnivals and the grisly *autos-da-fé* of the Inquisition. The palace that served as the headquarters for the Inquisitor-General once took up the north end of the square, a place occupied since the 1840s by the **Teatro Nacional Dona Maria II ⑫**. There is a statue of Gil Vincente (1470–1537), Portugal's foremost playwright, on the top. The two large fountains in the square were brought from Paris in 1890. When this book went to press, both the Rossio and the neighbouring Praça da Figueira (Figtree Square) were undergoing a major facelift, but should shortly be restored to their former (but more gleaming) glory.

Just to the east of the theatre is the **Largo de São Domingos** and the São Domingos church. The northern edge of the square is occupied by the **Palácio da Independência ⑬** (guided tours only, reserved in advanced, tel: 21-324 1470). The palace gained its name because here, in 1640, the Restauradores met to plan the retaking of Portugal. This 15th-century building retains several interesting architectural details, such as a fine terrace, carved porches and chimneys. The gardens are lined with beautiful tiles portraying mythological scenes. Today, the building is used as a centre to promote and maintain Portuguese culture and occasionally concerts are held there.

Coffee stop

If you are ready for a coffee, try the ever-popular **Café Nícola**, at the lower end of Rossio Square, where the Rua do Ouro begins. The first café on the site was founded by an Italian, over 200 years ago, and was a favourite of artists, politicians and intellectuals. The present one, which has been here for over 70 years, has attractive art nouveau decor and some fine original paintings on the walls. Needless to say, as in most of Lisbon's cafés, the coffee is excellent. ❑

Map
on page
124

THE ALFAMA

Hop on one of Lisbon's distinctive trams for part of this trip, which takes in the cathedral, the castle, some stunning viewpoints and the winding, picturesque alleys of the old quarter

This is a part of Lisbon that is hard to describe. Old, twisting, narrow, quaint, colourful – these few adjectives do not add up to the Alfama. You must enter on foot, and let yourself follow the tangle of alleys and staircases. The daytime is best for a visit, as there is a lot of activity; the night is not always safe, unless, of course, it is during the June festivals *(see page 89)*. You can take a map for reference – just don't bother trying to follow it.

The name Alfama has a Moorish origin, called after the hot springs once found near the Largo das Alcáçarias. The neighbourhood, however, is much older, dating from the time of the Romans and earlier settlers who first occupied this hillside. Under the Arabs and in the Middle Ages, many aristocratic mansions were built here; the first Christian churches in Lisbon were also consecrated in this quarter. Earthquakes, most notably the great one in 1755, destroyed most of the fine buildings, and the quarter was eventually abandoned to fishermen and the transient population.

PRECEDING PAGES:
the view from Largo
das Portas do Sol.
BELOW:
a Santa Luzia café.

Exploring the neighbourhood

Leaving from the east side of the Praça do Comércio, and walking along the traffic-filled Rua da Alfândega, you will come to the church of **Nossa Senhora da Conceição Velha** ⓮ (Our Lady of the Conception). The south façade is the only part of the original church to survive the 1755 earthquake. The fine Manueline carving on the doorway shows Our Lady of Mercy sheltering under her robe King Manuel I, Queen Leonor (who founded an almshouse on this site) and others in need of her protection.

Slowly wind your way up behind the church to the **Largo da Madalena**. Pass the church of Santa Maria Madalena, dating from the late 18th century but with a Manueline porch from an earlier place of worship, and continue up the Rua de Santo António da Sé to the **Largo de Santo António da Sé** with its many *tascas* (bars). In the corner of the square stands the **Igreja de Santo António** and the adjoining **Museu Antoniano** ⓯ (St Anthony's Church and Museum, museum open Tues–Sun 10am–1pm, 2–6pm, closed public holidays; admission charge).

The church and museum are dedicated to Lisbon's favourite saint (better loved than St Vincent, the official patron), and stand on the site of the house where St Anthony is believed to have been born in 1195. The church steps are lined with people begging for alms; they know they can depend on the pilgrims and the devout local worshippers. Inside the building are paintings by Pedro Alexandrino de Carvalho, who decorated numerous churches after the earthquake. The vestry has some notable 17th-century tiles.

The cathedral

Just up from here is the **Sé de Lisboa** ⑯ (cathedral; open daily 9am–5pm). Begun soon after Afonso Henriques captured Lisbon in 1147, it has been altered greatly over the centuries, but careful restoration allows the visitor to experience the impact of the original structure: two crenellated towers present a formidable aspect, softened by the large rose window between. To the left as you walk inside is the baptismal font where St Anthony was christened in 1195. Nearby, in the first chapel on the left, is a beautifully detailed crèche, or nativity scene, by the sculptor Joaquim Machado de Castro.

The chancel is 18th century, but the ambulatory, pierced with lancet windows, was remodelled in the 14th century. The third chapel from the south side of the ambulatory contains the tombs of Lopo Fernandes Pacheco, a companion-in-arms to Afonso IV (1325–57), and his wife, Maria Vilalobos. The details on the tombs are very fine: his hair is beautifully rendered, she reads a small book, and both are sculpted with their dogs at their feet.

The ruined cloisters, entered from the chapel just to the right, are well worth the small entrance fee. There are lovely bits and pieces of stone here, including some intriguing bas-relief figures spiralling up a damaged column just to the right as you enter. Also note a well-preserved 13th-century wrought-iron grill. Long-term excavations are taking place here and the remains of Moorish buildings, constructed on top of a Roman street, have been uncovered.

In the sacristy off the south transept you can see a casket containing the relics of St Vincent, patron saint of Lisbon, brought here by order of Afonso Henriques. Legend has it that two ravens accompanied the boat that carried the relics, and for centuries the birds' descendants were cared for by the church.

There are many fine pieces of sacred art in the cathedral.

LEFT:
the cathedral's ancient ceiling.
RIGHT:
the towers and rose window bathed in evening light.

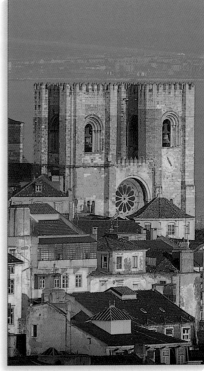

TIP

The Espaço Oikos is
run by a co-operative
dedicated to alleviating
poverty in the less-
developed world. They
have a small but good
selection of world
music and *fado* CDs.

Santa Luzia

The **Limoeiro**, on the street of the same name leading on up from behind the cathedral, was once a royal palace. It later became a mint and from the 15th century served as a prison. After the death of Salazar in 1974 the prison, which had been used to house political prisoners during his regime, was closed. Just above the Limoeiro is the **Espaço Oikos** (open Tues–Sat 11am–7pm), installed in the stables of the 17th-century Bishop's Palace. With its cobbled floor and 23 stone mangers, this is an attractive exhibition space for paintings and handicrafts by artists from under-developed countries. On the pavement in front of the building are three southern nettle trees. Just up on the left in Rua da Saudade are the ruins of a Roman theatre.

Continue on up past the antique shops to **Santa Luzia**, a pretty neighbourhood church and the **Miradouro de Santa Luzia** ⓱ behind it. There are some fine *azulejo* panels on the external walls of the church, one showing the heroic soldier Martim Moniz (who died while assisting Afonso Henriques to capture the city) and another of the Praça do Comércio. On the old Moorish walls supporting the little *miradouro* there is an exquisite wall tile painting depicting old Lisbon as seen from the Tejo river.

This belvedere provides a wonderful rest stop, filled with flowers and sunshine, and edged with a tile-and-vine-covered arbour. You can sit on one of the benches tucked in the arbour and enjoy panoramic views of the Tejo and the Alfama, while you recover your strength after climbing the steep, narrow streets. Immediately below, among the fading, interconnecting roofs, you may peek into the tiny yards and gardens of Alfama houses – complete with vegetable plots, various pets and children at play.

BELOW: neighbours
sit and talk in
the Miradouro de
Santa Luzia.

Portas do Sol

Immediately around the corner is the **Largo das Portas do Sol** ⑱, an attractive square named after the Sun Gate, one of the original city gates that once stood here. A statue of St Vincent overlooks the city. This square, with its soft-toned buildings and welcoming café terraces, is a popular photo-stop as it provides a stunning view from the Alfama down to the river. The towers and cupola of São Vicente de Fora can clearly be seen to the east.

Situated in a corner of the square is the **Museu de Artes Decorativas** ⑲ (Museum of Decorative Arts; open Tues–Sun 10am–5pm; admission charge), which forms part of the Ricardo do Espírito Santo Silva Foundation. This collection of Portuguese furniture and decorative arts, hand-picked by the founder, is housed in the transformed 17th-century Palácio Azurara. The interior is a highly characteristic if somewhat sombre evocation of an urban palace, with blue-and-white *azulejo* panels and painted ceilings. Furniture, tapestry and distinctive objects combine in the different rooms, to recreate the style and atmosphere of different historical epochs. Alongside the museum are workshops, where artisans practise such traditional crafts as gilding, cabinet-making, carpentry, wood-carving and bookbinding.

The Museu de Artes Decorativas is housed in a 17th-century palace.

Castelo de São Jorge

Continuing up the narrow streets you come to what may be the most beautiful view of the city and the river – from the *miradouro* on the ramparts of the **Castelo de São Jorge** ⑳ (gardens and ramparts open Mar–Oct, daily 9am–9pm, Nov–Feb, daily 9am–6pm; free), which crowns the first hill east of the city centre. The striking view is an ideal way to get to know Lisbon's layout.

BELOW: ignoring the view at the Castelo de São Jorge.

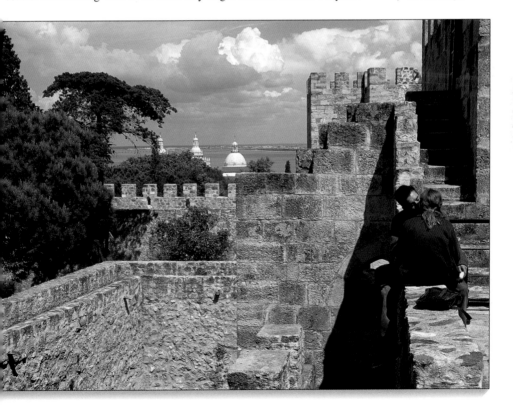

Peacocks lord it over the gardens of the Castelo de São Jorge.

BELOW:
a ride on one of Lisbon's old trams is not to be missed.

The castle itself can be seen from almost everywhere in Lisbon, serving as an apt and romantic reminder of the capital's ancient roots. Although the Roman settlement had a fortification on the site, many of the castle walls and towers are from the later Moorish stronghold. After the Portuguese drove out the Moors in 1147, the Paço de Alcáçova, which had been the residence of the Moorish governor, became the royal palace. King Dinis (1279–1325) added romanesque touches and King Manuel (1495–1521) embellished the structure with gothic details and additions, although he also moved the royal residence to a harbour site. Several decades later, the bellicose young King Sebastião, preferring the military fortification to the elegant waterside palace, briefly returned to the castle's heights. Much later, under Spanish rule, the castle was converted into a barracks and prisons, but in 1939 it was freed from any official duties.

Look and learn

Climb the towers and walk along the ramparts, look out over the Alfama to the busy harbour, with the 25 de Abril bridge stretching into the distance and the statue of Christ (Cristo Rei) on the far bank; or across the old town to Bairro Alto on the opposite hill. Stroll along the newly renovated paths, relax in the gardens by ponds and fountains, with peacocks strutting around, or just sit in the shade of the trees and gaze at the stunning views.

If you are interested in finding out more about the city, both past and present, you could also visit the **Centro de Interpretação de Lisboa-Olissipónia** (Multimedia Exhibition; open daily 10am–1pm, 2–5.30pm; admission charge) and learn about Lisbon's history. Or, during the summer months, there's also the **Torre de Ulisses** (Tower of Ulysses; open mid-Mar–mid-Sept, Wed–Mon

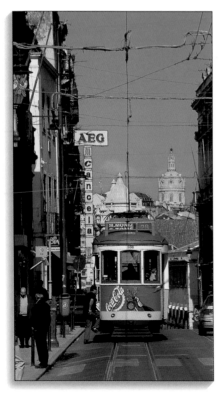

TRAVELLING BY TRAM

Lisbon's old-fashioned trams, with their brightly painted exteriors and wood-panelled interiors are the best, if not the fastest, way to get around. The system started in 1901 and has been going strong ever since. On some routes the antique trams have been replaced with, or are supplemented by, *eléctricos* – huge, articulated creatures festooned with highly coloured advertisements.

The most picturesque routes are the No. 15, which runs from the Praça do Comercio to Belém (old and new trams both work this route), and, best of all, the No. 28, which winds its way through the narrow streets of the Alfama – catch it in Praça da Figueira or Rua da Conceiçao in Baixa. Don't take this route if you are in a hurry, though, as parked cars and oncoming traffic – almost unbelievably some of these lanes have a two-way system – mean the journey is a slow one, giving a good opportunity to peer into tiny, dark shop doorways or admire the geraniums on the balconies.

The trams are part of the integrated CARRIS transport system, so you can buy a daily ticket for the equivalent of about £1.75/$2.50 and use the Metro, bus, tram and *elevadores* of Lisbon all day long. Four-day and seven day tickets are also available.

10am–1pm, 2–5.30pm; admission charge), a *camera obscura* where images of the city viewed through a periscope are projected on to a horizontal screen.

Map on page 124

Outside the walls

Return to the Largo das Portas do Sol through the little streets lined with gift shops and cafés. From here you can either plunge straight into the Alfama district by taking the steps on the right or continue up Rua do Salvador to the **Miradouro da Graça** (which gives a wonderful view of the castle) and the **Igreja Nossa Senhora da Graça ㉑**, a church with fine *azulejos* in the sacristy and an extravagant high altar. This is one of Lisbon's oldest churches; the Augustinian convent to which it was once attached dates from the 13th century, but has been much altered and now serves as an army barracks.

Continuing from the Largo da Graça, where the church stands, take the Travessa São Vicente which leads into Rua Voz do Operário, then turn right towards the large church and monastery of **São Vicente de Fora ㉒** (open Tues–Sun 10am–6pm; free; admission charge to cloisters). Its name described its original position outside the city walls (*fora* means outside), but its construction encouraged the growth of a new, wealthy neighbourhood. It was built on the site of a 12th-century monastery dedicated to St Vincent, commemorating the battle fought by the Crusaders to take Lisbon. Of this once-opulent building, nothing remains.

The present white limestone building with short twin towers was designed by an Italian architect, Filipo Terzi. The central dome collapsed in the 1755 earthquake and was replaced by a more modest one. The interior has a beautiful coffered vault and a baroque organ with gilded woodwork. The **cloisters** are covered with 18th-century *azulejos* depicting La Fontaine's *Fables*.

TIP

The castle has a shop (open 10am–1pm, 2–6pm) in the Governor's House near the entrance that sells better-than-average souvenirs.

BELOW: São Vicente, with his church in the background.

Off the cloisters is the former refectory which serves as the **Royal Pantheon**. Portuguese rulers, from João IV (who died in 1656) to Manuel II, Portugal's last king, are entombed here. There is a surprisingly eerie sight of a modern, life-sized stone figure praying at the centre tomb of King Carlos and his son Luís Felipe, assassinated in the city in 1908. The exiled King Carol II of Romania (1893–1953) is also buried here.

Work on the Santa Engrácia church started in 1682 but was not completed until 1966. Consequently, the Portuguese idiom for a project never finished is "obras de Santa Engrácia".

Bric-à-brac and baroque

Leave the square behind the church, and follow the road, passing under an archway into a large open area known as the **Campo de Santa Clara**, where the **Feira da Ladra** (Thieves' Market) ❷ takes place on Tuesday and Saturday from very early in the morning until around 1pm. There's some interesting bric-à-brac and quite a lot of junk in this flea market, and it's probably a better place for soaking up the atmosphere than finding real bargains.

Just below the square is the baroque **Igreja de Santa Engrácia** ❷ (open Tues–Sun 10am–5pm; admission charge) which is now the national pantheon (for non-royalty). The building is in the compact, satisfying shape of a Greek cross, with a central dome. The interior is covered in beautiful, multicoloured slabs of polished marble and has a pleasing feeling of space. However, the symbolic tombs of famous Portuguese figures – Vasco da Gama, Henry the Navigator, Luís de Camões – are somewhat sterile and have the unmistakable stamp of General Salazar and his cultural void.

BELOW: fish sold in Alfama is fresh and delicious.

Alfama atmosphere

From Santa Engrácia, weave your way down through the labyrinth of narrow winding streets and immerse yourself in the atmosphere of the real Alfama. Here there are steep staircases leading through arches into blind alleyways and inner courtyards, and narrow houses with crumbling ochre-coloured exteriors and blue-and-white tiles. From the geranium-decked balconies above, washing dries in the hot sun, and birds sing loudly in too small cages. Women hold loud conversations across the dividing alleyways and the appetising smell of garlic cooking in olive oil wafts down to street level. Down below, groups of elderly men sit smoking and chatting in the doorways, when they are not whiling away the day playing draughts or cards in the dark and smoky little *tascas*.

The fruits of local labour can be enjoyed by venturing down **Rua de São Pedro** where the market comes to life very early in the morning, its stalls selling freshly grown vegetables and fruit, and where fisherwomen sell a wondrous variety of fresh fish each day.

In a street so narrow that two people can barely pass, they carry their heavy baskets of fish on their heads calling "*sardinhas, vivinhas*" (fresh sardines), as fish sellers have done for centuries. If you'd like to sample the day's catch, simply step into one of the many little restaurants along the way. These tiny rooms, with just a couple of tables, are often below street level. The food is fresh, delicious and cheap.

Picturesque but poor

The Alfama has been the setting for films and the inspiration for the *fado*; it has influenced poets and novelists, and has an intangible quality that has to be experienced to be truly appreciated. One who was beguiled by it was the writer Pierre Kyria, who, in his book *Lisbonne* (Paris, 1985), described it lyrically as "a magical labyrinth, full of hidden corners, traversed by winding stairs, lined by dollhouses with façades decorated by drying laundry, a birdcage, pots of geraniums, or with tall walls where ivy creeps across *azulejos* that appear even more blue in the moonlight".

As in many other cities, picturesque scenes mask a great deal of poverty, and many of the houses in the area are in serious need of attention. Some of their inhabitants, who have lived here all their lives and retain a strong sense of community, are aware that an increasing number of wealthier people are keen to invest in these properties. Gentrification of the Alfama may be on its way.

Local landmarks

If you resist the *tascas* and continue to wander through the neighbourhood, look out for some local landmarks. At the corner of Beco das Cruzes and Rua da Regueira stands an 18th-century house with upper floors supported by carved ravens. A 16th-century mansion in Largo do Salvador has an elaborate baroque balcony. The church of São Miguel, its interior graced with beautifully carved woodwork, stands in the nearby square. The Largo de São Rafael is enclosed on one side by the ruins of a Moorish tower, and throughout the old quarter, although they are sometimes difficult to identify, are bits and pieces of the walls that ringed the Alfama some 1,500 years ago. ❑

Map on page 124

Men like to play draughts in the streets of Alfama.

BELOW: hanging out the washing and keeping an eye on the street below.

Map
on pages
144–5

RIVERSIDE LISBON

You will need more than a day to fully appreciate all the riverside sites, which range from the superb 16th-century Jerónimos monastery and Belém tower to the lively, renovated dockside area

The margins of the Tejo offer a continuous array of beaches, docks, forts, monuments and museums. The central Praça do Comércio *(see page 123)* is Lisbon's primary face to the river. Acknowledged as one of Europe's most beautiful squares, it is a fitting tribute from the city to the river. It also provides a convenient starting point from which to explore the riverside eastwards to the Museu do Azulejo, or westwards towards the World Heritage sites around Belém. Because there is so much to see and do, this chapter has divided up the route into three suggested trips, each starting from the Praça do Comércio. The Parque das Nações to the east has a short chapter of its own *(see page 158)*.

Heading east

PRECEDING PAGES: an old frigate and a colourful fishing boat in dock at the Parque das Nações. **BELOW:** entrance to the Museu da Água.

As you face the River Tejo, leave the Praça do Comercio to the left in the direction of the Estação Fluvial do Terreiro do Paço (ferry terminal) from where boats go to Barreiro on the south shore and trains leave for the Algarve and Évora. At least, trains are advertised as leaving from here, but in fact train passengers cross as foot passengers to join their train on the other side. "Lisbon from the River" sightseeing trips also leave from here *(see Travel Tips)*.

Across the Avenida Infante Dom Henrique in Rua dos Bacalhoeiros you will find the famous **Casa dos Bicos ❶** (House of Pointed Stones; open Mon–Fri 9.30am–5.30pm). The façade of this 16th-century building is extremely unusual, being made entirely of carved pyramidal stones, capturing beautifully the style of 16th-century Mediterranean Europe and the Age of the Discoveries. Brás de Albuquerque, a counsellor to King João III and illegitimate son of the first Portuguese viceroy of India, had it built. Like so much else, the house was partially destroyed in the 1755 earthquake. The first two floors are original, but have been restored. The top two have been reconstructed, based on details from several early engravings. Today, the building houses temporary exhibitions.

The king's fountain

Continue along Rua do Cais de Santarém until you reach the Largo do Terreiro do Trigo. By the pathway on your left, look for the 13th-century **Chafariz d'el Rei** (Fountain of the King), once the major source of the city's water supply. The nearby **Largo do Chafariz de Dentro ❷** (Square of the Fountain Inside the Walls), the largest square in the quarter – and not particularly large as squares go – is a favourite spot for locals to sit on benches and while away the hours.

Up a tiny alley off the square, the Beco do Mexias *(beco* means alley), the local women used to congregate to gossip and do their washing in the fountain

Situated in the square itself is the **Casa do Fado e da Guitarra Portuguesa** (House of Fado; open Wed–Mon 10am– 6pm; admission charge). It includes a museum with audio-visual installations, temporary exhibitions on the subject of *fado,* Lisbon's own music, *(see page 83)* and an auditorium that stages shows and debates. Altogether, it's a fascinating way to learn about the history of *fado,* and more generally about the Portuguese guitar.

Weapons and water

Eastwards along Rua de Jardim do Tabaco is the **Museu Militar ❸** (Military Museum; open Tues–Sun 10am–5pm; admission charge). This collection has found a proper home in what was, until 1851, the national arsenal. Here, appropriately enough, the 18th-century *azulejo* panels depict scenes of battle. The ceilings are painted with various allegorical figures that reinforce the notions of patriotism, valour and loyalty. The museum charts Portugal's military history, with paintings by 19th- and early 20th-century artists, as well as a large collection of armaments: light arms manufactured in the arsenal, and bronze and iron weapons of various periods; cannons, of course, and a room devoted to World War I artefacts. The armour room is usually popular with children.

The Museu Militar has a suitably forbidding doorway.

Beyond the Museu Militar, on the waterfront, is the **Estação Santa Apolónia** – the mainline railway station. From the Largo dos Caminhos de Ferro in which it stands, catch a bus No. 35, 104, 105 or 107 to Calçada dos Barbadinhos for a visit to the **Museu da Água ❹** (Water Museum; open Mon–Sat 10am–6pm; admission charge) in Rua do Alviela. The museum is located within the walls of an ex-convent where, in 1884, Lisbon's first pumping station was built to distribute water from the River Alviela for use in the city. Those keen on steam

BELOW: the Casa dos Bicos and its neighbours.

engines will find their hearts pumping faster when they set eyes on the four beautifully preserved 1880s models on display. Although not large, the museum is imaginatively designed and won a Council of Europe prize in 1990.

The art of *azulejos*

After visiting the Water Museum return to the bus stop and catch a No. 104 or 105 in the direction of Rua da Madre de Deus for a visit to the **Museu Nacional do Azulejo ❺** (National Tile Museum; open Wed–Sun 10am–6pm, Tues 2–6pm; admission charge). It is installed in the Manueline cloisters of the beautiful church of **Madre de Deus**, so has the added advantage of a setting as interesting as the museum itself.

The church was originally part of a convent founded in 1509 by Dona Leonor, widow of João II. Of its exterior, only the carved Manueline doorway survived the Great Earthquake. The 18th-century interior of the main church is a breathtaking combination: gilded woodwork, blue-and-white Dutch *azulejos* and lovely paintings high on the walls and on the ceilings. The paintings on the coffered vault represent the Life of the Virgin; those on the left wall are scenes from the life of St Clare; and on the right, St Francis. The extraordinarily ornate rococo altarpiece was installed after the earthquake.

The altar of Madre de Deus. The church is worth visiting, as well as the museum housed within it.

Be sure to take in the chapterhouse, sacristy and Chapel of St Anthony, which house a wonderful collection of paintings. Leading from the chapel, which contains tiles dating from 1780 depicting the saint's life and a number of paintings, is the nuns' choir, with lots of gilt and reliquaries.

Tracing the progression

In the museum itself the clearly designed progression of tiles illustrates the development of this notable art form so popular in Portugal. There are examples from the early Moorish origins, through to the vast polychrome carpet panels of the 17th century, the blue-and-white narrative panels of the 18th century, and the relief tiles of the 19th century. The collection follows the development of the *azulejo* right up to the late 20th century where it found new expression in major

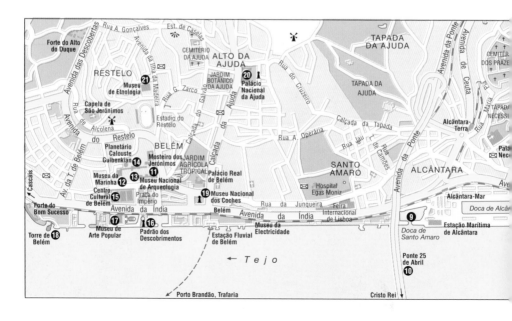

projects such as the Metro. One of the most remarkable pieces on show is the horizontal blue-and-white panel (1735) representing a panoramic view of Lisbon seen from the river before the 1755 earthquake.

The museum's small restaurant, which serves reasonably priced salads and snacks, is tiled with *azulejos* depicting poultry and game, giving it the air of a traditional farmhouse kitchen.

From the museum, you can return to the Praça do Comércio on any bus going in the direction of Cais do Sodré; or you can go further east, to the Parque das Nações *(see page 158)*.

Map on pages 144–5

Going west

A short walk from the Praça do Comércio along Rua do Arsenal, just opposite the Lisboa Welcome Centre, lies the **Praça do Municipio**. In the centre of the square is a twisted column surmounted by a banded sphere, a typical Manueline architectural device and symbol of municipal authority. From the balcony of the 19th-century Town Hall (Município) on the east side of the square, the Republic was proclaimed on 5 October 1910.

A few metres from here, turn up Rua Serpa Pinto and on the right you will find the **Museu do Chiado ⑥** (open Tues 2–6pm; Wed–Sun 10am–6pm; admission charge). This recently renovated and well-designed museum (it was closed for years after the Chiado fire in 1988) includes a fine and representative collection of paintings and drawings by Portuguese artists from 1850 to 1960. It used to be known as the Museum of Contemporary Art, and some of its temporary exhibitions are far more contemporary than the permanent collection.

Playful sculpted figures outside the Museu do Chiado.

Just above the museum on the left is the **Teatro Nacional de São Carlos ⑦**. Built in 1792, it was clearly inspired by Italian architecture, particularly the San Carlos opera house in Naples and La Scala in Milan. Some good operatic performances are staged here as well as ballet and symphony concerts *(see Travel Tips)*. This is where Lord Byron was supposed to have been struck for making a pass at a gentleman's wife. True or not, its splendid rococo interior would have made the perfect setting for aristocratic flirtations and jealous outbursts.

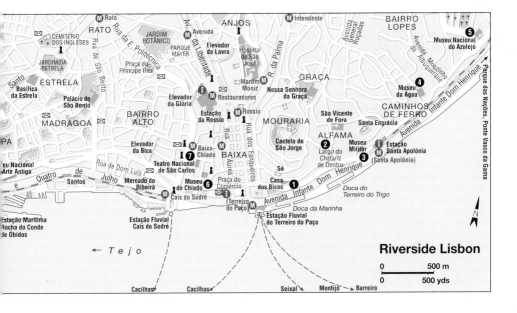

Riverside Lisbon

0   500 m
0   500 yds

Go back down to Rua do Arsenal and turn along to the right towards Praça Duque Terceira, where there are numerous bars favoured by visiting sailors. Here, at **Cais do Sodré**, is an important interface for buses and Metro, tram and ferry lines. From the railway station trains run the 30 km (18 miles) along the coast to Cascais and the Atlantic *(see page 198)*, while at the ferry terminal both passenger and car ferries cross the river to Cacilhas. It has been a working quay for many centuries – when George Borrow arrived in Lisbon in 1835 he noted, "We again anchored at a short distance from the Caesodré (sic), or principal quay of Lisbon."

Ancient art

Continuing west along the traffic-filled Avenida 24 de Julho (take the Eléctrico, a big double-jointed modern tram, No. 15 or 18 and alight at Cais da Rocha), the next major riverside stop is the **Museu Nacional de Arte Antiga ❽** (National Museum of Ancient Art; open Tues 2–6pm; Wed–Sun 10am–6pm; admission charge). This gallery, also known as the **Museu das Janelas Verdes** (Museum of the Green Windows), is installed in the 17th-century palace of the Count of Alvor. The baroque Chapel of St Albert, part of the Carmelite monastery that once occupied this site, has been maintained intact within the museum. The modern wing, in which the main entrance is situated, rests happily alongside the original palace, which opens on to a pleasant garden.

There is so much of interest in this museum that only a few items can be highlighted here. Of the numerous 15th- and 16th-century Portuguese altarpieces and painted panels, the most famous is the *Polyptych of St Vincent*, attributed to Nuno Gonçalves. Much controversy has surrounded this superbly

BELOW:
Ecce Homo in the
Museu Nacional
de Arte Antiga.

executed work. The panels depict the adoration of St Vincent, the patron saint of Lisbon, and include excellent portraits of many contemporary figures, including King Afonso V and Prince Henry the Navigator. Another outstanding, but anonymous, work of the same period is the sombre and poignant *Ecce Homo*.

In addition to Portuguese paintings, both religious and secular, there are numerous fine Italian, French, Spanish, German, Flemish and Dutch works, including a macabre and fascinating triptych, *The Temptation of St Antony*, by Hieronymus Bosch, and Lucas Cranach's *Salomé*.

More than just paintings

This museum also has a fine collection of decorative art and silverware. The numerous items of Portuguese liturgical silverware include the romanesque processional cross of King Sancho I and the renowned Manueline Monstrance of Belém, which was made from the first shipment of gold brought home by Vasco da Gama. The collection of French 18th-century silverware, especially the pieces by François Thomas Germain, is one of the finest in the world and includes over 200 pieces that once belonged to the Portuguese royal family.

Ceramics and glassware, ornately embroidered religious vestments, furniture from the reign of João V and José I, as well as that of Indo-Portuguese origin are among the other fascinating exhibits, as are Japanese *Namban* screens. *Namban* describes a 100-year phase in Japanese art corresponding to the period of trade between Portugal and Japan. The name originates in the nickname given by the Japanese to these foreigners who first set foot in southern Japan in 1543: "*Namban-jin*", barbarians coming from the south. The painted screens document the costumes and boats of the time in delicately executed trading scenes that even include some Portuguese Jesuits.

Map on pages 144–5

Floating docks

From the nearby gardens – Jardim 9 de Abril – from which there are extensive views over the river and the port, take the steps leading down to the Avenida 24 de Julho. Cross the wide road and railway line and turn right along Avenida de Brasília, past the yachts moored in the docks, to **Doca de Alcântara**. Here, in 1887, in a grand celebration with fireworks, military bands and thousands of spectators, King Luís launched the first stone into the river to begin the foundations for the current system of floating docks. Alcântara and the cosmopolitan neighbouring **Doca de Santo Amaro** ❾ (sometimes collectively known as "the docas") are fast becoming one of the most lively areas of Lisbon. Bars, cafés, clubs and restaurants, some of them in smartly converted warehouses, line the docksides, which buzz with life.

At the **Estação Maritima de Alcântara** (Marine Terminal) there are 14 large mural panels which were completed in 1949 by the Portuguese modernist painter José Almada Negreiros. These are vivid, Cubist-inspired works depicting the life of the port from the time of the discoveries right up to the construction of the terminals in which they are housed.

Selling handmade model boats in the Doca de Santo Amaro.

BELOW:
the Doca de Santo Amaro is a pleasant place to sit and admire the boats.

BELOW:
the Mosteiro dos
Jerónimos has
been classified as a
World Heritage Site.

Just west of Doca de Santo Amaro, visible from anywhere along this stretch of the coast, is one of Europe's longest suspension bridges, **Ponte 25 de Abril ⑩**. This slender structure, 2,300 metres (2,500 yds) long, and with a central span of 1,013 metres (1,108 yds), was started in 1962 and finished four years later. It was called the Salazar Bridge until the 1974 Revolution. It carries traffic to Setúbal and the Algarve, and its central section is some 70 metres (231 ft) above the water level, giving ample clearance for even the tallest ships. In 2000 a railway was added to the lower deck of the structure, providing the first rail link across the Tejo. Although only serving commuter traffic at present, there are plans to connect this line to the main Algarve route, thereby enabling the first through trains to run to the south.

From here you could catch a bus No. 14, 32, 43 or 28 to take you back to the centre. Alternatively, carry on towards Belém; take bus No. 27, 28, 29, 43, 49 or 51 or Eléctrico 15 tram.

Belém

West of Lisbon proper is the neighbourhood of Belém, Portuguese for Bethlehem. Here the Tejo begins to open up to the Atlantic, and here Vasco da Gama embarked on his journey in 1497, praying in a small chapel built by Henry the Navigator. That chapel was levelled shortly afterwards and in its place arose the **Mosteiro dos Jerónimos ⑪** (open May–Sept, Tues–Sun 10am–6.30pm, Oct–Apr, Tues–Sun 10am–5pm; admission charge to cloisters only) which was classified as a World Heritage Building in 1984.

Manuel I ordered its construction, which was begun in 1502, under the supervision of the French architect Diogo Boytac. The building is the perfect symbol

of the extravagant Age of Discoveries. The money used to build the edifice came from the sale of the spices and gold brought back by the explorers, which is why it was said to be "built of pepper". The Manueline architecture seems to rise from the sea, twisting and leaping with carved cables, coral, sea creatures, anchors and other nautical motifs.

This exuberance can be seen clearly in the south porch, facing the river. Designed by João de Castilho (who succeeded Boytac in 1517), it is decorated with numerous statues, climbing up to the top, capped by the cross of the Order of Christ, the knights who financed and manned many of the expeditions. The figure in the south doorway just below the cross is Nossa Senhora de Belém; below her in a canopied niche is a figure said to be Henry the Navigator.

Internal delights

The vast interior with its large octagonal columns covered with vines and shoots and strange creatures is equally delightful. The many-ribbed vaulting that fans out from the tops of the columns resembles a jungle canopy or towering palm fronds. Note, too, the remarkable star vaulting, seeming to hover without support above the transept crossing. Just inside the west portal is the l9th-century tomb of Vasco da Gama who died in Cochin and another opposite it honours Luís Camões, although the great poet was actually buried in a pauper's grave in 1580. The choir, entered from the cloisters, has particularly fine stalls that date from 1660.

The cloisters are magnificent, with beautiful detail on every arch, each crowned with a different decoration. The rounded arcade openings show a Renaissance influence, although most of the architectural structure here is

> **Map on pages 144–5**

> **BELOW:** a shop in Belém, near the monastery, sells religious objects.

late-gothic. It is thought that Boytac designed the cloisters, but Castilho actually carried out the work. The corner canopies, the columns and even the walls are decorated with the exuberant, rich Manueline motifs.

The chapterhouse is also in the cloisters, with the tomb of Portugal's greatest historian and historical novelist, Alexandre Herculano (died 1877); so is the refectory, which has beautiful vaulting and 18th-century tiling. The western annexes of the monastery now house the large Maritime Museum and the National Museum of Archaeology.

Maritime history

If one considers Portugal's geographical position, hemmed in by Spain and bordered by the Atlantic Ocean along its entire western margin, the sea's predominant role in the history of this nation is immediately comprehensible. That the **Museu da Marinha** ⑫ (Maritime Museum; open Jun–Sept, Tues–Sun 10am–6pm; Oct–May, Tues–Sun 10am–5pm; admission charge) should be housed in a wing of the Jerónimos Monastery is no coincidence. The monastery is close to Vasco da Gama's point of departure when he set off on his momentous sea journey to India in 1497, and the building itself is an imposing reminder of the period of maritime expansion.

Many objects and documents relating to Portugal's earlier maritime history were destroyed during the 1755 earthquake and the French invasions; a huge fire in 1916 in the museum, which was then housed in the Naval School, claimed much more, so the collection contains few truly old pieces. However, one private collection, donated in 1948, compensates for some of the losses and greatly enriches the whole museum.

BELOW: manicured box hedges in the botanical garden.

GREEN SPACES

Not far from Jerónimos, tucked behind the Palácio Real de Belém on Calçada do Galvão, is the Jardim Agrícola Tropical, sometimes known as Jardim do Ultramar. The garden started life as a research centre, and is now a haven of peace where you can wander among tropical and subtropical greenery. The dragon tree *(Dracaena draco)*, a native of Tenerife, which can live to a great age, is one of the most fascinating specimens. There is also a lovely Oriental garden with delicate bridges arching over streams.

There is a Museu Tropical in the grounds, too, with a huge collection of specimens, but it can be visited only by appointment. Check with the Tourist Office, or tel: 21-362 02 10 if you are interested.

The Jardim Botânico da Ajuda lies about 500 metres or so away, up the Calçada da Ajuda, close to the palace of the same name. This formal, Italianate garden, with the manicured box hedges typical of the style, was designed by Pombal in the 1760s. Here you'll find another of the strange, gnarled dragon trees.

Close by is the little Igreja da Memória, a neoclassical church that King José I had built on the spot where he survived an assassination attempt in 1758.

Following the discoverers

Proceeding from the main entrance, the visitor follows the story of the Portuguese discoveries – the sea journeys to the East and the New World. The wooden figure of the Archangel St Raphael is the oldest object in the museum. It accompanied Vasco da Gama to India and was brought back to Lisbon in 1600 by one of his great-grandsons. In addition to the large collection of model boats, displays of naval uniforms and a small but choice collection of objects from the Orient, there are charmingly naïve painted ex-votos (small images offered to a saint in gratitude for a safe sea journey), maritime paintings and numerous ships' prows. Though some of the prows represent women, in Portugal, as in the rest of southern Europe, prows were more customarily male. The visitor is also given a glimpse of life on a yacht at the turn of the 20th century through the reconstruction of a plush, softly lit, wood-panelled cabin from the royal yacht *Amélia*, named after Portugal's last queen.

Like many of Lisbon's museums, this one has quite a good café and gift shop (near the exit) but when you've stopped for a drink you are not quite finished with maritime things: be sure not to miss the collection of magnificent royal barges housed in the modern building across the square. These were the craft that once gave the Tejo a Venetian flavour.

Map on pages 144–5

A boat modelled from silver in the Museu da Marinha.

From the ancients to the stars

The **Museu Nacional de Arqueologia** ⑬ (National Archaeology Museum; open Tues 2–6pm, Wed–Sun 10am–6pm; admission charge) was founded by the eminent Portuguese ethnographer Leite de Vasconcelos in 1893, and was installed in the southern wing of Jerónimos Monastery in 1903. Although the

BELOW: a painting in the archaeological museum depicts St Anthony with farm workers.

Q.FEZ S.ANTONIO,A JOSE PREIRA, DO CAYOUCO). VINDO AS VACAS E O CARRO POR O CAMINHO, DE REPENTE FUJIRAM ÁS TRAZEIRAS,E CAIR DE UMA PAREDE ABAIXO; E S.ANTÓNIO LHE VALLEU QUE NADA E PERIGO. EM 1878. *O Pintar. Manoel Duarte.*

TIP

An easy way to get a general view of Belém's architecture and museums is to take the miniature train, which departs hourly from in front of Jerónimos. The route takes in all the important sites but does not allow you to stop and visit.

museum has long dedicated its activities more to archaeology and ethnology, there are also items representing Portuguese popular and religious culture included in the collection. In fact, certain areas – such as ceramics, archaeology and ethnology – seem to blend into each other.

The collection includes some beautiful pieces of archaic Portuguese jewellery: bracelets, rings, diadems, necklaces and earrings. In the section displaying sculpture from the Iron Age to the Middle Ages are some Roman pieces, such as the Quadriga (a group of four horses used to draw a chariot) atop a lion's head, discovered in Óbidos, north of Lisbon. The mosaics in the collection are from Roman villas throughout Portugal. There is also a display of African art and Egyptian pieces, with beautifully painted, majestic sarcophagi.

Close by (at the back of the monastery) is the **Planetário Calouste Gulbenkian** ⓮ (Calouste Gulbenkian Planetarium) where you can observe the universe, the stars and the moon (presentations Wed–Thur 11am, 2.30pm, 4pm; Sat–Sun 3.30pm, 5pm, plus Sun 11am special free performance for children; admission charge).

Cultural Centre

Integrated in the architectural complex of Jerónimos, on the west side of Praço do Império, is the **Centro Cultural de Belém** ⓯ (Belém Cultural Centre; open daily 9am–10pm). Starkly modern, although made of the same stone as the monastery (designed by Italian architect Vittorio Gregotti and his Portuguese colleague Manuel Salgado), it was extremely controversial when built as the headquarters of the European Presidency. It became a culture centre in 1993 and most people have now got used to its stark lines. Exhibitions and a variety of musical performances are held here, and free street performances bring the place to life at weekends. You can have lunch here with spectacular views over the Tejo and the Belém gardens.

The complex also houses the **Museu do Design** (open daily 11am–8pm), with a good collection of modern furniture and glassware, including some Charles Eames chairs.

Monument to the Discoveries

Leaving the Centro Cultural, cross over to the riverfront using the pedestrian underpass and visit the enormous **Padrão dos Descobrimentos** ⓰ (Monument to the Discoveries; open Tues–Sun 9.30am–6.30pm; admission charge). This graceless piece of "nationalistic" sculpture was built under Salazar's regime in 1960 to commemorate the 500th anniversary of the death of Prince Henry the Navigator. Constructed in the shape of the prow of a caravel thrusting towards the sea, it has the figure of Henry standing at its tip, followed by a number of his contemporaries: prominent among them are Afonso V, the explorers Vasco da Gama and Ferdinand Magellan, the poet Camões and the painter Nuno Gonçalves.

An attractively designed compass and map are set in the pavement in front of the monument, and there's a good view from the balcony at the very top – a lift whisks you up the 52-metre (170-ft) structure.

BELOW: the clean lines of the Centro Cultural de Belém.

Torre de Belém

Next, walk west along the riverfront to the **Museu de Arte Popular**
(Museum of Popular Art; open Tues–Sun 10am–12.30pm, 2–5pm; admission
charge). It contains a collection of Portuguese folk art from all over the country – pottery, tapestries, clothing, leather saddles, basketware, agricultural
implements and votive images all grouped by region.

Continuing in the same direction, walk along by the Doca do Bom Sucesso
until you come to the famous **Torre de Belém** ⑱ (open Tues–Sun 10am–5pm).
Originally called the Castle of St Vincent, the tower was made a World Heritage
Site in 1983, and is one of the best-known sights in the city. Like the Jerónimos
Monastery, it is a marvellous example of Manueline architecture, although the
lines here are heavier. It was built from 1512 to 1521 by Francisco de Arruda to
defend this part of the harbour, called Restelo. Originally the fortress sat out in
the river, surrounded by water, but the Tejo has changed its course since then and
washed the tower up on to its shore. From 1580 to 1828 it was used as a state
prison, with offenders housed in the damp dungeons.

*Woven tapestries are
on display in the
Museu de Arte
Popular.*

Francisco de Arruda spent some time in Morocco and his architectural flourishes seem more Moorish than European. But, of course, the edifice is a Christian one – note the countless crosses of the Order of Christ which circle it. On
the second-storey terrace, which looks out over the river, the centrepiece is a
statue of the Virgin (Our Lady of Safe Voyages), carrying the Christ Child.
There are elaborate carvings in the central section, including a whimsical crea-
ture playing a violin. Inside, spiral staircases lead to higher levels: on the next
floor a room with a corner fireplace; three storeys up, a vaulted room with
"whispering gallery" qualities; at the very top, an open roof with a great view.

BELOW: the famous
Torre de Belém.

Map
on pages
144–5

Two very different museums

Head east again now, along Avenida Brasília, back past the *docas*. Just beyond the Estação Fluvial de Belém (Ferry Terminal) is the **Museu da Electricidade** (Electricity Museum; open Tues–Sun 10am–12.30pm, 2–5.30pm; admission charge). The museum is situated in the old thermal power plant next to the river and houses machines used in the production and supply of the city's electricity during the first half of the 20th century.

Leaving the river behind you at Belém station, cross over the footbridge to the Praça Afonso de Albuquerque, past the central statue of the Viceroy to the East Indies, atop a tall column. Beyond is the old **Palácio Real de Belém** (Belem Royal Palace). This pale-pink building was erected in 1700 by the Count of Aveiro. King João V acquired it in 1726, thinking it would make a healthy summer palace. After earthquake damage in 1755, its present neo-classical façade was added. The building now includes the official residence of the President of the Republic of Portugal, although the part facing the square was originally the stables and riding school.

It was Queen Amélia, wife of King Carlos I, who inaugurated the **Museu Nacional dos Coches** (National Coach Museum; open Tues–Sun 10am–6pm; admission charge), which is situated in the former riding school of the Royal Palace. The queen's swirling, dusky-pink velvet cloak, which she presented to the museum in 1936, long after she had been forced into exile, is in a showcase in the room dedicated to her. The building was redesigned by Italian architect Giacomo Azzolini, after a Royal Decree in 1786 ordered the demolition and rebuilding of the riding school. The ceilings are decorated with enchanting paintings by Portuguese artists of the period.

TIP

From the Estação Fluvial de Belém there is a regular passenger ferry service across the river to Porto Brandão and Trafaria.

BELOW:
a magnificent coach in the Museu Nacional dos Coches.

The collection of vehicles is, perhaps, the finest of its kind anywhere – one imagines the larger, more ornate coaches proceeding regally down Lisbon's Praça de Liberdade on state occasions, or the smaller ones criss-crossing the gardens of the royal palaces on sunny mornings. Especially imposing are the huge carriages commissioned by King João V – one for his own use, and three for the Grand Legation to Pope Clement XI – with their extravagant groups of carved and gilded baroque-style figures. The coach used by King José I, the berlin made for the Queen Maria I for the inauguration of the Basilica da Estrêla, a delightful 18th-century French litter and the miniature carriage used by King Carlos I as a child are just a few of the delights offered by this museum.

Map on pages 144–5

Royal palace

Climb up the Calçada da Ajuda, the steep street that runs alongside the Coach Museum (or take a tram or bus No. 14 or 73), to the Largo da Ajuda where stands a large neoclassical building designed by the Italian architect Fabri. This is the **Palácio Nacional da Ajuda** ⓴ (open Thur–Tues 10am–5pm; admission charge). This enormous palace was started in 1802 under João VI. It was meant to replace a wooden structure that had been built on the site, complete with opera house, as temporary royal residence after the 1755 earthquake, but which burned to the ground in 1795. The permanent palace was never finished, but it was used by the royal family – Queen Maria Pia lived here until 1910.

It is fascinating to see how lavishly, yet awkwardly, the family inhabited its royal chambers. If you take the offered tour, which is occasionally given in English, there is much to see, including tapestries, portraits and many rare examples of decorative arts. There is an amusingly elaborate birdcage, and

LEFT: inside the Palácio da Ajuda.
RIGHT: the doorway of the little Capela de São Jerónimos.

Map
on pages
144–5

A delicate figure displayed in the Museu de Etnologia.

BELOW: soldiers queuing for tarts at the Antiga Confeitaria.
RIGHT: the Padrão dos Descobrimentos.

furniture made of Saxe porcelain. The state dining room is still used for large banquets and many rooms have wonderful ceilings, each one different. The famous library, on the ground floor, cannot be visited, but it is used by researchers and scholars who have obtained special permission.

Cultural booty

Slightly off our route but not far away (bus No. 32 from Rua Jardim Botânico), in Avenida da Ilha da Madeira, is the **Museu de Etnologia** ㉑ (open Tues 2–6pm, Wed–Sun 10am–6pm; admission charge). This starkly modern building, with a cool, spacious interior, forms part of an anthropological research institute and contains a valuable and fascinating collection of objects from various cultures around the world – African, Asiatic and South American – collected mainly during missions to these areas.

Tastefully displayed in spotlit showcases are items such as large, colourful, feather ritual masks from Brazil, African tribal sculptures and the musical instruments of various ethnic groups. The museum also owns an outstanding collection of Portuguese ethnographic items.

Very close to the Ethnological Museum is the **Capela de São Jerónimos** in Rua Pêro da Covilhã. With lovely views of the Belém Tower and the river this little chapel, built in 1514 at the same time as the Jerónimos Monastery, is also in Manueline style. Although historically important, it is often overlooked. It was here that the navigators held prayers and vigils before setting sail on their epic voyages.

From here, head back down to the monastery but, before returning to the city centre, don't forget to visit the Antiga Confeitaria de Belém *(see below)*. ❏

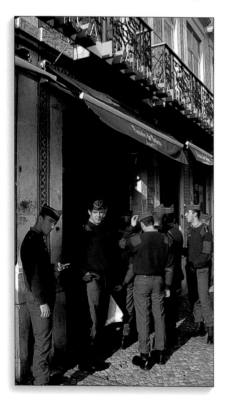

SECRET TARTS

You can't go to Lisbon and not sample one of the *pastéis de Belém*, creamy custard tarts made to a special and, of course, secret recipe. These tarts, generically known as *pastéis de nata*, can be found all over the city, but those from the Antiga Confeitaria de Belém are the *crème de la crème*. The story is that they used to be made by the monks of Jerónimos Monastery, just a few steps away, and that when the monasteries were dissolved in the 1830s the recipe was passed on to a local baker. It is also said that only three bakers at any one time know the recipe, which they pass on to someone else on retirement. Obviously, they can't all go on holiday at the same time.

Because it is such an institution the café gets very busy in the summer months, particularly at weekends. Open from 8am until 11pm or sometimes midnight, it never stops buzzing. It's a huge place, although you wouldn't know it from outside. A warren of rooms, all lined with blue-and-white *azulejos* hides behind a small shopfront. Here locals and visitors alike drink good coffee and enjoy the delicious little tarts, topped with a sprinkling of cinnamon and sugar from the old-fashioned shakers that the waiters plonk unceremoniously on the table.

Map on page 120

PARQUE DAS NAÇÕES

Expo '98 provided an opportunity to revitalise a run-down area of the city. Lisbon rose to the challenge, employing innovative architects to create a site that is now a popular leisure area

BELOW:
the Vasco da Gama tower with cable cars in motion.

The **Parque das Nações** (Park of Nations) was created for Lisbon's **Expo'98**. Prior to Expo, the site was a petrol refinery (one of the refinery's towers remains as a reminder) and a generally derelict industrial area, which also included the old seaplane terminal. It totals 60 hectares (148 acres) and is located at the eastern end of the Lisbon waterfront on the Tejo estuary. It has been highly successful in revitalising a run-down part of Lisbon that many locals had never visited.

For many people in Portugal, the hosting of Expo'98 was the final confirmation that the years of dictatorship were truly in the past and the country had assumed a position as a dynamic, modern economy among the Western European democracies.

The exhibition was a significant national success, even if it did not attract huge numbers from overseas (due in part to an indifferent publicity campaign). Through its oceanic theme, linking the ex-Portuguese colonies with concern for their future, it provided an appropriate bridge between a colourful history and the new Portugal.

The concurrent building of the impressive new bridge, **Ponte Vasco da Gama** alongside, gave an added dimension to this concept. A second Tejo bridge had become necessary to reduce the pressure of traffic on the Ponte 25 de Abril, further west, but funds had not previously been available.

Stunning architecture

The site retains all its fine modern buildings and facilities, put to good new uses. Most people arrive at the park via the Metro which surfaces at the mainline station, the **Estação do Oriente**, designed by Spanish architect Santiago Calatrava. This is one of the most stunning buildings of the development and is well worth a visit, even if you aren't going to catch an overland train. Its graceful structures provide an unforgettable entry point to the park.

The **Oceanário** (open daily 10am–7pm; admission charge), designed by American architect Peter Chermayeff, is the largest in Europe. This fascinating aquarium recreates different marine habitats and has fine displays of each ocean's distinctive fauna. In itself, it's a good reason to visit the site; children love it, but adults are usually hooked, as well.

Feast for the eyes

There are numerous places to eat and drink, and new ones seem to be opening all the time, since Lisboetas have got into the habit of frequenting the site. For a meal with a view, there's a swish restaurant at the top of the **Torre Vasco da Gama**. The tower itself, made of concrete, is the highest building in Lisbon at 145 metres (575 ft). The panoramic terrace sits above the restaurant, which is 100 metres (330 ft) up the tower.

Another splendid way to see the park and get fine views over the river and city is to take a ride in the **Teleférico** (cable car) which runs the full length of the site, parallel to the river.

The **Vasco da Gama Shopping Centre** is thriving, with most of the outlets even the keenest shopper could hope for – currently there are about 160 stores.

Prize pavilions

Other notable examples of contemporary architecture include the **Pavilhão do Conhecimento** (Pavilion of Knowledge), an interactive science and technology museum, and the **Pavilhão da Realidade Virtual** (Pavilion of Virtual Reality), a multimedia experience that focuses on varying subjects.

The **Pavilhão de Portugal**, designed by leading architect Álvaro de Siza Vieira, now houses government department offices so it cannot be visited but its exterior is splendid.

There's culture here, too: plays in the magnificent **Teatro Camões** and regular concerts in the **Pavilhão Atlântico**, a building with good accoustics and a space-age aspect. The pavilion hosts sporting events such as the World Indoor Athletics Championships. There is also a bowling alley, a lively atmosphere around the restaurants and bars, and a busy market all day on Sunday.

The Parque das Nações has been accepted by local people as a place to visit and enjoy, and it makes an interesting trip for visitors, as it shows such a completely different aspect of Lisbon. ❑

TIP

You can reach the Parque das Nações by Metro from Alameda Station, but if you decide to drive instead, there is a large car park at the shopping centre.

BELOW:
the Oceanário recreates an undersea world.

Map on page 124

EATING OUT

Whether they are standing elbow to elbow at a lunchtime counter, sitting in the sun by the river, or splashing out in a chic restaurant, the people of Lisbon love their food

In Lisbon, eating out is not just a special treat, or an experience for visitors: everyone dines out, and often. Consequently, you'll find locals crowding all of the more modest eateries both at lunchtime and in the evening. It's hard to go wrong with the local food, which is fresh, filling and full of flavour.

Traditionally, the Lisboetas are known as *alfacinhas* (little lettuces), a word with Moorish origins that has been their nickname since the 19th century, because of the amount of salad eaten by the inhabitants at that time. However, they've branched out a bit since then.

In recent years, traditional dishes from the Portuguese regions, always available in the capital, have been supplemented by a range of international cuisines, especially from Portuguese-speaking ex-colonies in Africa, Asia and South America. Coupled with this has come the inevitable arrival of the fast-food culture, increasingly popular with young people here as elsewhere in the world.

Riverside haunts

From the expensive Restaurant Torre T, with unsurpassed views from Lisbon's highest building, the Torre Vasco da Gama in Parque das Nações, along to the lively collection of restaurants in the Doca de Santo Amaro, and the up-market Vela Latina Restaurant in Belém, you can't fail to find somewhere that will suit your appetite and your pocket without even moving away from the riverside.

With its proximity to the sea and a river, the abundance of fish and seafood inevitably influences Lisbon's cuisine. Try the *arroz de marisco*, a delicious seafood rice dish, or the splendid *caldeirada de peixe*, a seafood stew, that was once a means of using up any leftover fish but is now one of Lisbon's most typical dishes. But there is nothing to compare with charcoal-grilled freshly caught sardines *(sardinha assadas)* for lunch, eaten while you sit out on an esplanade in the sun, with views of the river and the city, all topped with a bottle of wine.

Bairro Alto

The Bairro Alto is the most popular place to eat out and it is here that you will find a wide range of good restaurants. One of the best known in the district is **Tavares**. The walls are covered with mirrors and gilt and crystal chandeliers hang from the high ceilings. Service is attentive and the staff speak English. On the menu there may be fillets of sole with champagne or crabmeat in a crêpe with cheese sauce.

Occasionally the string trio from the Gulbenkian Foundation Symphony will turn up and play for customers. The dining room is not large, so reservations are recommended.

PRECEDING PAGES: cafés and restaurants on the Doca de Santo Amaro are always buzzing with life.
BELOW: a traditional Alfama restaurant.

Other Bairro Alto restaurants that offer sophisticated menus are **Pap´Açorda** or **Consenso**, and the elegant **Clara-Jardim Restaurant**, just off nearby Rossio. On the hill opposite, **Michel's**, famous for its French cuisine, is tucked into the outer wall of Castelo de São Jorge. For a more Portuguese flavour and fine views, try the **Casa do Leão** within the castle walls. But for a real treat Lisboetas take the ferry across the Tejo to Calcilhas. There on the wharf is **Atiro-te au Rio** (Throw Yourself in the River), a trendy restaurant with a great view of the city.

The *tascas*

If you want to experience the real pleasures of eating in the city, you must go to the *tascas*. These tiny restaurants usually consist of just one room with tables and chairs set close together. The kitchen, mostly staffed by various family members, is behind a counter or wall along the back. Service is invariably pleasant and attentive, and you can linger for hours over your meal. This is the source of true, unadulterated Portuguese food. Servings are generous and the ingredients are always fresh.

To start the meal there is usually bread, butter and *queijo* (a soft cream cheese), and sometimes olives, vegetable pâté or fragrant herb butter, and *presunto*, thin slices of cured ham. Or you might try *pipis* as an appetiser; this is made up of parts of animals that one would not normally think of eating but, tastily marinated in lemon juice or wine, it goes down surprisingly well with the traditional *soloio* bread.

When ordering wine, you will probably be pleased with the quality of *um garrafa de casa de vinho*, a bottle of the house wine, whether *tinto* (red), *branco* (white) or *verde* (green), which is also white, but very young and slightly fizzy.

TIP

You could finish off a meal with a visit to the Solar do Vinho do Porto at 45 Rua de São Pedro de Alcântara (open Mon–Sat 2pm–midnight). Here, in their comfortable lounge, you can sample a glass or two from over 200 varieties of port.

BELOW: a dish of clams and a bottle of white wine... sometimes simple things are best.

For soup, the most obvious choice is *caldo verde*, which originated in the northern province of Minho and is now popular throughout Portugal. This shredded cabbage soup with a potato base is usually served with exactly one slice of sausage floating in each bowl. As with much of Portuguese food, thriftiness has become a tradition. Another excellent choice for soup is *açorda á Alentejana*. An *açorda* is a bread soup, and this one is made with lots of coriander and garlic, and whole poached eggs.

Your next course will traditionally be fish, followed by meat, but you can always skip one course, or order one of each and split them with a companion. Fish is almost always good, particularly the *espadarte* (swordfish), *linguado* (sole) and *tamboril* (monkfish).

As already mentioned, the seafood is delicious, but some of it, lobster in particular, is expensive. However, the small clams called *amêijoas* are very tasty and inexpensive – try them with garlic and fresh coriander *(amêijoas a bulhão pato)*, and you will almost certainly end up mopping up the sauce with bread, just like the locals. If you like squid, try them stuffed *(lulas recheadas)* or simply grilled as a kebab with prawns *(espetada de lulas com gambas)*.

The national dish

The notable exception to fresh ingredients is the ubiquitous *bacalhau* – salt cod. The Portuguese claim to have 365 ways of preparing their national dish, one for every day of the year. Simply grilled, *bacalhau* retains its cardboard consistency, but there are many savoury ways it can be dished up, such as *bacalhau à Gomes de Sá* (casseroled with potato and onion), or *à brás* (with scrambled eggs, onion and potato), making this local staple well worth sampling.

TIP

Cervejarias are bars specialising in beer, but they usually serve snacks as well, often to be eaten standing at the counter.

BELOW:
barbecuing in the streets of Alfama.

Meat courses

Beef is increasingly popular, although it may be tough. Chicken is good when barbecued on a spit, a widespread practice here. Still, you may want to stick with pork, which is particularly sweet and tender. Be sure to try *carne de porco á Alentejana*, pork marinated in wine and served with small clams – it's an unexpected and delicious combination. If you want to splurge, many of the more expensive restaurants serve *leitão assado*, a roast suckling pig dish from central Portugal. Another pork dish is the classic *cozido á Portuguesa*, a hearty plate of boiled cabbage with sausages, ham, sometimes beef, and the occasional pig's foot tossed in. More typical of Lisbon is *iscas a Portuguesa*, marinated liver cooked with smoked ham and potatoes. Game includes quail *(codorniz)*, partridge *(perdiz)* and, in season, wild boar *(javali)*.

Sweets and cheeses

The Portuguese have a sweet tooth, which makes some of their desserts, *sobremesas*, a bit much for many visitors. However, the *pudim* (crème caramel) is often good, and some restaurants have an orange custard that will make you glad you squeezed it in. Then there is chocolate mousse, which is especially dense and rich. To cut the sweetness, try the Portuguese trick of pouring a shot of dry white port or *aguardente* (local brandy) into a hollowed centre.

After all this, if you still have an appetite, sample some Portuguese cheese. The most famous, from the central Serra da Estrela, is made from ewe's milk and can be served fresh (best in spring) or cured. Cheese often comes served with *marmelada*, a quince jam. Finally, round things off with a coffee (a *bica* is a small, strong black one) and, if you're not driving, an *aguardente velha*. ❏

Map on page 124

TIP

Vegetarians (if they don't eat fish) have a bit of a rough deal in Lisbon. The vegetable soups aren't to be trusted (meat stock may be added), and omelettes and plain salads are usually all that are on offer.

BELOW: an ornate pastry shop in Bairro Alto.

LOCAL CUSTOMS

Breakfast *(pequeno almoço)* in Lisbon is a light meal; usually just coffee and a roll or pastry. For those who need something more substantial to fortify them for a day's sightseeing, some hotels include a large, buffet-style breakfast in the price of the room.

Lunch *(almoço)* is a major event, eaten between 1 and 3pm, and dinner *(jantar)* doesn't usually start until about 9pm. Restaurants do open earlier (around 7pm), but you will find yourself sharing them only with other non-Portuguese visitors if you eat early.

Many places do a lunchtime *ementa turística*, a tourist set menu, which offers a cheap two- or three-course meal, often with wine included. Some are great value, others a bit on the mean side. If one is available, a *prato do dia* (dish of the day) can be worth trying if you want to be a bit adventurous.

Service is usually included on the bill and in some places you may see IVA (VAT) itemised. On the whole, you can eat – and drink – pretty cheaply in Lisbon, except in the obviously smart and pricey places. When you ask for the *contazinha* (literally, the little bill), that's usually what it is.

For a selection of restaurants and a glossary of useful gastronomic terms, see Travel Tips.

SHOPPING

Lisbon has some shiny new shopping centres and smart up-town boutiques, but many visitors find browsing in the street markets or discovering the small speciality shops is more rewarding

Map on page 124

O ne-stop shopping has only recently arrived in Lisbon. Most of the city's shops are small, traditional, family affairs, selling a limited range of products, so local people have to visit a number of different places for their weekly shop. This may be time-consuming for residents, but it does make shopping into a kind of social event, with people meeting in habitual places and stopping to chat. For the visitor, it also helps to give the bustling streets of the Baixa and Bairro Alto an old-fashioned air. However, Lisbon has entered the second millennium with a flourish. There has been a revolution and – apart from football – shopping has become the favourite pastime.

Commercial revolution

The frontrunner in the mid-1980s was the (then) daring, post-modern **Amoreiras** complex to the northwest of the city, considered huge with its 250 shops, restaurants and cinemas. More recently, the largest shopping centre in the Iberian peninsula has opened. **Colombo**, located in the new part of the city (Colégio Militar Metro station), with more than 400 shops, 60 restaurants and a 10-screen cinema complex, is a world in itself. Colombo also offers a Tourist Card, which gives a discount in some shops and restaurants.

On the other side of the city, overlooking the Tejo, is the newly opened **Centro Vasco da Gama** complex, located in the Parque das Nações (the former site of Expo'98; *see page 158*). Walking around this well-designed shopping centre feels almost like being on board a cruise ship. There are about 160 shops, including many of the big international chains, and some 30 restaurants serving Portuguese and international cuisine, as well as the ubiquitous fast food. There's also a vast car park, so there's no problem with transport for people who get carried away with their purchasing.

A smaller, élite shopping centre can be found in the Avenidas Novas area *(see page 184)*. Via Veneto on Avenida João XXI, which intersects Avenida de Roma, has more than 40 shops selling high-quality goods – mainly fashion. It is open Monday to Saturday from 10am to 8pm. In Avenida de Roma itself there's an Ana Salazar boutique; she's one of Portugal's best-known fashion designers – good but pricy.

Rising from the ashes

For centuries the commercial heart of the city has been the Baixa and the Chiado, on the edge of the Bairro Alto. But in August 1988 a terrible fire savaged the area, destroying dozens of shops, including Grandella, an old-fashioned department store. Slowly, a new district has risen from the ashes,

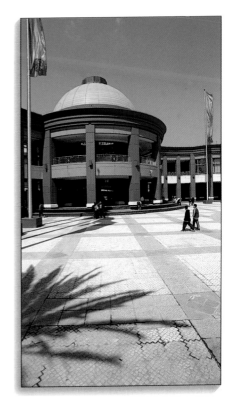

LEFT: the Centre Vasco da Gama.
BELOW: Colombo Shopping Centre has more than 400 shops.

bringing with it a return to the golden days of the Chiado. The shopping complex called **Os Armazens do Chiado**, with its 40 shops and a dozen restaurants, is a pleasure to visit.

Visitors will find the flat streets of the Baixa *(see page 125)*, where most of the shops are located, the easiest places to stroll and shop. **Rua dos Fanqueiros** is filled with clothing and fabric stores. **Rua da Prata** and **Rua do Ouro**, although no longer specialising in silver and gold, as their names suggest, do have a number of good jewellers' shops. **Rua Augusta**, one of the busiest traditional shopping streets in the Baixa, has just about everything, including a small arts and crafts market at its southern end.

For a closer look at modern Portuguese fashion and accessories while you are in the Baixa area, you could pay a visit to the **Modalisboa Design Centre**, situated in the new Lisboa Welcome Centre off Praça do Comércio *(see page 124)*. Here up-and-coming Portuguese designers show off their skills.

Shops in the main streets of the Baixa have tasteful window displays.

Traditional crafts

The most interesting purchases, however, are traditional Portuguese handicrafts. From hand-carved toothpicks to wicker furniture to regional costumes, there is an enormous range of crafts produced in Portugal, from the Minho region to the Algarve. The most famous handicrafts include hand-painted tiles *(azulejos)*, pottery, Arraiolos carpets and rugs, embroidery and lace work and filigree jewellery from the Minho. Portuguese crystal is also of high quality. Leather goods – handbags, belts and shoes – are good value. Although the selection of items is greater and often of better quality in the regions in which they are produced, most handicrafts are available in Lisbon *(see Travel Tips section)*.

BELOW: pottery in the Feira da Ladra.

Ceramics

Pottery is produced in almost every area of the country. The range of items is wide – from mugs, bowls and dishes to the ubiquitous Barcelos Rooster, one of the symbols of Portugal. You will probably encounter two terms no matter where or what you buy: *faience* and *barro*. *Faience* pottery is made of high-quality white clay; *barro* is a more earthy, red-brown clay. *Barro* pottery may be glazed and painted or unglazed. It is generally destined for day-to-day, practical purposes, and is less expensive than the more decorative *faience*. If you buy unglazed *barro* pottery and intend to use it in an oven or over direct heat, be sure to let it soak overnight in water before use, otherwise, it may crack.

Regional ceramics are extremely varied. Vista Alegre, which comes from a town near Aveiro, is one of the best known. Pottery from the Alentejo often features paintings of fruit or flowers. The best-known Coimbra pottery – copies of 16th-century work that show a clear Oriental influence – comes from the Conimbriga area. Viana do Castelo pottery is blue and white, and distinctive black pottery comes from Viseu and Bisalhões, near Vila Real.

Rugs and needlework

Beautiful, geometric hand-woven Arraiolos rugs and carpets are available in Lisbon. Some claim the craft goes back to the Middle Ages; others say it dates from the 17th century. Persian rugs brought back from early trading expeditions may well have lent their patterns to these rugs; the soft colours, though, are pure Portuguese. There is a wide variety of designs to choose from, or you may order your own; most stores are familiar with shipping goods overseas.

Much of the lovely needlework you see in Portugal comes from Madeira, and includes crocheted bedspreads and tablecloths, embroidered place mats, linen and fine laces. Mainland work is beautiful, too, and you'll find it sold not only in the shops but on the streets as well.

Atlantis, Portuguese crystal, is internationally known for its high quality. Lead crystal comes in several grades, depending on the percentage of lead oxide. In Portugal, you'll find superior-quality lead crystal, which is at least 30 percent. The best can be distinguished by its weight, clarity and shine.

Markets

The city's main food and flower market, a cheerful, colourful affair, is the **Mercado da Ribeira** near the Cais de Sodré station, held from Monday to Saturday from dawn until about 2pm. The **Feira da Ladra**, at Campo Santa Clara, near the Alfama, gets its name (Thieves' Fair) because many of the goods are rumoured to be stolen. It's a large flea market and the range of items is enormous, from toy boats to antique telephones, from old prints to army surplus. Some of the most intriguing stalls sell antique books and thousands of vintage postcards. The Feira da Ladra operates on Tuesday and Saturday morning; Saturdays tend to be very crowded. Every Sunday from 10am to 7pm there is a market at **Parque das Nações**, with each Sunday having a particular theme, ranging from collectors' items to street art and antiques. ❏

Map on page **124**

TIP

Buy a Lisboa Shopping Card at a tourist office and you will get discounts of between 5 and 20 percent at shops in Avenida da Liberdade, Chiado and the Baixa.

BELOW: shopping in food markets has changed little over the years.

NORTHERN HEIGHTS

Shady parks and botanical gardens, ornate palaces and the famous aqueduct would be reason enough for visiting the northern areas of Lisbon, but the Gulbenkian Foundation makes a trip essential

Map on page 174

T he northern neighbourhoods of Lisbon are sometimes overlooked by visitors, but they shouldn't be, as they have a lot to offer. For a start, they are a delight for anyone who enjoys plants and flowers. Although Portugal's capital is a sizable city, dominated by tile, brick and stone, it has managed to preserve some attractive green spots and open spaces, very welcome on a hot summer day. There are also a number of excellent museums and galleries, including the Gulbenkian Museum; additionally, it is an area where some serious shopping goes on. This chapter will take you on a tour of the most interesting sites in the upper part of the city.

The museum in the garden

In the hot summer months the **Jardim Botânico ❶** (Botanical Garden; open Apr–Sept, Mon–Fri 9am–8pm, Sat–Sun 10am–8pm; Oct–Mar till 6pm; admission charge) is a good place to get away from the noise and heat of the city. Leave the Rato Metro station in the busy Largo do Rato and walk past the antique shops and small art galleries of Rua da Escola Politécnica, where the garden is situated, or take a No. 58 or 100 bus to Praça do Príncipe Real.

The main entrance to the 4 hectares (10 acres) of gardens is along a dusty alley lined with tall palm trees, beside the old academic buildings that now contain the cheerful and child-friendly **Museu de Ciência** (Museum of Science; open Mon–Fri 10am–1pm, 2–5pm, Sat 3–6pm; admission charge). Its aim is to make science fun, and it succeeds, without being patronising. It can get busy when school groups are visiting, but their enthusiasm is infectious.

Weird Australian trees greet you as you enter the gardens, their colossal trunks twisting and bending in the oddest way, as do their trunk-sized roots. Follow the black-and-white paved path on a restful downhill stroll. The garden is filled with rare trees and plants, all labelled for easy identification.

Jardim da Estrela

Returning to Largo do Rato, you will find the **Jardim da Estrela ❷** (Estrela Gardens) in Largo da Estrela at the opposite end of Avenida Pedro Álvares Cabral. These gardens are officially called the Jardim Guerra Junqueiro, but not many local residents are likely to be aware of their true name.

This is very much a neighbourhood park: children are brought to play in the spacious, well-equipped areas designated for them, and older residents pass the time chatting on the shady benches.

The European trees (most of which are planes and elms) and the neat flowerbeds and shrubs are fenced

PRECEDING PAGES: the Palácio dos Marquêses de Fronteira. **LEFT:** Sunday in the Parque Eduardo VII. **BELOW:** the Basílica da Estrela.

in so that you can look but not touch as you stroll along the pathways. A small lake, with a statue of a young girl in the middle, has the obligatory goldfish, carp and ducks. Next to it there is an open-air café with plenty of tables at which to stop and have a drink. The highlight of the park is a delightful wrought-iron gazebo, its elegant arches decorated with delicate fretwork.

Not far from these gardens is the Anglican **Cemitério dos Ingleses** (English Cemetery), where the great 18th-century novelist and playwright Henry Fielding was buried in 1754.

The gardens of the Jardim da Estrela are full of well-kept flower beds.

Basílica da Estrela

Walking through the gardens, you can't fail to be impressed by the sight of the imposing **Basílica da Estrela ❸** (open daily 6.30am–1pm, 3–8pm), with its large twin bell towers and finely shaped dome – remarkable for being made not of lead but of solid stone. The basilica, which was commissioned by the devout Maria I to fulfil a vow she had made for the birth of a son, was

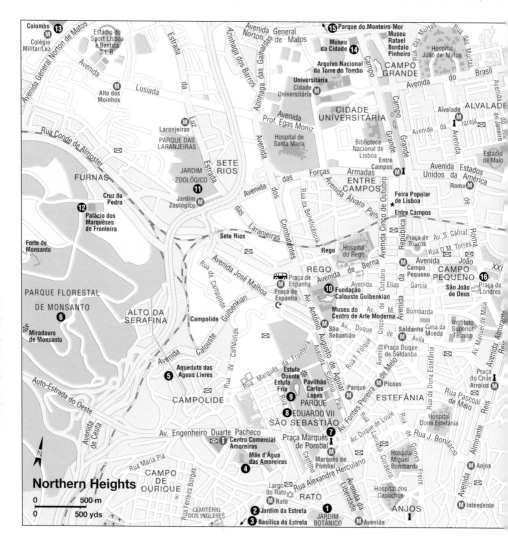

erected in the 1780s. Designed by architects of the Mafra School, the exterior is neoclassical, the interior a dignified baroque, with pale, gleaming marble in blues, yellows and pinks. Tucked in a small room is an enormous nativity scene carved by Machado de Castro, composed of over 500 cork and terracotta figures.

Map on page 174

The tomb of Inacio de São Caetano, a man who rose from nothing to become confessor to the queen, is here, as is that of Maria I herself, who died insane in 1816 in Brazil. Her tomb is a particularly morbid affair of black marble, decorated with a writhing serpent, mourning angels and marble skulls.

Bringing water to the city

On the far side of the Largo do Rato, in Rua das Amoreiras, is the impressive **Mãe d'Água das Amoreiras** ❹ (open Mon–Sat 10am–6pm; admission charge), which once supplied the city with water from its reservoir. There are magnificent views from here over the city. Adjacent to the aqueduct, and housed in a former silk factory, is the **Fundação Arpad Szenes-Vieira da Silva** (open Mon and Wed–Sat noon–8pm, Sun 10am–6pm; admission charge). The foundation is dedicated to the modernist works of Maria Helena Vieira da Silva, born in Lisbon in 1908, and her Hungarian husband, Arpad Szenes, both regarded in Portugal as important painters.

At the upper end of the Rua das Amoreiras, overlooking the Alcântara valley, is the enormous pink edifice of the Centro Comercial Amoreiras, a modern complex of offices, shops, restaurants and cinemas.

About 1km (½ mile) northwest, but well worth the diversion if you have time, is the **Aqueduto das Águas Livres** ❺ (guided tours, Mar–Nov). Leaving the three pink towers of the commercial centre behind you, cross the Avenida Engenheiro Duarte Pacheco, into the cobbled street of Prof. Sousa da Câmara. Continue along this street for a short distance, and then bear left into Calçada da Quintinha.

This remarkable structure was built between 1729 and 1748; by centring an arch over a fault in the ground, the designers created a truly sound structure that was tested a few years later when it emerged triumphantly whole after the Great Earthquake. The aqueduct is 18 km (11 miles) long, and still brings fresh water to the city. There used to be a walkway open along the top of it but, deemed dangerous, it was closed in 1844. If you take one of the tours, you get easy access to Monsanto Park.

BELOW: the Aqueduto das Águas Livres.

Parque Florestal de Monsanto

Stretching uphill to the west of the city, the **Parque Florestal de Monsanto** ❻ is the largest park in Lisbon, running from behind the Palácio Nacional da Ajuda as far north as the suburb of Benfica. It was established by Salazar, and may survive as his most positive legacy. There are public tennis courts with a nice bar, a jogging track (*circuito de manutenção*), and a children's playground containing the shell of a World War II fighter plane and a defunct tram car. Ninety percent of Monsanto is covered with eucalyptus, plane, cedar and oak trees, unfortunately overgrown and not very well cared for. Litter is strewn among the ferns, and hookers solicit openly by the roadside.

Much of the park is on high ground and two *miradouros* offer different perspectives of the city. **Miradouro de Monsanto** is well signposted, but another way to find it is to look for the tall television receiver that stands beside it. Here, a telescope aids the panoramic view across to the industrial south bank of the Tejo, the Ponte 25 de April, the Cristo Rei statue with the Arrábida mountains behind, the Castelo São Jorge and the dome of the Basílica da Estrela. You could also admire all this from the restaurant at the *miradouro*.

The **Miradouro de Montes Claros** is situated in a much prettier setting than the Miradouro de Monsanto, but its westerly vista is less impressive, marred somewhat by the ugly suburban tower blocks of Alfragide. **Montes Claros** is the highest point in Monsanto and much effort has gone into making it appealing. Flowering trees, an ornamental lake and an ivy-clad colonnade separate the viewpoint itself from the car park and restaurant. All the high spots give views over the grand proportions of the Aqueduto das Águas Livres, a sight that, more than any other in Lisbon, must be seen from a distance to be appreciated.

Lisbon's municipal camp site is also in Monsanto and it is considered to be one of the best organised and most attractive in Europe. Shops and amenities on the site make up for its out-of-town location.

BELOW:
swans are at home on the lake in the Parque Eduardo VII.

Parque Eduardo VII

For a very different look at north-of-centre Lisbon, start again at the **Praça Marquês de Pombal ❼**. The vast and busy square was, of course, named after the man responsible for rebuilding the city after the 1755 earthquake. In its

Map
on page
174

centre is a tall column crowned with a statue of the ubiquitous Pombal, posed with a lion at his side, which can be seen from far and wide.

To the north of the square, the luxurious Ritz and Meridien hotels overlook **Parque Eduardo VII 8**, the grand park that reigns over the heart of the city. The formally landscaped gardens were officially opened to the public in 1902, and named in honour of the English king who was in Portugal to reaffirm the Anglo-Portuguese alliance, which dates back to the Treaty of Windsor of 1386.

The sloped lawn is dotted with shady trees and centred on two boulevards paved in black and white, which stretch up to a belvedere at the top of a hill. Dividing the two avenues are formal clipped hedges, cut by horizontal pathways. The belvedere is sided by two massive concrete pillars. From here you can look over the park to the Pombal statue and right down the Avenida da Liberdade to Baixa. Opposite, in commemoration of the millennium, Lisbon erected a Roda (wheel), albeit the smallest in Europe (about 30 metres/100 ft high) from where you get more extensive views. Above is the Jardim Alto do Parque (Garden above the Park), with green spaces, paths, lake and another belvedere.

To the right of the park is the sports pavilion, recently renamed after the Olympic gold-medal marathon runner Carlos Lopes. The grand neo-baroque façade, with pillars, colonnade and statues, gives no hint that the purpose of the building is the pursuit of sports. Four lovely blue-tiled panels depict scenes from famous battles of independence in wars against the Moors and the Spanish. Above the pavilion is a lake-fronted restaurant and café with terrace tables.

The work of creating and maintaining the geometric patterned walks that are found here and all over Lisbon is a skilled job, done by craftsmen called calceteiros. They fit small stones together, rather like in a mosaic, then fill the cracks with sand and cement.

BELOW:
a graceful statue in the Estufa Fria.

Exotic flora

In the northwest corner of the park is the **Estufa Fria** (Cool House) **9** (open daily 9am–5.30pm; admission charge), a horticultural wonderland of exotic plants and flowers. It was undergoing a major facelift when this book went to press, but a visit is highly recommended when it reopens (check with the Tourist Office). To get to it from the belvedere, walk along to Rua Castilho and enter in front of the Meridien Hotel. From the park entrance, take the path to the left up through a grassy area. The Estufa Fria is entirely enclosed by green wooden slats which keep out the sun but allow the air to circulate. It is humid without being uncomfortable and absolutely still – not even the whisper of a breeze.

The structure is beautifully laid out: narrow paths wind between flowering shrubs, gigantic palms, exotic flowers and rare trees. Water is everywhere – ponds, small waterfalls, fountains and streams. You can cross these lilliputian obstacles over pretty Japanese bridges or stepping stones. The air smells wonderful, a combination of rich damp earth and delicate flower perfumes. Discreet labels identify the species and specify the country of origin: Australia, Africa, India, China, Java, South America. Some are recognisable houseplants, such as the rubber plant – except that it is the height of a two-storey house.

The peace and tranquillity are striking. Occasionally the silence is broken by the odd sucking, slurping

noises. The culprits are huge goldfish and Chinese carp who have yet to learn table manners as they feed noisily from around the stones and statuary in the ponds and streams. Most of the walls have been lined with rock, from which trickle down fine cascades of water. Grottoes have been created in corners, where cooling water forms strange calcified patterns.

The Cool House leads you to the smaller **Estufa Quente** (Hot House). It is laid out in a similar way to its cooler neighbour, but supports plants that need higher temperatures. Visually it is just as delightful, and there are exotic flamingos adorning the lotus-filled lake. Doves bill and coo in the small aviaries on the higher levels. It is very hot in here – in high summer it can be unbearably humid – but there is plenty of water to splash on your face.

Gulbenkian's legacy

The **Fundação Calouste Gulbenkian** (Calouste Gulbenkian Foundation) **⑩**, in addition to acting as the most important funding body for the arts in Portugal, has a museum and a centre of modern art. They can be reached from either São Sebastião or Praça de Espanha Metro stations, or on buses 16, 26, 31, 46 or 56. The foundation also has its own orchestra, choir and ballet company.

The **Museu Calouste Gulbenkian** (open Tues 2–6pm, Wed–Sun 10am–6pm; admission charge), in Avenida da Berna, contains a collection of around 6,000 items amassed over a period of 40 years by Armenian oil magnate Calouste Gulbenkian. He created the foundation shortly before his death in 1955, and donated all his treasures to the country that had given him refuge during World War II. The British were not so hospitable, even though he had been granted citizenship in 1902.

LEFT: a gilded Egyptian mask in the Gulbenkian Museum.
RIGHT: a piece from the René Lalique collection.

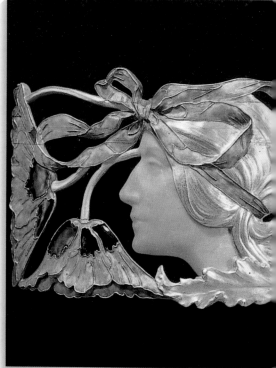

The museum, which was opened to the public in 1969 and substantially renovated and modernised in 2001, has cool exhibition rooms and large windows looking out on a landscaped garden, with a small lake, sculptures and an amphitheatre. The collection is clearly the expression of a singular taste – Gulbenkian is known to have collected works that afforded him great aesthetic pleasure, but not without first consulting experts and connoisseurs. This resulted in a collection that is as diverse as it is excellent.

In the Oriental, Far Eastern, Egyptian and Classical sections there are rare pieces of Chinese porcelain, Chinese jade and Japanese prints, Egyptian sculpture, Greek vases and coins. The European collection includes illuminated manuscripts, early European art and 18th-century French furniture, tapestry and textiles. The fine collection of later European paintings includes works by Rubens, Rembrandt, Degas, Gainsborough, Renoir, Manet and Monet. There is also a whole room full of art nouveau jewellery designed by René Lalique, a personal friend of Gulbenkian.

The gardens of the Gulbenkian Museum display sculpture in a natural setting.

The **Museu do Centro de Arte Moderna** (open Tues 2–6pm, Wed–Sun 10am–6pm; admission charge), situated at the other side of the park-like gardens, displays the work of 20th-century Portuguese artists and includes a collection of contemporary English art.

The next Metro stop is the place to head for if you want to visit the 100-year-old **Jardim Zoológico** ⓫ (Lisbon Zoo; open daily10am–6pm; admission charge). It is set in some 25 hectares (62 acres) that make up the Parque das Laranjeiras (Orange Tree Park). About 2,000 animals, from practically all over the world, are housed here in spacious enclosures amid rose gardens, shrubberies and ornamental ponds. Attractions include a children's farm, a cable car

BELOW:
Metro art at Campo Pequeno station.

ART ON THE METRO

Any visitor who has come to this northern part of the city will have become familiar with Lisbon's Metro system and noticed the efforts that have gone into making the stations more attractive. A number of well-known artists have collaborated in this *Arte no Metro* initiative, with some striking results. Of the northern stations, Campo Grande has blue and white azulejo designs, while Campo Pequeno, where the bullring is, has bullfighting scenes. Baixa-Chiado was designed by Álvaro de Siza Vieira, so is a work of art in itself; while Oriente, in the Parque das Nações, has an underground design to compete with Calatrava's overland station.

Even the names of the Metro lines are colourful: the blue line is called Gaviota (seagull), the green line is Caravela (caravel), the yellow is Girasol (sunflower), while the newest, red line is a bit of a come down, being called simply Oriente (east).

On a more practical note, the Metro is part of Lisbon's integrated transport system, as mentioned elsewhere, and combined tickets make travel cheap and simple. Do remember, though, that you have to validate tickets for each journey by inserting them into a small machine next to the ticket barrier.

Map on page 174

with views over the animal enclosures, a reptile house, dolphin aquarium, cafés, shops and a restaurant. Another feature of the park is an elaborate and curious dogs' cemetery.

Noble mansion

Well worth a diversion from the Zoo – but it is advisable to take a taxi – is the **Palácio dos Marquêses de Fronteira** ⑫ (open daily, guided tours booked in advance 10.30am–noon; tel: 21-778 3386; admission charge). Situated on the edge of Parque Florestal de Monsanto *(see page 175)*, the palace was built between 1650 and 1675 for the Mascarenhas family, and expanded and redecorated in the 18th century. It contains beautiful decorative *azulejos* depicting some famous battles scenes. The dining room is decorated with frescoed panels and oil paintings by great Portuguese artists, such as Domingos Sequeira. The chapel, built in the late 16th century, is adorned with shells, broken glass, scraps of porcelain, bricks and stone.

For many visitors, the lovely gardens and terraces, wonderfully designed in Italian Renaissance style, are the real attraction. There are topiary gardens, fountains, pyramid pavilions and an ornamental lake. Covered terraces display magnificent 17th-century tile panels – the best depicting life-sized knights on horseback. They purport to represent the "Doze de Inglaterra", 12 medieval knights who, according to legend, sailed to England to fight for the honour of 12 English maidens. Other 17th-century panels are less romantic but still beautiful, particularly the 10 with motifs devoted to science and art. Among the statuary, there are full-sized figures of the nine Muses, sculpted in marble (on one of the terraces), and white marble statues of the first 15 Portuguese kings.

BELOW: one of the 15 Portuguese kings whose statues stand in the gardens of the Palácio dos Marquêses de Fronteira.

VELVET REVOLUTIONARY

Dissident poet and political activist of the 1960s and 1970s Antonio de Cairu was born in the northern suburb of Alverca in 1941. By 1960, his avant-garde verse and public recitals had gained a wide following. His first collection of poems (1965) was critically acclaimed but banned by the fascist government, as it revealed him to be a communist and a homosexual, and he was promptly drafted to Africa. His harrowing experiences in Angola and Mozambique and the growing discontent of young soldiers forced to fight guerrilla wars inspired him to write his first novel, *In Search of Sunflowers*. By 1970 de Cairu was back in Portugal where he became an influential political campaigner, his recitals enjoyed by ever-larger crowds. He was tried and imprisoned, narrowly escaping deportation to the Azores thanks to a friend in the ministry.

After the revolution in 1974 *In Search of Sunflowers* became an instant bestseller and his dissident writings were published in several languages. Today, de Cairu continues to write and perform recitals and his works are studied in Portuguese schools. He lives in London and Lisbon, where you can sometimes catch him reciting in the piano bar, **Wireless**, his childhood home at 9 Av. Dr Miguel Bombarda, Alverca, on the way to the airport.

Change of scene

If you have had enough of culture and horticulture for now, and feel like a bit of shopping and cinema, take the Metro from Jardim Zoológico to Colégio Militar-Luz and one of Europe's largest commercial centres, **Colombo** ⓱. Here you can browse around the shops, have lunch or coffee and pastries at one of the many cafés and restaurants, or watch a film in one of the cinemas – there are 10 screens and nearly all films have subtitles.

City museum

Another interesting trip through the northern part of the city involves starting from Praça Marquês de Pombal and taking the Metro to Campo Grande. There you will find the **Museu da Cidade** ⓮ (City Museum; open Tues–Sun 10am–1pm; 2–6pm; admission charge) which is housed in the 17th-century Palácio da Pimenta (Pepper Palace), a fine manorial residence built during the reign of King João V (1706–50). It got its joky name because it was said to have been funded by the proceeds of the spice trade. Many of its walls are decorated in the blue-and-white *azulejos* typical of the period. At the entrance, the visitor is greeted by a celebrated portrait of the poet Fernando Pessoa, painted in 1954 (19 years after his death) by his friend, the multi-faceted painter and writer José Almada Negreiros. A decade later, Almada painted a replica copy which now hangs in the library of the Calouste Gulbenkian Foundation.

The museum charts the history of the city chronologically, from prehistorical archaeological remains, through the Roman and Moorish invasions, the opulence of the period of Portuguese overseas expansion and the reconstruction of the city after the catastrophic earthquake of 1755, and ends with the establishment of the

Map on page 174

Have coffee beneath the palms in the Colombo Centre.

BELOW: children enjoy the zoo.

First Republic in 1910. Panoramic views, objects of everyday use, ceramics and silverware, paintings, engravings and drawings combine to sketch a portrait of the changing face of the city. Special attention is given not only to historical events, but also to the various quarters, the riverfront before and after the Great Earthquake, and to local lore, customs and dress.

Anyone especially interested in ceramics may also enjoy a visit to the nearby **Museu Rafael Bordalo Pinheiro**, which is dedicated to the works of Bordalo Pinheiro, an extraordinary and eccentric 19th-century ceramicist and caricaturist. The museum was closed for renovation work when this guide went to press, so it would be advisable to check with the Tourist Office about current opening times if you are planning to visit.

Not far away, in the university complex on Alameda da Universidade, is the **Arquivo Nacional da Torre do Tombo**, an architecturally striking fortress-like building that houses the national archives.

To the east of the university complex is **Campo Grande**, a park that is very popular with Lisboetas. It is planted with tropical and European trees, and has a small lake with rowing boats for hire.

A great estate

Beyond Campo Grande lies the district of Lumiar, once an area of fashionable estates but now reduced to a rather dreary mass of suburban tower-block apartments with dense traffic on the busy roads.

Tucked away among it, however, is a jewel of a place, the **Parque do Monteiro-Mor** ⑮, an estate, more or less intact, which was once the property of the noble Palmela family and was bought by the state in 1975 (take bus No. 3

Map
on page
174

from Campo Grande Metro). The 18th-century **Palácio Angeja-Palmela** originally belonged to the third Marquês do Angeja (1716–88), the minister who succeeded Pombal.

Both the palace and the adjacent garden were purchased by the Duke of Palmela in 1840. Part of the terrain was then converted into an English-style garden with romantic enclaves, a tea-pavilion and small ponds. The spacious formal gardens are planted with fine old trees, which make it a cool and shady place, very popular with families from the nearby apartments. Picnic areas with tables and benches have been provided should you wish to lunch there, or you could eat in the café in the National Museum of Theatre, one of two museums in the park.

The exhibits in the **Museu Nacional do Teatro** (open Tues 2–6pm, Wed–Sun 10am–6pm; admission charge) include photographs, theatrical costumes, scenery, programmes, in fact everything apertaining to the theatre. It was set up in 1985 and most of the thousands of objects are gifts from private individuals. There is also a library and a section devoted to Amália Rodrigues, the *fado* singer and Portuguese icon (*see page 84*).

A collection of over 30,000 items is displayed in the **Museu Nacional do Traje** (National Costume Museum) nearby (open Tues–Sun 10am–6pm; admission charge), ranging from textiles and fashion accessories, to dolls and toys. A magnificent marble staircase sweeps up to the first floor in which the main collection is housed and where social history is revealed through the collection of vivid costumes dating from the 18th-century court to the Imperial period. The pink and powder-blue stucco, the frescoed ceilings and *azulejos* and the little chapel evoke the styles of the 18th century.

A security guard keeps a friendly eye on things in the Parque do Monteiro-Mor.

BELOW:
the Museu do Traje
is not all historical.

Map on page 174

The Camel Show is an enduring favourite at the Feira Popular.

BELOW:
equine statue on the Fonte Luminosa.
RIGHT:
the starkly elegant São João de Deus.

Popular pastimes

From here, head south on the Metro from Campo Grande and Avenida da República to **Campo Pequeno**, where the large red-brick, neo-classical 19th-century bullring stands in the **Praça de Touros**. This ring is still used regularly and has a small museum dedicated to the *tourada (see page 92)*.

Across the Avenida da República from the bullring is the **Feira Popular de Lisboa** (open Mon–Fri 7pm–1.30am, Sat–Sun and holidays 3pm–1.30am; the admission charge is donated to a children's charity). With its roller-coasters, swings, amusements, kiosks and restaurants, this is a good, old-fashioned fair, and is still the favourite recreational park for city families.

Avenidas Novas

While you are in the north of the city, it might be interesting to explore some streets that most visitors never discover – especially if you are interested in fashion or trends in modern architecture and social engineering. The route starts from the **Roma Metro station** at the junction of Avenida de Roma and Avenida dos Estados Unidos da América. The surrounding area is dominated by striking tower blocks that date from the 1940s and 1950s. The stark austerity of the buildings is softened only by the trailing greenery on the concrete balconies.

A stroll south along **Avenida da Roma** takes you past numerous elegant shops, fashionable boutiques and chic home furnishing stores – this is a street trying to live up to its name. At the end, where it crosses Avenida João XXI, is Via Veneto, a shopping centre with some 40 small up-market stores.

In the middle of the 20th century, a grand plan for the new suburbs of Lisbon was devised by the Salazar regime. The principles that guided it are much in evidence in the **Praça de Londres** ⓰. The residential quarters were designed with a distinctly rural character, intended to be villages in the heart of the city with detached one-family houses, their own neighbourhood church and school.

Just off the square, the **Igreja de São João de Deus**, an eye-catching structure built in 1948, stands in a prominent position at the entrance to an estate called Arco Cego. The proportions of the narrow, turreted tower contrast with the unshapely body of the church. The large structure behind it is a postmodern temple of a different kind – the headquarters of Caixa Geral de Depósitos (the major savings bank), built in 1992.

Nearby towers the pinnacle of 1940s architectural achievements. The **Instituto Superior Técnico** looks down over a park from inside a horseshoe-shaped arc. At the lower end of the park stands a huge, sometimes illuminated, fountain, the **Fonte Luminosa**.

It is usually possible to cross the campus of the Instituto Superior Técnico to reach Avenida João Crisóstomo, a quiet thoroughfare. On the right is the mint, the **Casa da Moeda**, another austere piece of functional architecture. Follow the avenue and cross the wide Avenida da República where you can have a well-deserved break at the *pastelaria* called the **Café Versailles**. With its attractive, old-style interior, this is a place still redolent of old Lisbon, and cheerfully retains its own atmosphere. ◼

Map on page 196

Lisbon

TALES OF THE TEJO

The port on the Tejo was the launching pad for the Portuguese discoveries. These days it is still important for cargo and industry, but it is increasingly used for leisure as well

The chronicler Luiz Mendes de Vasconcellos noted of Lisbon at the beginning of the 17th century: "Because of the port there do throng to it from all parts Ships, bringing provisions and things necessary to life. And thus this commodity has caused this port to be frequented, and hence this City to grow…"

The Rio Tejo – known in English as the Tagus – is truly the *raison d'être* for Lisbon as a capital. Not only does it provide an ideal port, with many sheltered anchorages and wide bays, but it has also made Lisbon Europe's nearest major port to the continents of Africa and the Americas.

Wayfarers of antiquity, including, according to legend, Ulysses, were drawn to the place which held so much promise. After the Phoenicians, the Romans settled and developed the fishing industry, which is still thriving. At the end of the 15th century, Vasco da Gama returned after two years at sea with news of the sea route to India, and Lisbon became the European centre of commerce, a frantically busy port. Not long afterwards, detailed charts began to be made of that century's voyages, with one of the earliest known dated 1560. In 1583 a Dutch chart was one of the first to feature soundings of the Tejo.

The river's source is in the Montes Universales in Spain, not far from Cuenca. In the Portuguese section of its 840-km (525-mile) path to the sea it flows through some beautiful landscapes. Near the end of its journey the Tejo broadens into an estuary to the east and south of Lisbon.

The mouth of the Tejo is defined by two structures, the Torre de São Julião and the Torre do Bugio. Between them is the main channel into the port. The **Torre do Bugio**, a round stone fort with a central tower built on an island in the river off Oeiras, was begun during the reign of João III in the 17th century and was originally made of wood.

The southern part of the estuary – **Mar de Palha** (Sea of Straw) or "Jackass Bay" to English sailors of old – is Lisbon's harbour proper. The river then curves around the city's extensive docks and western suburbs and heads west into the Atlantic Ocean, officially ceasing to be a river at the **Torre de São Julião**, built on a spur of land near **Oeiras**, about halfway between Lisbon and the fishing village and popular resort of **Cascais** *(see page 198)*.

View from above

Looked at from above, the river estuary is large, but the water actually travels through a relatively narrow (although very deep) channel, the Corredor, to the sea. The Mar de Palha, it has been calculated, is large enough to contain all the warships in the world. That is unlikely to be tested, but in the middle of the 16th century there were well over 1,000 river craft working

BELOW: work goes on in the dockyards.

between the various Tejo ports. In 1730, an English visitor, the Rev. John Swinton, noted "almost an infinite number of small Portuguese fishing boats" on the river. Today, from virtually any point along its shores can be seen cargo vessels, pleasure craft, ferries, liners and oil tankers as well as the occasional warship and aircraft carrier.

The estuary is some 25 km (16 miles) long, and varies in width between just over 2 km (a mile) in the Corredor and 14 km (9 miles) across the Mar de Palha. Most commercial activity is centred on the north shore, which has about 14 km (9 miles) of docks and wharves, compared with 3 km (2 miles) on the south bank. More than 15 million tons of cargo pass through the port each year.

The port authorities employ some 60 pilots, whose job is to conduct ships safely in and out of the harbour. It is often a family tradition, and some of them are third-generation pilots. All are highly skilled, and need to be; they may find themselves aboard a 300-ton ship in the morning and a 300,000-ton vessel in the evening, with several tug boats in attendance.

In the estuary north of Lisbon there are large sandbanks called mouchões, and further east is the protected Reserva Natural Estuário do Tejo.

Sea of Straw

The Mar de Palha acts as a vast reservoir, and when the tide is going out the water creates a very strong current in the Corredor, which maintains the down-stream channel and its normal depth. The fastest surface currents have been measured at between 4 and 3 metres (12 ft and 10 ft) a second for the ebb and flood tides respectively. A float put into the river 30 km (18 miles) from the river mouth, near the high-water time of a spring tide, reached the bar channel at an average speed of 5 kph (3 mph). The largest ships to use the port are moved only when tidal conditions allow, but the smaller can sail at any time.

BELOW:
a Tejo tugboat.

There are several wrecks in the estuary. These are marked on the navigation charts used by the pilots, not for historical interest but as places where anchoring should be avoided, to avoid entanglement. The river water isn't clear enough for divers to see much of them.

There are thousands of bass swimming along on the sea bed around the docks but you can't eat them. Local people say they're like vacuum cleaners, sucking up the oil as they feed.

Fishing

Fishing is mostly done either upstream or downstream of Lisbon where the waters are clear and fresh. *Sargo* (sea bream), *robalo* (bass), sole and mullet can all be caught. Fish are to be found the length of the river, of course, but not all are recommended for eating. Portuguese fishermen, whose boats and nets can be seen all along the coast to Cascais, mostly go to the river mouth and beyond, where, as well as *robalo, sargo* and sole, they catch crabs, using special baskets.

Along the south bank

In centuries past the southern shore of the Tejo, the inlets of the **Coina** and **Judeu** rivers, were the sites of shipbuilding yards and moorings. They offered particularly good shelter, allowing shipbuilding to continue during winter, and the abundance of pine and cork trees encouraged the industry to flourish. The smaller size and shallow drafts of ships in those days meant these places could be used, though they are no longer suitable for any serious commercial shipping.

At **Porto Brandão**, sheltered by the hills and situated opposite Belém, there is the **Lazareto**, a curious building where in times past visitors from plague areas were kept for 40 days before they were judged not to be infected and were ferried over the river to Lisbon. In Portuguese, "40 days" is "*quarenta dias*", the origin of the word "quarantine".

BELOW:
sunset over the
Ponte 25 de Abril.

To the east, at **Almada**, and overlooking the Sea of Straw, is an old ruined fort and, nearby, the docks of **Cacilhas**. To the west, facing the Atlantic Ocean, is the **Costa da Caparica**, broad, easy-to-reach beaches which are much favoured by the Lisboetas (*see page 215 for more on the south bank*).

Map on page 196

Rediscovering the old view

For centuries the vast majority of travellers to Lisbon arrived by sailing up the Tejo, and were presented with a wonderful view of the city, rising on its hills: the Praça do Comércio at the front, with the castle, churches and houses ranged behind, the ships and boats passing in the foreground. Today's visitors, whose first view of Lisbon is usually from the air, can rediscover the old view by taking one of the ferries or driving across the Ponte 25 de Abril.

As Fernão Lopes noted during the reign of King Fernando: "And so there did come from divers places many ships to Lisbon, in such a manner that with those that did come from abroad and those that were in the Kingdom, there did often lie before the City 400 and 500 merchant ships…"

Car ferries take commuters and visitors across to the other side.

Enjoying the riverside

Today, although the Tejo is no longer the sole economic lifeblood of the city, it continues to shape the character of Lisbon. There have been changes to the riverside, reflecting contemporary lifestyles: Expo '98 opened up an area to the east, on a site where the Parque das Nações now flourishes. And in the centre of town, the Docas de Alcântara and Santo Amaro are lively spots, lined with cafés and restaurants. The people of Lisbon today are taking advantage of the river as a place for leisure as well as for commerce and industry. ❑

BELOW: the docks are now a place for leisure as well as work.

EXCURSIONS FROM LISBON

*The following chapters highlight some key sites for visitors
with time to venture beyond the city limits*

The remainder of this guide concentrate on some towns, resorts, beaches and monuments outside Lisbon. Many visitors with more than a few days to spare choose to hire a car (or take a train or coach) to explore the area beyond the city. There are also numerous people who make their base in Estoril or Cascais and explore the city from there. The electric train makes the short (29-km/18-mile) trip into Cais do Sodré Station.

Elegant Estoril, once a well-known spa town, Cascais, a royal resort in the 19th century, and Sintra, with its wonderful palaces, form what is known as the Golden Triangle. A little further west lie the beaches of the rocky Atlantic coast.

Further north, about 100 km (60 miles) from Lisbon, is the pilgrimage site of Fátima and, close by, two UNESCO World Heritage Sites, the monastery at Batalha and the Cistercian Abbey at Alcobaça. An efficient new motorway system means they are easily reached by road, and some companies organise coach trips.

Finally, by crossing the River Tejo by ferry, road or rail you come to the Arrábida Peninsula, with broad beaches, fishing villages and the ancient town of Setúbal. Also to the south of the Tejo, and easily reached these days by the E1 motorway, is the beautiful town of Évora, with its pretty houses, Roman remains and some impressive Romano-gothic architecture.

So, if you have time to explore, there is much to see and do without going very far. Public transport is regular and inexpensive but you will of, course, have far more freedom if you travel by car. ❑

PRECEDING PAGES: a bird's eye view of the great monastery at Batalha.
LEFT: Castelo dos Mouros, near Sintra.

ESTORIL AND CASCAIS

Close to Lisbon, these neighbouring resorts are well connected to the city, convenient for exploring as far north as Sintra, and favoured by windsurfers, sunseekers and golfers

Map on page 196

H andily located for **Lisbon ❶**, south-facing Estoril and Cascais are the most significant coastal resorts outside Algarve, although neither is especially large. They grew to prominence as a playground for Lisboetas, but recent years have witnessed a role reversal: these resorts and their environs are dormitories for Lisbon commuters, and are often the preferred places to stay for many visitors whose main intent is to explore the capital.

The electric train offers the quickest and most convenient way of making the 29-km (18-mile) journey into Lisbon. It arrives in Cais do Sodré Station on the west side of town, close to the riverside. As part of the infrastructure improvements for Expo '98, Lisbon's Metro was extended to connect Cais do Sodré to central Lisbon. The mainline train also stops at Belém which is especially convenient for visiting one of the capital's most fascinating areas.

A network of new motorways makes driving into Lisbon somewhat easier than in recent years, although signposting is often confusing and accurate maps hard to obtain. Parking is considerably easier in the city now that metering is widespread – Portuguese motorists *hate* paying for parking. The *Marginal* route along the riverside, once regarded as a delightful drive, suffers from the modern contagion of congestion at busy times. Travelling this route out of Lisbon leads through Belém to the elegant hillside neighbourhood of Restelo, the location of many embassies and diplomatic residences. **Algés** is the first town outside the city limits, and it is here that taxi drivers turn off their meters and start calculating by kilometres.

A string of small riverside towns follow. **Dáfundo** has several splendid old mansions standing in rather sad contrast alongside dilapidated rent-controlled housing. It also has the **Aquário Vasco da Gama** (open Tues–Sun; admission charge), with its fascinating world of sea turtles, eels, barnacles and all kinds of fish.

Cruz Quebrada is the site of a stone-seated stadium built for soccer matches, while **Caxias** is known for its flowering villas, 18th-century gazebos and an infamous hillside prison-fort. In **Oeiras** you'll find a fine 18th-century baroque church, a lovely park, modern apartment blocks and an austere 16th-century fort.

Just beyond lies the 17th-century fortress of **São Julião**, marking the point where the Tejo meets the Atlantic. **Carcavelos** has several moderate hotels and a broad sandy beach.

Elegant Estoril

Estoril ❷ is the first point of what has often been called the Golden Triangle, and includes Cascais and Sintra. A flowering, palm-lined, pastel-coloured resort, it first gained fame at the turn of the century for its

LEFT: one of many elegant houses in Estoril.
BELOW: enjoying the sun on the palm-lined prom.

TIP

The train service
between Lisbon and
Estoril and Cascais is
frequent, and the
journey takes only
about half an hour.

therapeutic spring waters. During World War II, Estoril became known as the haunt of international spies. Later, this corner of the Atlantic, with its mild weather and gracious lifestyle, became a home-from-home for European royalty and other refugees fleeing the political upheavals after the war. Among the Triangle's illustrious residents were former kings Simeon of Bulgaria and Umberto of Italy, and Bolivia's ex-leader, Antenor Patiño.

With changing times, local aristocrats are selling or renting their villas. More and more Portuguese and foreigners come to the Triangle to live, retire or keep summer homes. Estoril has now become a cosmopolitan playground with its celebrated casino, first-rate hotels, restaurants and a range of popular international tennis and golf tournaments. There is no brashness here: the sophisticated image remains untarnished by rashes of modernity like fast-food outlets, kiosks, kiss-me-quick hats and the like. It is not that sort of resort.

Estoril's fine sandy **Tamariz** beach is attractively set with a touch of the picturesque added by a castellated private house surrounded by palms at the

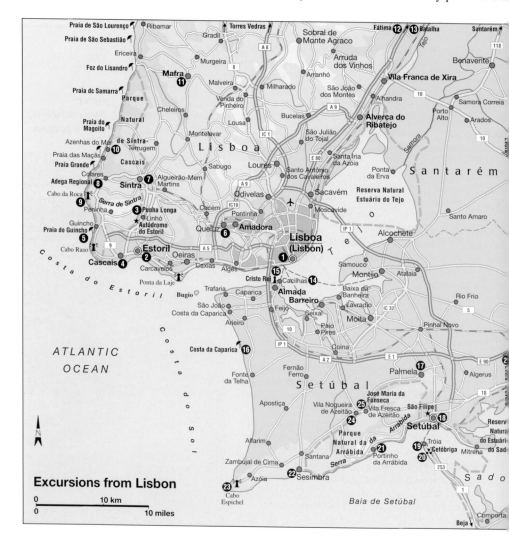

Excursions from Lisbon

0   10 km
0   10 miles

eastern end. Even this Atlantic location has suffered from water pollution in recent years, although the situation is improving, with continued investment in the infrastructure. But the beaches further west offer reliably safer waters.

The **Casino** is a low, white modern building with immaculately kept gardens. You need a passport or identity card to get in, and the minimum age limit is 18. Some people come to the Casino just to see the show, usually a colourful international extravaganza. There is also an elegant dining room, an art gallery, a cinema and a bar.

Festivals and rallies

The **Estoril Music Festival** takes place from mid-July to mid-August. Concerts and recitals are held in Estoril Cathedral, Cascais Cidadela (fortress) and other impressive settings. The **Handicrafts Fair** has become a major production, lasting throughout the months of July and August. Located near the railway station, the fair features arts and crafts, food, wine and folk music from all over the country.

There is a lot to do in the way of sports in the Triangle. The **Autódromo do Estoril**, the automobile race track located inland on the road to Sintra, used to draw large crowds for the Formula One Grand Prix races but, much to the dismay of local traders and hoteliers, the track fails to meet current safety requirements for Formula One racing and has been dropped from the list. There is no prompt movement to upgrade the track, and arguments revolve around funding. It is also the site for the start and finish of the annual international Port Wine Rally. A huge shopping development nearby with parking for 3,000 vehicles has attracted some major international stores.

Map on page 196

Estoril's Casino has lots to offer those who don't want to gamble.

BELOW: where golfers feel close to paradise.

GOLF IN THE GOLDEN TRIANGLE

The so-called Golden Triangle is a paradise for golfers. The Estoril Golf Club's 9-hole course, on the outskirts of Lisbon, is one of the loveliest in Europe. It was laid out by McKenzie Ross on a hillside dotted with pine trees and eucalyptus groves. The smaller Estoril-Sol Golf Course is located in a pine wood at Linhó near Sintra. Quinta da Beloura, which was designed by William Roquemore and opened in 1993, lies beneath the hills of Serra de Sintra. Six lakes provide golfers with plenty of watery challenges.

Penha Longa, built with Japanese finance, is more than a golf course; it is a country club with a whole range of sporting activities, and includes a five-star hotel. The 18-hole course, designed by Robert Trent Jones Jr, embraces natural woodland and rocky outcrops, and is located between Serra de Sintra and the Atlantic.

Finally, overlooking the Atlantic coast just west of Cascais is the Quinta da Marinha, also designed by Robert Trent Jones, with swimming pools, tennis courts and riding facilities as well as an 18-hole course. This attractive course weaves through umbrella pines, water features and wind-blown sand dunes. *(See Travel Tips section for telephone numbers and other details.)*

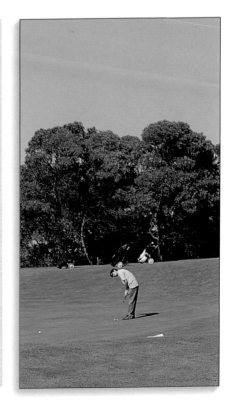

Mild winters and summers tempered by cool westerlies provide ideal conditions for golf all year around. There are five courses on the north side of the Tejo and four within easy reach on the south. **Penha Longa ❸** *(see box on page 197)* is one of the best.

Cascais: resort of kings

Although it was once a royal resort, **Cascais ❹** has all the glitter but none of the reputation of Estoril. In 1870, King Luís I established his summer residence in the 17th-century citadel on the Bay of Cascais. Before that, it was known only as a fishing port. Locals claim that a fisherman from Cascais, Afonso Sanches, actually discovered America in 1482, and Christopher Columbus merely repeated the trip 10 years later and got all the glory, but Sanches is not internationally known. In 1580, the Duke of Alba attacked Cascais when Spain was laying claim to Portugal. And in 1589 the English arrived here in retaliation for the Spanish Armada's 1588 foray. The fishing port still remains, with the comings and goings of the colourful fishing boats in the bay, the noisy nightly auction at the central fish market, and good shopping and restaurants.

Around the port has grown a resort with all the vibrancy that Estoril lacks, and yet it has managed to avoid spilling beyond its original boundaries. Pedestrianised streets paved with traditional black and white *calçada* blocks recreating dynamic wave patterns may make seamen feel at home but can make landlubbers a little queasy. They are colourful for all that, especially where the cafés spill out on to the streets and the traders set up stalls. A Wednesday market, where you can buy fresh fruit and vegetables as well as handicrafts, is repeated on a smaller scale on Saturday morning.

Estoril and Cascais are joined by a pedestrianised promenade that is a delight to walk. It passes by the beaches, and there are snack bars and restaurants all along the way.

BELOW: fishermen mend their nets at Cascais.

There are several lovely old churches and chapels in Cascais, including the 17th-century **Nossa Senhora da Assunção** with its plain façade, lovely tiles and marble nave. It contains several paintings by the 17th-century artist Josefa de Obidos. On the outskirts of town, in an exotic garden, is the **Museu Castro Guimarães** (open Tues–Sun 9am–1pm, 2.30–5.30pm; admission charge). Housed in the former residence of the Conde de Castro Guimarães, this museum displays 17th-century Portuguese silver, tiles and furniture, and some good 19th-century paintings, as well as prehistoric finds.

Cascais has its own bullring, although few fights are scheduled: it's usually too windy. There are also opportunities for horse riding at the Escola de Equitação de Birre on the road to Sintra, and at the Centro Hípico da Marinha, inland from the beach at Guincho *(see below)*.

The main beaches lie between Cascais and Estoril; there is a small beach to the west, **Praia de Santa Marta**, but it's barely big enough for a game of volleyball. Take a short walk beyond, along the main road, and you will come to the **Boca do Inferno** ("Mouth of Hell"), a narrow inlet with arches and caverns. Waves crash into the inlet with some ferocity, especially when the Atlantic swell is running high. An informal flea market around the Boca do Inferno has been regularised with custom-built stalls selling colourful woven rugs, sheepskin carpets and craft work, which has taken over as the main attraction.

Beyond here lies the rocky Atlantic coast. Lisboetas flock here at weekends to enjoy seafood at several popular restaurants. Some also swim at the broad, clean beach of **Praia do Guincho ❺**, where the waves can be wild and the undertow fierce. Windsurfers love it. Some people, however, simply like to take the road to Sintra, through the pines and along the open coast. ❏

Map on page 196

Pottery is for sale in the Cascais market on Wednesday and Saturday morning.

BELOW: Lisboetas come to the Cascais beaches at weekends for seafood, surf and sun.

SINTRA

Map on page 196

Known by the Romans as the Mountains of the Moon, the Serra da Sintra has a delightful collection of palaces and monuments along with some splendid beaches

With its lush forests and gentle surrounding plain, Sintra has long been a favourite summer resort for Portuguese and foreign visitors. People delight in the area because of its sheer natural beauty and it was declared a World Heritage site by UNESCO in 1995. Lord Byron, who could find little good to say about the Portuguese, was enamoured of Sintra and likened it to "Elysium's gates". In *Childe Harold*, he wrote: "Lo! Cintra's glorious Eden intervenes in variegated maze of mount and glen."

Some 32 km (20 miles) to the northwest of Lisbon, Sintra is another world with its own special climate – a clash of warm southerlies and moist westerlies over the Serra da Sintra – and an almost bucolic way of life. The most practical way to go is by train from Rossio Station. If you drive, rush-hour traffic should be avoided if at all possible. It seems that most of the inhabitants of Sintra commute to Lisbon on weekdays and vice-versa at weekends. The road to Sintra from Lisbon starts at the Praça Marquês de Pombal and is well marked. Avenida Duarte Pacheco runs into the *auto-estrada* or super highway that leads out of town, past the Aqueduto das Águas Livres, up the hill through Parque de Monsanto, turning right to join the highway to Sintra.

LEFT: the Quinta de Monserrate.
BELOW: tiled signpost at Sintra.

Queluz Palace

A slight detour to visit **Queluz ❻** is well worthwhile. The town has become a rather drab Lisbon dormitory, but its rose-coloured palace is anything but dull. The **Pálacio** (open Wed–Mon 10am–1pm, 2 –5pm; admission charge) was built as a simple manor for King Pedro II in the mid-1600s and was enlarged when the court moved there. Most of the palace, including its magnificent façade, is baroque, but the courtyard and formal gardens were modelled on Versailles.

In summer, concerts are sometimes held in the Music Room. At other times, the public may visit the lavishly decorated Throne Room with its fine painted wood ceiling, the Hall of Mirrors, the Ambassador's Room, and others. The great kitchen, with stone chimney and copperware, has been turned into a luxury restaurant called **Cozinha Velha**. Palace and gardens are a spectacular stage during August and September for **Noites de Queluz** (Nights at Queluz), enchanting musical recreations of 18th-century court life.

Back on the main road continue along rolling hills, past modest whitewashed villages and rich *quintas,* or manors, to arrive at the Serra de Sintra. At the base of the mountain lies the village of **São Pedro de Sintra**, where on the second and fourth Sunday of each month, a wonderful country fair takes place. On display are all kinds of crafts from primitive wood carvings and ceramics to fine antique furniture, as

well as the latest lines in plastic utensils and polyester tablecloths. São Pedro is also known for its popular tavernas, which serve spicy sausages, hearty cod dishes and heady wines.

Sintra Vila

The famous swan ceiling in the Palácio Nacional's Sala dos Cisnes.

The road now climbs slightly and curves around the mountain to reach **Sintra Vila** ❼, the historic centre of Sintra. Here lie the Tourist Office and, on the upper floor, the municipal art gallery, the **Museu Regional** (open Mon–Fri 10am–noon, 2.30–5pm, Sat–Sun 2.30–5pm; admission charge). The road to the left, Rua Gil Vicente, leads down to **Museu Ferreira de Castro**, which is dedicated to the works of the great Portuguese novelist Ferreira de Castro (1898–1974). A little further on is the **Hotel Lawrence**, formerly Estalagem dos Cavaleiros, where Lord Byron stayed in 1809, and now restored as an inn under its original name.

The centrepiece of Sintra is the royal palace, the Paço Real, now called the **Palácio Nacional**, parts of which date from the 14th century (open Thurs–Tues 10am–1pm, 2–5.30pm; admission charge). Broad stairs lead up to the stately building with gothic arches, Moorish windows and two extraordinary chimney cones. Of special interest on the guided tour of the palace are: the Sala dos Brasões, with remarkable ceiling panels painted in 1515, which show the coat-of-arms of 71 Portuguese noble families (that of the Távoras was removed after the conspiracy against King José in 1758); the Sala dos Arabes, with marble fountain and 15th-century Moorish tiles; and the Sala dos Cisnes, an enormous reception hall with swans painted on the panelled ceiling; the Sala das Pegas, its ceiling covered with magpies brandishing banners reading "Por Bem". It is said

BELOW:
the palace and
gardens at Queluz.

that when Queen Philippa caught João I dallying with a lady-in-waiting he claimed it was an innocent kiss. "Por Bem", he said, which loosely translated means: "It's all for the best." Philippa's response is not recorded.

The other Sintra

Estefânia, is another district of Sintra where you can go to catch the train or a local bus to Lisbon. Walking in that direction from the historic centre, you pass the **Museu de Brinquedo** (Toy Museum; open Tues–Sun 10am–6pm; admission charge) and then the **Casa Museu Anjos Teixeira** (open Tues–Sun 10–noon, 2–5.30pm; admission charge), which houses an important collection of sculptures.

Shortly after this, on the left and before the bus and railway stations, is Sintra's Town Hall, which is often overlooked amid so much fine architecture. It has a square castellated tower with a steeple in an exuberant gothic style. Beyond the bus station, housed in a grand building, is the **Museu de Arte Moderna** (open Wed–Sun; admission charge).

Mountain retreats

Sintra's other palace-museum, the **Palácio da Pena** (open Tues–Sun 10am–1pm, 2–5pm; admission charge), dominates the town from the top of the mountain. The road winds up steep, rocky slopes through thick woods to the castle, built on the site of a 16th-century monastery: you can walk up, drive or take a bus. But some think Pena is better viewed from afar, from where the impression is of some medieval stronghold. Close at hand, the castle is an architectural monstrosity, a pot-pourri of various styles and influences: Arabic minarets, gothic towers, Renaissance cupolas, Manueline windows. It was commissioned by

Map on page 196

TIP

Red open-topped London buses run from the bus station along the Colares road to Ribeira, to connect with the electric tram to the coast at Praia das Maçãs.

BELOW: the Palácio Nacional, once the royal palace.

Prince Ferdinand of Saxe-Coburg-Gotha, husband of Queen Maria II, and built by German architect Baron von Eschwege around 1840.

At the entrance to the castle a tunnel leads to the ruins of the original monastery. The old chapel walls are decorated with fine 17th-century tiles and there is a splendid altar of alabaster and black marble by 16th-century French sculptor Nicolas Chanterène. But the best thing about the castle is the view. Below lies the **Parque da Pena**, with lakes and black swans, a wide variety of flora, tangled forest and tiled fountains.

Across the way are the ruins of another mountain-top castle, the **Castelo dos Mouros**, dating from about the 11th century. The fortifications visible along the mountain ridge were restored in the middle of the 19th century. To the southwest rises the highest peak, **Cruz Alta**, at 540 metres (1,772 ft) and marked by a stone cross. The mountainside is a luxuriant mass of vegetation – sub-tropical plants, boulders covered with moss, giant ferns, walnut, chestnut and pine trees, and rhododendron bushes. One of the strangest sights on the mountain is the **Convento dos Capuchos**, a 16th-century monastery built entirely of rocks and cork. Some say the monks lined their cells with cork to obtain absolute silence, but there is little noise here other than bird sounds. More likely, the cork helped insulate the monks from the long, bitter winters.

On the outskirts of Sintra Vila (on the way to Colares) stands the **Palácio de Seteais**, an obscure name thought to mean "the seven sighs". This was where the Convention of Sintra was signed in 1809, after the defeat of Napoleon by British and Portuguese forces. It is said that the terms of the treaty upset the Portuguese so much that the palace became known for their sighs of despair. Seteais was restored and turned into a luxury hotel and restaurant in 1955 and should be visited, if only for tea or a drink. The elegant rooms contain crystal chandeliers, wall-hangings, murals and antique furnishings. From the gardens you have a magnificent view of the surrounding countryside.

Almost opposite is the remarkable **Quinta da Regaleira** (open to visitors, enquire at the Tourist Office), built at the close of the 19th century as an assembly of gothic, Manueline and Renaissance styles that would be out of place anywhere but Sintra.

Nearby is the **Quinta de Monserrate**, a strange Moorish-type villa built in the 19th century. The villa is under renovation but the exotic garden and greenhouse are worth seeing for the trees and plants from all over the world: palms, bamboos, cedars, magnolias, cork-oaks, pines and giant ferns.

Once part of the Monserrate gardens, the **Quinta de São Tiago** is a 16th-century manor with a fine chapel, splendid kitchen, cell-like bedrooms, gardens and its own swimming pool. The owners found taxes and other expenses prohibitive and, in 1979, opened the *quinta* to paying guests. You can also stay in the nearby **Quinta da Capela**.

For a delightful excursion, the road to Colares leads through vineyards, whitewashed hamlets and stone walls to the sea. En route, it is possible to visit the **Adega Regional** ❽, a traditional winery. Colares grapes grow in sandy soil with a humid maritime climate. The wines are dark ruby and very smooth.

Mafra is the site of the church of Santo André. Pedro Hispano was priest here before he was elected Pope John XXI in 1276 – the only Portuguese pope in the history of the Vatican.

BELOW: strange architectural styles at Palácio da Pena.

Map on page 196

Cabo da Roca ❾ is a wild, desolate cape, which is the westernmost point of continental Europe, and visitors receive a certificate to mark their visit. Heading north, there are several beaches frequented mainly by the Portuguese: broad, sandy **Praia Grande** and **Praia das Maçãs**. The attractive fishing village of **Azenhas do Mar** ❿ has a natural-rock seashore swimming pool.

Magnificent Mafra

Following the road north towards the coast from Sintra, you reach the beach resort and fishing village of **Ericeira**. From here it is an easy 10-km (6-mile) drive inland to **Mafra** ⓫, a name shared by both a modest village and a vast palace-convent (open Wed–Mon 10am–5pm; admission charge) nearby, which rises like a dark mirage across the plain. The complex of buildings almost as large as Spain's Escorial was erected by João V in fulfilment of a vow. Work began in 1717 and took 18 years, drawing so many artists from so many countries that João founded the School of Mafra, making these talented men masters to local apprentices. The most famous teacher was Joaquim Machado de Castro, who also worked on Lisbon's Basílica da Estrela.

The limestone façade is 220 metres (720 ft) long. At its centre is the church, with two tall towers and an Italianate portico. The interior is decorated with the finest Portuguese marble, while the 14 large statues of saints in the vestibule were carved from Carrara marble by Italian sculptors. The church also contains six organs. Most impressive is the library, full of baroque magnificence and light. Among its 35,000 volumes are first editions of *Os Lusíadas* by Camões and the earliest edition of Homer in Greek. Other areas open to the public include the hospital, pharmacy, audience room and chapterhouse. ❑

A lighthouse stands on the westernmost point of continental Europe.

BELOW: the great baroque library at Mafra.

MONASTERIES AND SHRINES

The shrine of Fátima and two architectural jewels that have been nominated UNESCO World Heritage Sites make a trip to the north of Lisbon well worthwhile

Map on page 196

The sites described in this chapter may be a bit too far away if you have only a few days in Lisbon, but any visitor who is here for a longer stay and is interested in Portugal's history will find this an extremely rewarding trip. Fátima lies about 100 km (60 miles) from Lisbon, and Batalha and Alcobaça are just a few kilometres away from the shrine, towards the coast. Now that the motorways are so good it is an easy journey to make if you have a car. Several coach companies in Lisbon offer day tours to these destinations (enquire at the main Tourist Office for details), but with so much to see one day is really not enough to appreciate all that they have to offer. However, a day trip would allow you to get a glimpse of two UNESCO World Heritage Sites and the shrine which rivals Lourdes in importance for devout Catholics.

LEFT: the majestic portal of Batalha.
BELOW: Fátima, one of the great pilgrimage sites.

Fátima

Fátima ⑫ welcomes all those with a genuine interest, but it is not a place for non-believers, and there is even a notice to advise you of this. It is principally a place for pilgrims – of which there are up to 2 million a year. On 13 May 1917, three shepherd children had a vision of the Virgin here. Thereafter, she appeared before the children and, on one occasion, as a shining light to the townspeople who gathered with them on the 13th of the subsequent months. The two younger children died shortly after seeing the apparitions, but one, Lucia de Jesus Santos, lived well into her eighties in a convent near Coimbra. The processions that now take place each year draw thousands of people from around the world.

A vast white basilica, consecrated in 1953, was built in recognition of the importance of this site to pilgrims, but with little attention to aesthetics. The basilica is fronted by a huge esplanade large enough to hold 100,000 worshippers. Inside lie the tombs of the two visionary children who died, Jacinta and Francisco Marto.

Today, Fátima has capitalised on its massive appeal with ubiquitous merchandising of religious souvenirs. Many thousands of pilgrims still walk for days, suffering penitential hardship.

Batalha: an essential stop

Batalha ⑬ is one of Portugal's most beautiful monuments, which deserves its title as a UNESCO World Heritage Site. The origins of the **Mosteiro de Santa Maria da Vitória**, to use its full name, lie in Portugal's struggle for independence from Castile. One

The statue of Álvarez Pereira was not erected until the 20th century.

LEFT AND RIGHT: interior details of the church at Batalha.

of the decisive battles for autonomy was fought at Aljubarrota, which was not far from Batalha *(see page 30)*.

The Castilian king, Juan, who based his claim to the throne on his marriage to a Portuguese princess, invaded Portugal in 1385. The 20-year-old Dom João, Master of the Order of Avis and illegitimate son of Pedro I, promised to build a monastery to the Virgin Mary if the Portuguese won. With his young general, Nuno Álvares Pereira, João defeated the Castilians, and became João I. In fulfilment of the vow, the monastery was constructed between 1388 and 1533. Álvares Pereira's statue stands outside, although it was erected only during Salazar's time.

Interior elegance

You enter the monastery through the majestic front portal. Inside, the arches sweep upwards to a sculpture representing the hierarchy in the heavenly court, as it was perceived in the Middle Ages. In the centre is Christ surrounded by the four gospel writers, Matthew, Mark, Luke and John. Although the outside of the monastery is ornate, the interior is endowed with a simple gothic elegance and dignity. Vaulted ceilings arch above a slender nave which is illuminated through stained-glass windows.

To the right is the **Capela do Fundador** (Founder's Chapel), built around 1426 by João I, and here you will find the tombs of João and his English queen, Philippa of Lancaster, with their effigies eloquently holding hands. Tombs of their children, including that of Prince Henry the Navigator, are set into the walls under regal arches. The room is topped by a dome supported by star-shaped ribbing.

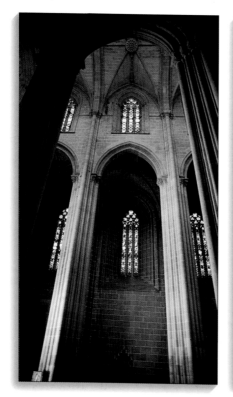

The Claustro Real

On the other side of the building you may enter the **Claustro Real** (Royal Cloister). Arches filled with Manueline ornamentation surround a pretty courtyard and are patterned with intricate designs. The **chapterhouse** is the first room off the cloister. It has an unusual and beautiful ceiling, with no support other than the walls. The impression is of precarious balance.

The chapterhouse window is filled with a stained-glass figure of Christ on the Cross, which is remarkably rich in colour. This chamber holds the tombs of two unknown soldiers, whose remains were returned to Portugal from France and Africa after World War I. The emotive sculpture entitled "Christ of the Trenches" was given by the French government. An armed guard of honour seems out of place in this peaceful setting.

Capelas Imperfeitas

To reach the **Capelas Imperfeitas** (Unfinished Chapels), you have to go outside the monastery. The octagonal structure of the building is attached to the outside wall and its rooflessness comes as an abrupt shock. The chapels were commissioned by King Duarte I to house the tombs of himself and his family, but although they were begun in the 1430s their construction was never finished, and no one is quite certain why.

However, the building fulfils its original purpose: the shell contains simple chapels in each of its seven walls. The chapel opposite the door holds the tomb of Duarte and Leonor, his wife. The eighth wall is a massive door of limestone, with endless layers of beautifully detailed ornamentation in the intricately carved Manueline style.

Map on page 196

BELOW: the Capelas Imperfeitas.

Map on page 196

An exquisite Calvary scene in the Mosteiro de Santa Maria.

RIGHT: the monastery cloister.
BELOW: detail on the façade of the monastery.

Alcobaça

Twelve km (8 miles) south of Batalha is the town of **Alcobaça**, named after two rivers, the Alcoa and the Baça. At its heart is the magnificent Cistercian **Mosteiro de Santa Maria** (open daily 9am–5pm, till 7pm in summer; admission charge), another UNESCO World Heritage Site. The first king of Portugal, Afonso Henriques, founded it to commemorate the capture of Santarém from the Moors. He laid the foundation stone himself in 1148.

The Cistercian monks were energetic and productive. Numbering, it is said 999 ("one less than a thousand"), they diligently tilled the land around the abbey, planting vegetables and fruit. In Sebastião I's reign, the exceedingly wealthy and powerful abbey was declared by the Pope to be the seat of the entire Cistercian Order.

Although monks of the Cistercian Order generally lived a simpler life than their Benedictine contemporaries, those at Santa Maria were known particularly for their lively spirits and lavish hospitality. They ran a school, one of the first in Portugal, and a sanctuary and hospice as well. In 1810, however, the abbey was sacked by French troops, and during the Liberal Revolution of 1834, when all religious orders were expelled from Portugal, it was again pillaged.

Doomed love

The long baroque façade, which was added in the 18th century, has twin towers in the centre, below which are a gothic doorway and rose window, surviving from the original façade. Directly inside the serene and austere church, the largest in Portugal, three tall aisles and plain walls emphasise the clean lines. In the transepts are the two well-known and richly carved tombs of the doomed lovers, Pedro I and Inês de Castro. Inês, it will be remembered, was murdered in 1355 on the orders of Dom Afonso IV, because, as a Spaniard, her motives were suspect. Off the south transept are several other royal tombs, including those of Afonso II and Afonso III, and a sadly mutilated 17th-century terracotta of the Death of St Bernard. To the east of the ambulatory there are two fine Manueline doorways that were designed by João de Castilho.

Claustro de Silencio

An entrance in the north wall of the church leads to the 14th-century **Claustro de Silencio** (Cloister of Silence). Several rooms branch off the cloister, including the chapterhouse and a dormitory. There is a kitchen, with an enormous central chimney and a remarkable basin through which a rivulet runs: it supposedly provided the monks with a constant supply of fresh fish. Next door is the refectory, with steps built into one wall leading to a pulpit. To the left of the entrance is the **Sala dos Reis**, with statues, probably carved by monks themselves, of many of the kings of Portugal. The panel in the same room, which tells the history of Alcobaça Abbey, is a rare example of a manuscript *azulejo* panel.

Alcobaça today is the centre of a porcelain and pottery industry. There are many shops around the central square, and some factories welcome visitors.

THE ARRÁBIDA PENINSULA

Map on page 196

New transport options make the Arrábida Peninsula increasingly popular with visitors. And while you are on "the other shore" it is easy to visit the ancient and beautiful town of Évora

Lisboetas call it *Outra Banda*, the other shore, meaning the southern bank of the Tejo, long neglected because of the inconvenience of getting there. This changed after 1966 with the completion of what was then Europe's longest suspension bridge, the Ponte 25 de Abril, and changed yet again with the opening of the rail link in 1999. A second, even longer bridge, the Vasco de Gama, opened in 1998 to relieve pressure on the first. The region, known as the Arrábida Peninsula, has developed rapidly and not always wisely.

Directly across the river is the unassuming ferry port of **Cacilhas** ⓮. Its main charm is a string of riverfront fish restaurants with a grand view of Lisbon. About 5 km (3 miles) west of Ponte 25 de Abril is **Trafaria**; the whole town was burned to the ground on the orders of Pombal in 1777 as punishment for resisting press gangs, but was later rebuilt. Most visitors tend to drive through the neighbouring industrial town of Almada without stopping, except those who want to examine the **Cristo Rei** ⓯ (Christ the King monument) at close hand. You can go to the top of the pedestal – so high it seems to dwarf the figure on top – by elevator and then stairs, for a magnificent view of Lisbon.

Most people avoid the *Outra Banda* dormitory district by taking the super highway leading directly from the bridge. After a few kilometres, a turn-off leads to **Costa da Caparica** ⓰, a series of broad Atlantic beaches with moderately priced hotels and restaurants. This popular resort is cleaner than the Estoril/Cascais coast, and the currents are safer than those of the Atlantic north of the Tejo.

On to Palmela

Continuing south on the highway, you pass new factories. The road marked **Palmela** ⓱ leads to a small town with a great medieval castle. This has been restored and converted into a luxury *pousada,* with a lounge in the cloisters, and an elegant dining-room in the old refectory. The attached church is a beautiful Romanesque structure, its walls covered with 18th-century tiles.

Built by the Moors, the castle was reconstructed in 1147 as a monastery and the seat of the Knights of the Order of Saint James. In 1484, the bishop of Évora was imprisoned in the dungeon for his role in the conspiracy against João II. He died a few days later, probably poisoned. The castle was badly damaged by the 1755 earthquake, but was rebuilt and monks remained there until the abolition of religious orders in 1834.

Just outside Setúbal rises another great castle turned *pousada*, **São Filipe**, with a magnificent view of the Sado estuary. Philip II of Spain ordered its construction in 1590, to keep a watch over the area – Portugal

PRECEDING PAGES: Serra da Arrábida, a nature reserve by the sea. **LEFT:** Ponte 25 de Abril. **BELOW:** snack bar in Cacilhas.

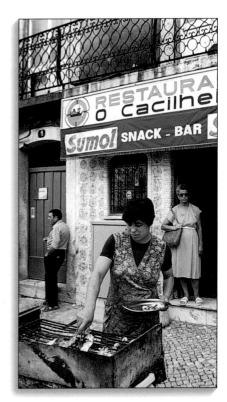

The entrance to Diogo Boytac's spectacular Igreja de Jesus.

was under Spanish rule at the time. The chapel is decorated with tiles that recount the life of Saint Philip (*not* Philip of Spain), signed by the master painter Policarpo de Oliveira Bernardes, and dated 1736.

Setúbal and the Tróia peninsula

According to local legend, **Setúbal** was founded by Tubal, the son of Cain. It is said that Phoenicians and Greeks, finding the climate and soil of Arrábida similar to their Mediterranean homelands, started vineyards. Setúbal is known to have been an important fishing port since Roman times. Today it is an industrial town, a centre of shipbuilding, fish-canning and the production of fertilisers, cement, salt and moscatel wine.

Setúbal's pride is the **Igreja de Jesus**, a spectacular monument dating back to 1491. The church was designed by Diogo Boytac, one of the founding fathers of the Manueline style of architecture. The narrow building has a high arched ceiling supported by six great stone pillars that look like coils of rope; its apse is etched with stone and lined with tiles. Arrábida marble was used, and the pebbled, multicoloured stone gives it a distinct appearance. There are also lovely tiled panels along the walls. The cloister houses a museum, the **Museu de Cidade** (open Tues–Sun 10am–12.30pm, 2–5pm; admission charge).

Nearby you'll find the **Praça do Bocage**, laid out with palm trees and a statue honouring one of Setúbal's illustrious sons, 18th-century sonneteer Manuel Barbosa du Bocage. Off the square stands the church of **São Julião** with a handsome Manueline doorway, built in 1513. The inside walls are decorated with 18th-century tiles showing fishing scenes and the life of the saint. Also of interest is the **Museu Etnográfico** with models depicting the main

industries: fishing, farming and textiles (open Tues–Sun 10am–noon, 2–5pm; admission charge).

Setúbal's harbour is fascinating, especially in the morning when brightly painted trawlers arrive, loaded with fish. There's a continual show, as fishermen mend nets and work on their boats. Best of all is the lively fish auction.

Setúbal is the main point of departure for the peninsula of **Tróia ⓯**, a long, narrow spit jutting out into the Sado estuary. Ferries make the 20-minute crossing frequently in season. On the northern end of the peninsula, there is a rather unattractive modern beach resort. The Tróia Golf Club has an 18-hole course designed by Robert Trent Jones. On the southern end of the peninsula, however, there are still miles of pine forest and glorious empty beaches and dunes. Tróia is said to be the site of the Roman town of **Cetóbriga ⓴**, destroyed by a tidal wave in the 5th century. Substantial ruins have been found but little has been excavated except for a temple and some tombs. Underwater, you may see remains of the walls of Roman houses.

Serra da Arrábida

A delightful excursion from Setúbal goes along the ridge of the **Serra da Arrábida** which rises to 600 metres (2,000 ft). As you leave the city, the only sight that mars the natural beauty of the coast is the cement factory, usually spitting out black smoke. A road descends to **Portinho da Arrábida ㉑**, a popular bathing beach with transparent waters, white sand and the splendid **Gruta da Santa Margarida**. Hans Christian Andersen, who visited the region in 1834, marvelled in his diaries at this cave with its imposing stalactites. Scuba diving is very popular here.

Map on page 196

TIP

From Cetóbriga you could choose to return to Setúbal via Alcácar do Sal, a drive of some 120 km (75 miles), though of course it is much quicker to take the ferry from Tróia.

BELOW: pushing the boat out at Tróia beach.

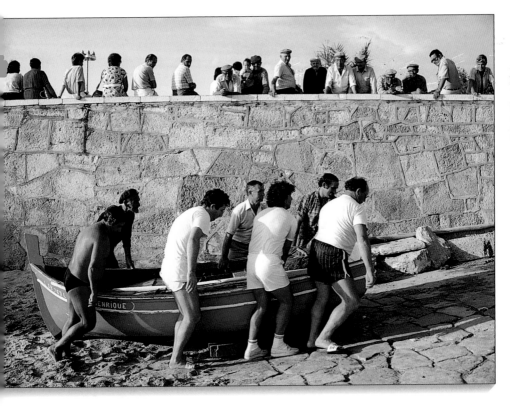

But it was the poet and historian of the Peninsular War Robert Southey (1774–1843) who consecrated Arrábida for English readers, calling it "a glorious spot". He tells of going swimming at the base of the mountain and writes: "I have no idea of sublimity exceeding it."

Regaining the ridge, continue along the skyline drive. The next turn-off leads to **Sesimbra** ㉒, a lovely fishing village and resort with several notable sights. The castle above the village, although known as Moorish, has been entirely rebuilt since that time. Afonso Henriques captured it in 1165, but the Moors utterly razed the structure in 1191. King Dinis almost certainly helped with the rebuilding, and King João IV again added and repaired in the 17th century. Inside the walls are ruins of a Romanesque church, Santa Maria, and the old town hall. King João IV also ordered the fort of São Teodosio built, to protect the port from pirates. But the most fascinating sight is the port, which is always busy. There are several simple bistros nearby: swordfish is the local speciality.

Going westward about 11 km (7 miles), the road ends at **Cabo Espichel** ㉓. This promontory, and the shrine of **Nossa Senhora do Cabo**, used to be an important pilgrimage site, as shown by the long rows of dilapidated pilgrims' quarters on either side of the church. There is still a fishermen's festival here each October. On the edge of the high cliff is the small fishermen's chapel of Senhor de Bomfim, in a rather desolate state but with a breathtaking view.

Olive tree village

The road back to Lisbon goes through **Vila Nogueira de Azeitão** ㉔, sometimes simply called Azeitão, which means "large olive tree". In the centre of this charming village is the stately Palácio Távora, where the Duke of Aveiro and his

Map on page 196

friends are said to have plotted to overthrow King José. They were burned at the stake in Belém in 1759. Lovely baroque fountains border the town's main street. The Igreja São Lourenço has been restored and has beautiful 18th-century altars, paintings and tile panels.

The Azeitão fair, held in the central square on the first Sunday of the month, became so popular that it caused havoc and had to be moved to the outskirts of town. Less picturesque now, it is still a major attraction offering everything from shoes and pottery to furniture, plus a large section devoted to livestock.

In the village is the original **José Maria da Fonseca Winery ⓭**, founded in 1834. The old family residence, which now houses a small museum, stands nearby. The winery still produces one of Portugal's best red table wines, the soft rich Periquita, as well as Setúbal's popular moscatel wines. Visitors are welcome to tour the factory and see its assembly-line production.

Not far from town stands one of the oldest inhabited manors in the country, the **Quinta da Bacalhoa**, built in 1480. It had fallen into ruins and was saved by an American woman from Connecticut, Mrs Herbert Scoville, who bought it in 1936. The gardens, open to the public, are admirable with their clipped boxwood in geometric designs, orange and lemon groves and pavilion with beautiful tile panels. One of these scenes, showing Susanna and the Elders, is dated 1565, and said to be the earliest-known panel in Portugal.

Another attractive manor, the **Quinta das Torres**, stands just outside the neighbouring village of **Vila Fresca de Azeitão**. This 16th-century *quinta*, decorated with tile panels and set in a romantic garden, has been converted into a cosy inn and restaurant. In the village, there is yet another pretty church, São Simão, with more ancient tile walls and polychrome panels.

BELOW:
a shady restaurant
in Sesimbra.

Évora: Alentejo's city

As you enter **Évora** ❷ on the main Lisbon road, there is a small tourist office just before the Roman walls, where you can pick up a street map marked with suggested walks that take in the most important sights. The best place to park is outside the walls and walk to **Praça do Giraldo** at the centre of the city. This large square is arcaded on two sides and has a 16th-century church and fountain at the top. From here you can explore the inner city with ease.

The city's history can be traced back to the earliest civilisations on the Iberian peninsula. Evora derives its name from *Ebora Cerealis*, which dates from the Luso-Celtic colonisation. The Romans later fortified the city, renamed it *Liberalitas Julia*, and elevated it to the status of *municipium,* which gave it the right to mint its own currency. Its prosperity declined under the Visigoths, but was rekindled under Moorish rule (711–1165). Much of the architecture, with arched, twisting alleyways and tiled patios, reflects the Moorish presence. Évora was liberated from the Moors by a Christian knight, Geraldo Sem-Pavor ("the Fearless"), in 1165, in the name of Afonso Henriques I, Portugal's first king.

For the next 400 years Évora enjoyed great importance and wealth. It was the preferred residence of the kings of the Burgundy and Avis dynasties, and the courts attracted famous artists, dramatists, humanists and academics. Great churches, monasteries, houses and convents were also built. The splendour peaked in 1559, when Henrique, the last of the Avis kings (and also Archbishop of Évora), founded a Jesuit university. In 1580, following the annexation of Portugal by Spain, Évora's glory waned. The Castilians paid little attention to it, except as an agricultural and trading centre, and even, after Portuguese independence was restored in 1640, it did not regain its former brilliance.

BELOW: a view of historic Évora.

Évora: the sights

The oldest sight in Evora is the **Temple of Diana (Templo Romano)**, off Praça do Giraldo, which dates from the 2nd or 3rd century. The temple is presumed to have been built as a place of imperial worship. The Corinthian columns are granite, their bases and capitals hewn from local marble. The façade and mosaic floor have disappeared completely, but the six rear columns and those on either side are still intact. The temple was converted into a fortress during the Middle Ages, then used as a slaughterhouse until 1870, an inelegant role that nevertheless saved it from being torn down.

From a good viewpoint in the shady garden just across from the rear of the temple, you can look down over the lower town and across the plains: the tiny village of Evoramonte is just visible to the northeast. To the right of the temple is the **Convento dos Lóios** and the adjacent church of **São João Evangelista**. The convent buildings have been converted into an elegant *pousada* but the church is still public. Founded in 1485, its style is Romano-gothic, although all but the doorway in the façade was remodelled after the 1755 earthquake. The nave has an ornate vaulted ceiling and walls lined with beautiful tiles depicting the life of St Laurence Justinian, dated 1771 and signed by António de Oliveira Bernardes. There are guided tours of the church, cloisters and chapterhouse.

The Cathedral

The nearby **Sé** (Cathedral) is a rather austere building. Its granite Romano-gothic-style façade was built in the 12th century, while its main portal and the two grand conical towers – unusual in that they are asymmetric, with one tower adorned with glittering blue tiles – were added in the 16th century. Before you

Map on page 196

POUSADA DOS LOIOS

The Pousada dos Loios, a good place for a meal, is housed in the former convent.

BELOW: the Temple of Diana.

go inside, take a close look at the main entrance, which is decorated with magnificent 14th-century sculptures of the apostles. With three naves stretching for 70 metres (230 ft), the cathedral has the most capacious interior in Portugal, and the vast broken barrel-vaulted ceiling is stunning.

Once you've seen the cathedral, it is worth paying the nominal sum to visit the cloisters, choir stalls and **Museu de Arte Sacra** (open Tues–Sun 10am–12.30, 2–5pm). The latter, in the treasury, contains a beautiful collection of ecclesiastical gold, silver and bejewelled plate, ornaments, chalices and crosses. The Renaissance-style choir stalls, tucked high in the gallery, are fashioned with a delightful series of wooden carvings with motifs both sacred and secular. From the choir stalls you get a good bird's-eye view of the cathedral. The marble cloisters are 14th-century gothic, large and imposing, more likely to inspire awe than meditative contemplation.

Next door to the cathedral is the **Museu de Évora** (open Wed–Sun 10am–12.30pm, 2–5pm, Tues 2–5pm; admission charge), formerly the Bishop's Palace and now home to a fine collection of paintings, both Portuguese Primitives and Flemish. There is also some interesting local sculpture and furniture.

More Évora landmarks

At the old **Jesuit University**, some elegant and graceful cloisters are visible. You have to follow a short road down to the east of the city to reach it. The marble of the broad cloisters seems to have aged not at all since the 16th century, and there is still the peaceful atmosphere of the serious academic.

The classroom entrances at the far end of the cloister gallery are decorated with *azulejos* representing each of the subjects taught. If you take a slow walk

During the last week of June, Évora is filled with visitors who come to enjoy the annual Feira de São João. This huge fair fills the grounds opposite the public gardens. There's a handicraft market, an agricultural hall and open-air stalls, as well as folk singing and dancing, and restaurants serving typical cuisine.

LEFT: the marble, Gothic cloisters.
RIGHT: Manueline remains in Évora.

back up the hill and head for the Igreja São Francisco, you'll pass another church, the **Misericórdia**, noted for its 18th-century tiled panels and baroque relief work. Behind it is the Casa Soure, a 15th-century Manueline-style house formerly part of the Palace of the Infante Dom Luís.

As you walk, take notice of the houses. Nearly all have attractive narrow wrought-iron balconies at the base of tall, rectangular windows. An odd tradition in Évora, as elsewhere in Portugal, is that visiting dignitaries are welcomed by a display of brightly coloured bedspreads hung from the balconies.

When you reach the Misericórdia church, take a brief detour to **Largo das Portas de Moura**. The gates mark the fortified northern entrance to the city, the limit of construction and safety as it was in medieval times. This picturesque square is dominated by a Renaissance fountain, built in 1556.

Heading west along the Rua Miguel Bombarda, keep an eye out for the church of **Nossa Senhora da Graça** (Our Lady of Grace), just off the Rua Miguel Bombarda. Built in granite, it is a far cry from the austerity of the cathedral. A later church (16th-century), its influence is strongly Italian Renaissance. Note the four huge figures supporting globes which represent the children of grace.

The most interesting thing about the **Igreja de São Francisco** is the Capela dos Ossos, the Bone Chapel, but the chapterhouse that links the chapel to the church is worth seeing, too. It is lined with *azulejos* depicting scenes from the Passion and contains an *altar dos promessas* (altar of promises) on which are laid wax effigies of various parts of the body. Ailing people, or their friends and relatives, go to the altar and pray for a cure. If it is granted, then an effigy of the relevant part is placed in thanks on the altar. The church also has an interesting Manueline porch. ❏

Map on page 196

The region is known for brightly coloured bedspreads and rugs.

LEFT: statue of a pregnant Madonna in the Sé. **RIGHT:** in the Capela dos Ossos.

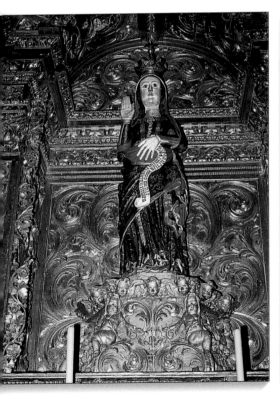

INSIGHT GUIDES
Travel Tips

Insight Guides Website
www.insightguides.com

*Don't travel the
planet alone.
Keep in step with
Insight Guides'
walking eye,
just a click away*

Probably the <u>most</u> <u>important</u> TRAVEL TIP you will ever receive

Before you travel abroad, make sure that you and your family are protected from diseases that can cause serious health problems.

For instance, you can pick up *hepatitis A* which infects 10 million people worldwide every year (it's not just a disease of poorer countries) simply through consuming contaminated food or water!

What's more, in many countries if you have an accident needing medical treatment, or even dental treatment, you could also be at risk of infection from *hepatitis B* which is 100 times more infectious than AIDS, and can lead to liver cancer.

The good news is, you can be protected by vaccination against these and other serious diseases, such as *typhoid, meningitis* and *yellow fever.*

Travel safely! Check with your doctor at least 8 weeks before you go, to discover whether or not you need protection.

Consult your doctor before you go... not when you return!

SB
SmithKline Beecham
VACCINES

Produced as a service to public health

CONTENTS

Getting Acquainted

The Place

Area: Lisbon occupies 3 percent of Portugal's total surface area of 88,940 sq km (32,561 sq miles)
Population: 1,835,380 (1998 – Greater Lisbon)
Language: Portuguese
Religion: Roman Catholic
Time Zone: GMT + 1 hour; Eastern Standard Time + 5 hours. Clocks are advanced one hour for summer time
Currency: The Euro (€)
Weights and measures: metric
Electricity: 220 volts, two-pin plug
International dialling code: + 351 + number

The Climate

Lisbon is Europe's most westerly city and the climate is generally warm and sunny. It was built on seven hills on the northern bank of the Rio Tejo (River Tagus) just a few miles from the Atlantic. The breeze from the ocean fans the city and prevents the heat becoming too insufferable during July and August. Winters are mild and rainfall usually measures 700mm (28 inches) throughout the year. The city is at its most beautiful during spring and autumn and the best time to visit is probably during May or June. Even so most tourists tend to arrive during the summer months.

Average daily temperatures (°C/°F):

Air temperature:

January–March:	17/63
April–June:	21/71
July–September:	26/79
October–December:	15/53

Sea temperature:

January–March:	14/58
April–June:	17/63
July–September:	19/67
October–December:	16/60

The Economy

Portugal joined the European Union in 1986 and committed itself to a process of fundamental change. A huge inflow of European cash from central funds and private investment transformed the face of the country in the following decade. It can be one of the cheapest countries in Europe to live in, and qualified for entry into the single currency and introduction of the Euro in 2002.

About 15 percent of the labour force works in agriculture, but there is little real investment in farming. Major crops are wheat and maize, along with tomatoes, potatoes, cork and forestry products. Grapes are cultivated for wines – table wine as well as port and Madeira.

Apart from local produce, the main exports are textiles and clothing. Other products include footwear, processed food and, increasingly, electrical appliances and petro-chemicals.

Tourism accounts for 10 percent of the GNP and 25 percent of foreign investment.

Lisbon has experienced dramatic development and growth in recent years; the hosting of Expo'98 provided a significant impulse in this and playing host to the European football championships in 2004 will continue the trend.

The Government

The Portuguese president is elected every five years by popular vote. The 230 members of the Assembly (parliament) are directly elected every four years. The president appoints a prime minister from the majority party in the Assembly, and the prime minister appoints a Council of Ministers.

In 1974, the Salazar regime, the longest-running dictatorship in any European country in the 20th century, fell. The Social Democratic Party (PSD), led by Cavaco Silva, formed the first clear majority government and remained

Ten Facts about Lisbon

1. Oldest shrine: The remains of St Vincent, Lisbon's patron saint, who was martyred in Spain in AD 287, are preserved in a shrine in Lisbon's cathedral.
2. Farthest point: Continental Europe begins and ends 40 km (25 miles) west of Lisbon at Cabo da Roca.
3. Most moving moment: Grândola, Vila Morena, sung by José Afonso, which started the 1974 revolution.
4. Poetic quarter: The Chiado district, at Lisbon's commercial heart, was named after the poet António Ribeiro who used Chiado as his *nom de plume*.
5. Trichological note: More men have moustaches in Lisbon than in any other European city.
6. Culinary point: The people of Lisbon used to be known as *Alfacinhas*, or lettuce-eaters.
7. Cod almighty: Dried cod *(bacalhau)* is Lisbon's favourite fish and there is said to be a different way of cooking it for every day of the year.

8. Worst drivers: in annual surveys on the worst drivers in the European Union, the Portuguese frequently come out on top.
9. Reel break: Some Lisbon cinemas still have an intermission of 15 minutes during the film.
10. Biggest investment: Over £2 billion was spent on building the Expo'98 complex (now the Parque das Nações) on what was a derelict site.

in power until 1995 when the socialist (PS) government of António Guterres came to power. Currently (2001) Jorge Sampaio is president, serving, like his predecessor, Dr Mario Soares, a second term. The government must have the confidence of the president and the parliament, which sits in the Palácio Assembleia Nacional on the western side of the Bairro Alto.

Public Holidays

1 January:	New Year's Day
27 February:	Carnival
March/April:	Good Friday
25 April:	1974 Revolution Day
1 May:	May Day
Early June:	Corpus Christi
10 June:	Camões Day
15 August:	Feast of the Assumption
5 October:	Republic Day
November 1:	All Saints' Day
1 December:	Independence Day
8 December:	Immaculate Conception
25 December:	Christmas Day

Planning the Trip

What to Bring

CLOTHING

In summer bring light clothes, but take sweaters or a jacket as the evenings can be cool. The winter can be wet so pack some rain-proof clothing. In general, dress tends to be more stylish than formal even in the smartest of restaurants. Comfortable shoes are particularly important for the mosaic pavements and cobbled streets.

FILM

Film is expensive, so it is best to bring your own, plus camera batteries, too. Film processing costs and standards are comparable with anywhere else in Europe.

Health and Insurance

Although the Portuguese health service has reciprocal emergency treatment arrangements with other European Union countries (take your E111 form with you), it is advisable to have additional health insurance. Take sufficient supplies of any prescription medication you are using. It is a good idea to check that you are covered for polio and typhoid before you go. The water in Lisbon is drinkable.

Entry Regulations

European Union nationals may enter Portugal with a national identity card. Citizens of Great Britain and Australia need nothing more than a valid passport for a

three-month stay. The same applies to Americans and Canadians staying for 60 days or less. Citizens of the EU can stay for three months before applying for a resident's visa; Canadians and Americans can stay for two months. Extension visas can be obtained from a Portuguese embassy before the visit or, once in Lisbon, from the Serviço de Estrangeiros, Avenida António Augusto de Aguiar, 20, tel: 21 358 5500.

Customs

The standard European Union customs allowances apply to Portugal if you are arriving from outside the EU. You can bring in as much currency as you like. Non-EU members can bring in 400 cigarettes or 50 grams (1oz) tobacco, one bottle of spirits, two bottles of wine.

Money

Barclays Bank and the major international banking groups are in Lisbon. You will be able to use Visa and Access cards in most ATMs (Automatic Teller Machines), usually called *Multibanco*, if you have a PIN number. This is the easiest way to obtain cash. Traveller's cheques are another way of bringing your non-Euro currency.

Tourist Offices

Canada: Portuguese Trade and Tourism Commission, 60 Bloor Street West, Suite 1005, Toronto, Ontario M4W 3B8. Tel: 416 921 7376; fax: 416 921 1353.
United Kingdom: Portuguese Trade and Tourism Office, 22–52A Sackville Street, London W1X 1DE. Tel: 09063 640 610.
United States: Portuguese National Tourist Office, 4th Floor, 590 Fifth Avenue, New York NY 10036-4704. Tel: (212) 354 44003-8; fax: 764613.

Festivals

The year is filled with festivals, fairs and pilgrimages in and around Lisbon. Dates can vary, so check at the tourist office.

Carnival (late February): The biggest event is in Torres Vedras, north of the city, but there are costumed parades and lots of revelry elsewhere. The festival centres on Shrove Tuesday, so the date depends on Easter, but 27 February has now been made a public holiday.

Calvary: On 15 March there is a dramatic Procession of our Lord of Calvary through Lisbon's picturesque Graça district.

Book fair: For three weeks in May/June, Parque Edward VII is full of bookstalls.

Festas dos Santos Populares: The festival of Santo António (12–13 June) is a huge celebration with parades, fireworks, feasting and dancing.

Celebrations continue through most of the month, linking the festivals of São João (23–24 June) and São Pedro (28–29 June). The atmosphere is electric.

Boat burning: On the feast of São Pedro, 28–29 June, there is a fishing and farming festival at Montijo across the Tejo. Boats are blessed, bulls are run through the streets and finally a skiff is set alight in the river.

Red Waistcoat Fair: Vila Franca da Xira, 32 km (20 miles) up the Tejo, holds this festival of folk dancing and bullfights in early July, releasing bulls which run through the streets.

Wine harvest: In early September the harvest is celebrated in Palmela, in the Setúbal wine-growing area to the south of Lisbon, with song, dance, tastings and fireworks.

Embassies Abroad

United Kingdom: Portuguese Embassy, 11 Belgrave Square, London SW1X. Tel: 020 7235 5331; www.portembassy.gla.ac.uk
United States: Embassy of Portugal, 2125 Kalorama Road, NW Washington DC. Tel: 202 328 8610; www.portugalemb.org

Getting There

BY AIR

All flights land at Lisbon's Portela Airport. TAP Air Portugal is the national carrier. The city is also served by some 20 other airlines including British Airways and Continental. Operators from the US often include Lisbon in combined tours of Portugal and Spain.

TAP Air Portugal offices abroad:
UK: 38–44 Gillingham House, Gillingham Street, London SW1J 1JW. Tel: 0207 828 2092; reservations 0845 6010932.
US: 608 5th Avenue, 3rd Floor, New York, Tel: (toll-free) 800 221 7370.

BY RAIL

From the UK, rail travel is likely to be more expensive than a flight, though there are deals for extensive travel and for those under 26. For details, contact travel agents or the British Rail Travel Centre at Victoria Station, London. It takes about 40 hours to get to Lisbon from London. The usual route is Eurostar to Paris Gare du Nord; onward TGV twice-daily connections to Madrid, (changing trains at Hendaye/Irun), leave from Gare de Montparnasse; alternatively the night train departs daily from Austerlitz. Seat reservations are necessary. In Madrid change to the Lisboa Express. Trains arrive in Lisbon at Santa Apolónia station.

BY BUS

From the UK: the National Express bus company runs Eurolines to Lisbon several times a week from the London Victoria Coach Station, tel: 020 7730 8235. Although

cheap, it may not be as cheap as a charter flight. The journey takes about 36 hours. Tickets tend to be open, so make sure you book a seat for the return journey. In Lisbon you can buy tickets at Inter Centro, Serviço Internacional at the Central Rodoviária, Av. Duque Àvila, Arco Cego.

BY CAR

From Calais it is just over 1,770 km (1,100 miles) to Lisbon and the journey from London usually takes about three days, including overnight stops.

BY FERRY

The twice-weekly ferry from Plymouth to Santander, northern Spain, takes 24 hours and a couple of leisurely days driving from there. For ferry details in the UK contact: Brittany Ferries, tel: 0870 536 0360. Alternatively, the slightly longer P&O service travels from Portsmouth to Bilbao. For more information: tel: 0870 242 4999; or www.poportsmouth.com.

Practical Tips

Security and Crime

Lisbon has a low crime rate for a capital city, but it is still advisable to take precautions, especially on public transport to and from popular tourist locations. Hotels will usually provide a safe in your room or allow you to keep your valuables in their safe for no charge.
Police: tel: 112 (freephone)
Fire brigade: tel: 21 342 2222
Police station: In the event of theft, report it to the police within 24 hours to reclaim insurance. The main Policia de Segurança Pública (PSP) station dealing with foreigners who have been robbed is at the Palacio Foz, in the Praça Restauradores.
Lost property: All lost property turned in to the police ends up being dealt with at Olivais police station, Praça Cidade Salazar. You will need to wait 24 hours before trying to reclaim lost property, tel: 21 853 5403.

Medical Services

Emergency ambulance: tel: 112 (freephone)
Ambulance (Portuguese Red Cross): tel: 21 942 1111
24-hour Chemists: 118 (freephone)
National Poison Centre: tel: 21 795 0143
Linha Vida (for information of drug use and abuse): tel: 21 726 7766
Linha Sida (Aids line): tel: 800 201 040
Hospital da Cruz Vermelha, Rua Duarte Galvão 54 (behind the zoo), tel: 21 771 4000
Hospital de Santa Maria, Avenida Prof Egas Moniz (in the Areeiro district to the northeast), tel: 21 797 5171.

Lisbon United Kingdom Hospital (previously called **The British Hospital**), Rua Saraiva de Carvalho (notoriously overlooking the British cemetery near the Jardim de Estrêla), tel: 21 395 5067 has no casualty department, but takes outpatients and may be able to help as all staff speak English.
First Aid: make your way to the nearest Centro de Enfermagem or Centro de Saude.

Chemists

When closed, all chemists (Farmácias) have a list on their doors highlighting the nearest open chemist. Newspapers also publish a list of chemists open late each day. Chemists in Lisbon are open from 9.30am to 1pm and from 3pm to 7pm, Mon–Fri and Sat morning.

Business Hours

Shops: 9am–1pm and 3–7pm Mon–Fri and 9am–1pm on Sat. Some shops in the Bairro Alto open 2–9pm and for late-night shopping the shops in the big new commercial centres (Colombo, Vasco da Gama, Amoreiras and Chiado) stay open until 9pm–11pm daily.
Banks: 8.30am–3pm, closed weekends and holidays.

Etiquette

The people of Lisbon are, in general, smart and stylish dressers and visitors who want to blend-in are advised not to wear shorts or beachwear in town. If you are visiting churches and monasteries, dress appropriately.
   The Portuguese are very courteous, and they always say "please" (faz favor, pronounced fash fuhVOOR) and "thank you" (obrigado, if you are a man, obrigada if you are a woman).
   The Portuguese are the only nation apart from Britain to see any sense in orderly queueing. When introduced, the Portuguese shake hands. This form of greeting is common practice among friends, although more familiar

acquaintances greet each other with a kiss. Don't be surprised to see people spitting in public.

Tipping

Tips are expected but you don't have to be over-generous with hotel porters, waiters, hairdressers, shoeshine men, cinema or theatre ushers. Around 10 percent is usual for taxis. Restaurant bills usually include service; a small tip may be added if service has been particularly appreciated.

Religious Services

Roman Catholic: Dominican Church of Corpo Santo, Largo do Corpo Santo, 32. Mass in English on Sunday morning, 11am.
Anglican: St George's Church, opposite Jardim da Estrela, Rua de St Jorge 6, reached through the British Cemetery. Sunday service at 11.30am.
Presbyterian: St Andrew's Church of Scotland, Rua Arriaga, 13. Sunday service at 11am.
Jewish: Lisbon Synagogue, Rua Alexandre Herculano, 59.

Media

PRESS

APN, Anglo-Portuguese News, published in Estoril, is an English-language weekly, out on Thursdays. Hotels may have copies of magazines called Lisboa Step by Step, Follow me Lisboa and Agenda Cultural. These are available from the tourist office should your hotel not have copies
   International newspapers and magazines are on sale throughout the city, and foreign magazines are popular. Best stocked are TEMA International Press Centre, in the Xenon Cinema complex near the Palácio Foz in Praça Restauradores and in Centra Roma, Avenida Roma. The Livraria Artes e Letres in Largo Trindade Coelho in the Bairro Alto has foreign magazines and is open 8am–11pm seven days a week.

TELEVISION AND RADIO

RTP, the state-owned corporation, operates two national television channels (RTP 1 and RTP 2) as well as two regional stations for the Azores and Madeira, and one international station. There are two other commercial channels (SIC and TVI). European and American satellite programmes are available in most hotels.

The state-owned radio corporation, RDP, has four national and five regional radio stations with the usual mix of chat and pop. Antena 2 (94.4 FM) has classical music. The BBC World Service is on 648 KHz MW and 15.07 MHz SW. The Voice of America can be heard on 6040 on 49m short wave. There is also an English-language programme aimed at tourists on 558 to 720 KHz/87.9 and FM 95.7 broadcast between 8.30 and 10am.

Post

Post offices (CTT Correios) are open Mon–Fri 9am–6pm; smaller branches close for lunch, larger ones open on Saturday mornings. The most convenient post office is in the Praça dos Restauradores, 58 opposite the main tourist office in the Palácio Foz. It is open Mon–Fri 8am–10pm, Sat, Sun and holidays 9am–6pm. There is an automatic machine for stamps, into which you punch the details of what you are sending and it tells you how much money to insert. The Portuguese for a stamp is um selo and air mail, Via aérea, should be written on all mail. Express mail can be sent expresso, or correio azul; money orders are vales; registered post is registos and insurance is seguro.

Another large post office can be found in the northwest corner of the Praça do Comércio (Mon–Fri 8.30am–6.30pm). The post office at the airport is open 24 hours a day.

Poste Restante (Posta Restante) in Lisbon is also at the main post office in Praça dos Restauradores. The charge for collecting a letter is the same as for an inland stamp.

Telecommunications

Call boxes accept either coins or PT charge cards, which are widely available from newsagents and post offices. Some bars and most hotels have phones where you pay after making the call, but the price of a unit is likely to be double. Coin boxes only take small coins, so an international call is best made at one of two principal assisted booths, at the post offices in Praça dos Restauradores or Praça do Comércio.

International calls: dial 00, followed by the country's code (usually written in the booth): 44 for the UK, 1 for the US and Canada, 353 for Ireland, 61 for Australia. AT&T: 05017 1 288; Sprint: 050171 1 877.

Fax: the larger hotels and some shops have fax machines as do most post offices.

Tourist Offices

Main Offices
Lisboa Welcome Centre, Praça do Comércio. Tel: 21 031 2700.
Palácio Foz, Praça dos Restauradores. Tel: 21 346 3607 (which also provides information about the rest of Portugal).
Lisbon Airport: Tel: 21 845 0657; tel: 21 849 3689 for the rest of Portugal.
Santa Apolónia station: Tel: 21 882 11604.
Information kiosks: Rua Augusta (Baixa); Castelo de São Jorge (both during summer months only).

You can get a **Lisboa Card** at any of these outlets (see page 239).

Embassies

Canada: Avenida da Liberdade 196, 3º. Tel: 21 316 4600.
Ireland: Rua da Impresa a Estrela 1, 4º. Tel: 21 392 94 40.
United Kingdom: Rua São Domingos à Lapa 37. Tel: 21 396 1191.
United States: Avenida das Forças Armadas 16. Tel: 21 727 3300.
South Africa: Av. Luis Boliar 10-A. Tel: 21 319 22 00.

Getting Around

On Arrival

Lisbon's Portela Airport is only about 20 minutes from the centre of town by bus. The No 91 Carris Express (buy your ticket on board) goes through the centre of town to the Praça do Comércio and Cais Sodré, serving most of the Lisbon hotels along the way.

Carris bus numbers 44 and 45 also go to the Praça do Rossio in the centre of town. Taxis are inexpensive.

In Lisbon most airlines have offices in Avenida da Liberdade. In the UK tour operators include: Mundi Colour Holidays, tel: 020 7828 6021 and Portuguese Affair Limited, tel: 020 7385 4775. **Lisbon Portela Airport flight information:** Tel: 21 841 3700. **TAP-Air Portugal:** Rua Duque de Palmela, tel: 21 317 9100. **British Airways:** Avenida da Liberdade, tel: 21 321 7900. **Continental Airlines:** Rua Braamcamp, tel: 21 383 4000.

Public Transport

Lisbon's Metro is steadily being extended and the system is becoming a more attractive alternative to the taxis, buses and trams that are still the most popular way to get around.

Bus stops are clearly marked with shelters where there are maps of the direction the relevant bus takes. Some have a map of the entire city network.

Individual tickets can be bought on board or you can buy, quite cheaply, a day ticket from kiosks or Metro stations, valid for bus, tram or Metro and for the lifts (elevadors). These must be validated by being punched and dated by machine on entering the station or bus, etc.

The **Elevador Santa Justa** office also sells three-day and seven-day passes, or passe turístico, which are worthwhile if you are doing a lot of running around. These, too, are valid on trams, buses, elevadors and the Metro. Take your passport along if you want to get one of these.

TRAMS

A ride on one of these wonderful vehicles, some pre-World War I, made in Sheffield, should be an essential part of any holiday. The most popular routes are the 28 and 12. In summer they run special 2-hour city tours, leaving from Praça do Comércio, tel: 363 9343.

BUSES

Buses (autocarros), trams (eléctricos) and funiculars are run by **Carris**. Their information kiosks are scattered round the city, and they may have maps in stock. There is a central kiosk in the Praça de Figueira, the most easterly square in the Baixa, but the main information centre is located at the bottom of the Santa Justa lift (see below). Bus and tram stops are signposted Paragem.

FUNICULARS

Two funiculars and one elevador (lift) make the short haul up to the Bairro Alto. One funicular starts from beside Palácia Foz in Praça dos Restauradores and ascends the Calçada da Gloria to the miradouro of São Pedro de Alcântara. The other goes from near the Cais de Sodré station up São Bento, arriving just to the west of Praça Luis Camões. The Santa Justa lift goes from Rua de Santa Justa in the Baixa.

METRO

The Metro is clean and modern, and is easy to follow. The network has recently been extended and there is a new line, making four in total: **Line 1** (yellow) Rato to Campo Grande; **Line 2** (blue) Baixo-Chiado to Pontinha; **Line 3** (green) Cais de Sodré to Campo Grande, **Line 4** (red) Alameda to Oriente. New extensions are underway; the one that will be most useful to visitors (and will probably be completed first) will run from Baixo-Chiado to Praça do Comércio then on to Santa Apolónia main line station.

Name changes

A source of some confusion for visitors to Lisbon is that names appear to be somewhat fluid: the Praça do Comércio is often referred to as the Terreiro do Paço, and the square marked on maps as Praça Dom Pedro IV is invariably called by its original name, Rossio. There is also the Elevador Santa Justa, which is frequently known as the Elevador do Carmo. Most people soon get the hang of it.

TAXIS

The city's taxis are ubiquitous and inexpensive; nearly all are cream coloured but a few of the older black and green ones remain. They have a roof light and the letter 'A' or word 'Taxi' painted on the door. A 10 percent tip is normal; the fare is metered and all taxis display a printed table of current rates. A higher tariff applies 10pm–6am and luggage put in the boot will be charged as extra. Taxi drivers are usually very knowledgeable about the city. For journeys outside the city the driver may charge a flat rate per kilometre, and may charge the return fare (even if you don't take it). If you think you are being overcharged ask for a receipt (recibo) and take a note of the taxi number.
Central Radio Taxis, tel: 21 793 27 56.

TRAINS

There are four station terminals serving the suburbs and the country. Rossio, the neo-Manueline station at the bottom of Praça dos Restauradores, houses an Information Centre and is the most central place to ask for information or tel: 876025.

Estoril coast
Commuter trains to the west, stopping at Belém, Oeiras, Carcavelos, Estoril and Cascais, leave from Cais do Sodré. This is near the waterfront to the west of Praço do Comércio. Trains leave about every 15 minutes and take up to 45 minutes to reach Cascais.

Northwestern suburbs
Trains inland westward to Sintra leave from Rossio station in Praça dos Restauradores. The journey time to Sintra is about 45 minutes.

International and north
Santa Apolónia station, on the waterfront about 2 km (1 mile)) east of Praça do Comércio. Most of the trains leaving from Santa Apolónia also stop at the new Oriente station at the Parque das Nações before heading out of Lisbon.

South
Trains for Évora and the Algarve leave from Barreiro on the Tejo's south bank. Inclusive boat and train tickets are bought at the Sul e Sueste station, the furthest building at the Terreiro do Paço ferry terminal just west of Praço do Comércio.

FERRIES

Terreiro do Paço by the Praça do Comércio serves Barreiro, Seixal and Cacilhas (for the Christ statue).
Cais do Sodré takes vehicles to Cacilhas.
Belém has boats for Porto Brando and Trafaria.
All these have bus links to the Costa Caparica.

Private Transport

CARS AND CAR RENTAL

If you have no plans to leave the city, a car can be a handicap. The best-known hire car firms are at the airport and around the Avenida da Liberdade. Hotels and travel agents will have brochures, *Yellow Pages* has a dozen pages of *Automóveis-Aluger com e sem conductor* – Cars for hire, with and without driver. It's worth shopping around as prices vary.

Booking car hire from outside Portugal before you arrive can often save you money.

Driving in Lisbon can be a terrifying experience. Parking is not easy either and car parks rarely meet demand. The speed limits are: 50 kmh (37 mph) in town; 90 kmh (56 mph) out of town and 120 kmh (75 mph) on the motorway. Drivers must have a current licence, held for a year, and must be 21, in some cases 25.

Car Hire Companies

Car hire firms at the airport include:
Europcar tel: 21 940 7790
Avis tel: 00 34 93 344 3744
Hertz tel: 21 840 1496
Auto Jardim tel: 21 846 2916
Or, if you prefer two wheels contact:
Budget, Avenida da Brasil 92, tel: 21 793 0203.

Where to Stay

How to Choose

Lisbon has plenty of hotels in every category, but they do get crowded in July and August, so it is best to book. If you arrive without booking first, go to the Tourist Office at the airport or in the Palázio Foz in the Praça do Restauradores, tel: 346 3643/342 5231 (open Mon–Sat 9am–8pm, Sun 10am–6pm). They will help you choose a hotel and make the booking free of charge.

Categories and prices: Hotel categories are from 1–5 stars. The other categories and ratings are as follows: *Albergarias* are inns with 1–4 stars and serve meals. *Residencials*, which have an "R" above their name, do bed and breakfast only, as do *pensions*, which go from 1–4 stars. Breakfast is sometimes obligatory and included in the price. In most hotels children under 12 are usually free if sharing rooms with parents.

Prices for accommodation range from around €30 for a double room in a pension to around €300 in a good hotel. The Four Seasons Ritz, beside the Parque Edward VII, is one of the most expensive hotels.

Most of the smaller, cheaper hotels and *pensions* are found in the old town. Many of the newer hotels, anodyne and efficient to attract congresses, have been built further out of town. This is fine if you are being taken care of, but public transport in some places has yet to catch up, so it is a good idea to find out how far you might be from the centre of town when booking. The sheer convenience of being near the centre is worth a lot.

Hotels

5-STAR

Alfa Lisboa Hotel
Avenida Columbano Bordalo Pinheiro
Tel: 21 726 2121
Fax: 21 726 3031
E-mail: alfa.hotel@mail.telepac.pt
Modern hotel with fine views of the Aqueduto das Águas Livres and the Parque de Monsanto. Ten minutes from the international airport.
€€€€
Carlton Palace Hotel
Rua Jau 54
Tel: 21 361 5600
Fax: 21 361 5601
E-mail: ana.henriques@pestana.com
A luxurious hotel located in the newly restored 19th-century Valle Flor Palace. Peacefully situated with views over the River Tejo. €€€€
Four Seasons H. Ritz Lisboa
Rua Rodrigo da Fonseca 88
Tel: 21 383 1783
Fax: 21 389 0505
E-mail: ritzfourseasons@mail.telepac.pt
High-quality rooms and service. Overlooking Parque Edward VII. The top of the luxury range. €€€€
Hotel Altis
Rua Castilho 11
Tel: 21 310 6000
Fax: 21 310 6262
E-mail: reservations@hotel-altis.pt
Modern hotel overlooking the city with indoor swimming pool and sauna. €€
Hotel Avenida Palace
Rua Primeiro de Dezembro 123
Tel: 21 346 0151
Fax: 21 342 2884
E-mail: hotel.avpalace@mail.telepac.pt
A grand 19th-century building, recently modernised, smack in the old town centre, located on the Praça dos Restauradores, near the Rossio. €€€€
Hotel Le Méridien Park Atlantic Lisboa
Rua Castilho, 149
Tel: 21 381 8700
Fax: 21 389 0500
E-mail: reserves.lisboa@lemeridien.pt
Elegant, with usual French flavour, overlooking the Parque Edward VII just above the Ritz. €€€€

Holiday villas beyond indulgence.

BALEARICS ~ CARIBBEAN ~ FRANCE ~ GREECE ~ ITALY ~ MAURITIUS
MOROCCO ~ PORTUGAL ~ SCOTLAND ~ SPAIN

If you enjoy the really good things in life, we offer the highest quality holiday villas with the utmost privacy, style and true luxury. You'll find each with maid service and most have swimming pools.

For 18 years, we've gone to great lengths to select the very best villas at all of our locations around the world.

Contact us for a brochure on the destination of your choice and experience what most only dream of.

INTERNATIONAL
CHAPTERS

Toll Free: 1 866 493 8340
International Chapters, 47-51 St. John's Wood High Street, London NW8 7NJ. Telephone: +44(0)20 7722 0722
email: info@villa-rentals.com www.villa-rentals.com

Live it up!

Ride through the **past** in a **trishaw** and be welcomed into the **future** by **lions**.

For the time of your life, live it up in Singapore!
Explore historic back lanes and shop in malls of the future. Take part in a traditional tea ceremony at a quaint Peranakan house, then tee off for a birdie at one of our challenging golf courses.

Spice things up with some hot Pepper Crab and unwind in a world-class spa. Join a Feng Shui Tour to harness positive energy and later channel it into a night on the town. Come to Singapore and catch the buzz and excitement of Asia's most vibrant city.

Singapore
www.newasia-singapore.com

For more information, mail to: Singapore Tourism Board, Tourism Court, 1 Orchard Spring Lane, Singapore 247729 or Fax to (65) 736 942

Name: _____   Address: _____

Email: _____

Hotel Tivoli
Avenida da Liberdade 185
Tel: 21 319 8900
Fax: 21 319 8950
E-mail: htlisboa@mail.telepac.pt
Modern and luxurious, situated in Lisbon's main avenue, between the old and new parts of the town. €€€€

Lapa Palace
Rua Pau de Bandeira 4
Tel: 21 394 9494
Fax: 21 395 0665
E-mail: reservas@hotelapa.com
Glamorously restored 19th-century mansion in the best residential quarter. Traditional luxury. €€€€

4-STAR

Albergaria Senhora do Monte
Calçada do Monte 39
Tel: 21 886 6002
Fax: 21 887 7783
Beautiful views overlooking Castelo de São Jorge, Alfama and across the Tejo. €€€

Hotel Britânia
Rua Rodrigues Sapaio 17
Tel: 21 315 5016
Fax: 21 315 5021
E-mail: britania.hotel@heritage.pt
Small comfortable hotel, recently refurbished, on a quiet street parallel to the Avenida da Liberdade. €€€

Hotel Flórida (Residencial)
Rua Duque de Palmela 34
Tel: 21 357 61 45
Fax: 21 354 35 84
Near Praça Marquês de Pombal. Pleasant rooms, reasonably priced. €€€

Hotel Mundial
Rua D. Duarte 4
Tel: 21 884 2000
Fax: 21 884 21 10
E-mail: mundial.hot@mail.telepac.pt
Recently revamped with a good view of the old city from its restaurant. Handy for the Baixa. €€

Hotel Marquês de Pombal
Avenida da Liberdade 243
Tel: 21 319 7900
Fax: 21 319 7990
E-mail: info@hotel-marquesdepombal.pt
Contemporary hotel near Marquês de Pombal with gymnasium, sauna and Turkish bath. €€€

Price Guide

Price categories are based on the cost of a double room for one night in high season.
€€€€ above €225
€€€ €150–€225
€€ €75–€150
€ up to €75

Hotel Regency Chiado Hotel
Rua Nova do Almada 114
Tel: 21 325 6100;
Reservations: 21 325 6200
Fax: 21 325 6161
E-mail: regencychiado@madeiraregency.pt
Situated in the very heart of Lisbon, in Chiado. Decor in Portuguese style with a hint of Oriental art, influenced by the Age of the Discoveries. Very convenient for sightseeing, shopping, restaurants, cafés and theatres. €€€

Hotel Tivoli Jardim
Rua Júlio César Machado 7
Tel: 21 353 9971
Fax: 21 355 6566
E-mail: htjardim@mail.telepac.pt
A modern, comfortable hotel in a quiet location but with easy access to the centre. Access to the Tivoli Club with swimming pool and tennis courts. €€€

Pensão York House
Rua das Janelas Verdes 32
Tel: 21 396 2435
Fax: 21 397 2793
E-mail: yorkhouse@hlcmm.pt
In a class by itself: comfort and charm combined. Installed in the 17th-century Convento dos Marianos, a great favourite of, among others, Graham Greene. In an interesting neighbourhood, near the Museum of Ancient Art. It is about 10 minutes by bus or tram from the Praça do Comércio and it is advisable to reserve in advance. €€€

Pensão As Janelas Verdes
Rua das Janelas Verdes 47
Tel: 21 396 8143
Fax: 21 396 8144
E-mail: jverdes@heritage.pt
A very pleasant hotel situated on the same road as York House and located in a small 18th-century palace. €€€

3-STAR

Best Western Hotel Eduardo VII
Avenida Fontes Pereira de Melo 5
Tel: 21 356 8800
Fax: 21 356 88 33
E-mail: sales@hoteleduardovii.pt
Near the park with a beautiful view from the restaurant. Slightly dark, and small, rather like a club. €€

Hotel Botânico (Residencial)
Rua da Mãe d'Agua 16–20
Tel: 21 342 0392
Fax: 21 342 0125
E-mail: hotelbotanico@mail.telepac.pt
A pleasant and comfortable hotel, situated near the botanical gardens. €€

Hotel Da Torre
Rua dos Jerónimos 8
Tel: 21 361 6940
Fax: 21 361 6946
E-mail: hoteldatorre@mail.telepac.pt
In Belém, opposite the monastery, this hotel has a quiet, out-of-town feel. €€

Hotel Meliá Confort Oriente
Avenida D.João II, Parque das Nações
Tel: 893 0000
Fax: 21 893 0099
E-mail: melia.confort.oriente@isoterica.pt
An aparthotel located in the Parque das Nações, just a few minutes from Lisbon city centre. Convenient for the International airport, Gare do Oriente (railway station) and coach services. With extensive views over the Parque das Nações and the impressive Vasco da Gama bridge over the Tejo. €€

Hotel Métropole (Residencial)
Praça D. Pedro IV (Rossio)
Tel: 21 321 9030
Fax: 21 346 9166
E-mail: almeidahotels@ip.pt
Located in the heart of Lisbon with spectacular views of the Baixa, Alfama and the Castelo de São Jorge. €€

Hotel Miraparque
Avenida Sidónio Pais 12
Tel: 21 352 4286
Fax: 21 357 8920
E-mail: miraparque@esoterica.pt
A comfortable and peaceful hotel overlooking the Parque Edward VII. €€

Hotel President
Rua Alexandre Herculano 13
Tel: 21 317 3570
Fax: 21 352 0272
E-mail: hpresidente@mail.telepac.pt
A comfortable modern hotel in a quiet area close to the Praça Marquês de Pombal. €€

Sana Classic Rex Hotel
Rua Castilho 169
Tel: 21 388 2161
Fax: 21 388 7581
For those who can't afford the Ritz or the Méridien, the Rex is a nice hotel next door. €€

Hotel Veneza *(Residencial)*
Avenida da Liberdade 189
Tel: 21 352 2618
Fax: 21 352 6678
E-mail: hveneza@mail.telepac.pt
A comfortable modern hotel situated on the main avenue. €€

Price Guide

Price categories are based on the cost of a double room for one night in high season.

€€€€	above €225
€€€	€150–€225
€€	€75–€150
€	up to €75

2-STAR

Hotel Borges
Rua Garrett 108
Tel: 21 346 1951
Fax: 21 342 6617
A comfortable, mid-priced hotel in the heart of the Chiado. €

Hotel Ibis Lisboa Saldanha
Avenida Casal Ribeiro 23
Tel: 21 319 1690
Fax: 21 319 1699
E-mail: h2117@accorhotels.com
Situated near the Praça Duque de Saldanha with easy access by bus and Metro to the city. €

Hotel Ibis Lisboa Malhoa
Avenida José Malhoa
Tel: 21 723 5700
Fax: 21 723 5701
E-mail: h1668@accorhotels.com
Near Praça da Espanha Metro and the Calouste Gulbenkian Museum. Just 10 minutes from the airport. €

Hotel Internacional *(Residencial)*
Rua da Betesga
Tel: 21 346 6401
Fax: 21 347 8635
Not too many amenities, but a fine, newly renovated Art Nouveau hotel, right in the middle of the bustling Baixa. €

Hotel Portugal *(Residencial)*
Rua João das Regras 4
Tel: 21 887 581
Fax: 21 886 7343
In the Baixa but not on a main street. Pleasant and inexpensive. €

INEXPENSIVE

Pensão Ninho das Aguias
Rua Costa do Castelo 74
Tel: 21 885 4070
The name means "eagles' nest", though not all the rooms have fantastic views down from the top of the Alfama. Come for the charm if not the comfort. €

Pensão Praça da Figueira
(Residencial)
Travessa Nova de S. Domingos 9
Tel/Fax: 21 342 4323
E-mail: rrcoelho@clix.pt
Right in the middle of the city, handy for the Baixa. €

Residencial Florescente
Rua das Portas de Santo Antão 99
Tel: 326609
Simple, inexpensive and full of charm. Tiled hallways, clean rooms. Near Praçca Restauradores. €

Residencial Roma
Travessa da Glória 22
Tel/Fax: 21 346 9557
A *residencial* with many of the amenities of a hotel, including private bath and TV in every room. Don't let the rather shabby exterior put you off; the inside is well kept and clean. €

Residencial Dom João
Rua José Estêvão 43
Tel: 21 314 4171
Fax: 21 352 4569
In a quiet residential neighbourhood, slightly off the beaten track, but only a 15-minute walk to the Praça Marquês de Pombal.

Residencial Dom Sancho I
Avenida da Liberdade 202
Tel: 21 354 8648
Fax: 21 354 8042
Located on the main avenue, this *residencial* is clean and well furnished (Portuguese style) with the essential services. €

Casa de San Mamede
Rua da Escola Politécnica 159
Tel: 21 396 3166
Situated near the Largo do Rato, a friendly atmosphere in a small 18th-century refurbished palace. €

Youth Hostels

The city's **Pousada de Juventude**, which can cater for 200, is in the Rua Andrade Corvo 46, off Fontes Pereira de Melo east of Praça Marquês de Pombal, tel: 21 353 2696. **Pousada de Juventude de Catalazete**, at Forte do Catalazete, Oiras, tel: 21 443 0638, is between Belém and Cascais. You can get there by taking the train from Cais do Sodré.

Camping

The city campsite, **Lisboa Camping – Parque Municipal**, tel: 21 762 3106, is somewhat out of town on the border of the Parque Florestal Monsanto. This is on the north side of the Lisbon–Cascais motorway to the west of the city inland from Belém. It is fully equipped with showers, toilets, a children's playground, swimming pool and tennis courts. It also has a shopping area, including restaurant, mini-market and a bar.

Where to Eat

For both variety and price, Lisbon is one of the best cities in Europe for eating out. Typical dishes are given in the *Eating Out* chapter on page 162. As well as Portuguese cuisine, there are plenty of opportunities to sample the flavours of the former Portuguese colonies in Africa and Brazil.

Restaurants

The favourite place for an evening meal and a night out is the Bairro Alto. Some of the restaurants here are no bigger than a suburban front room, so it's best either to book or get there by 8pm, before they start to fill up.

The Baixo also has a number of good places to eat out. Rua das Portas de Santo Antão, running behind Praça dos Restauradores down to the back of the National Theatre, is full of eateries of every description. Parallel to Rua Augusta is Rua da Correiros, a street of sensible local restaurants serving nourishing Portuguese meals.

A little out of town there are excellent restaurants in Parque das Nações. On the waterfront to the west, the area around Doca de Santo Amaro has some lively eating places.

In Belém, there is a charming row of restaurants in Rua Vieira Portuense on the river side of the main road, and a couple of good, though pricey restaurants in the yacht marina.

At a reasonable price, Portuguese restaurants offer a *menu turistíco*. This is a fixed-price menu and includes a starter, main course (choice of fish or meat) and a dessert. A roll and butter, *vinho da casa* (or a beer or soft drink), service charge and tax are included in the price.

Below are a few recommended restaurants, but there are, of course, many more, and choosing a place to eat can be part of the fun.

Price Guide

The restaurants are divided into the following price categories based on a meal for one, including wine:
€€€ above €40
€€   €20–40
€   below €20

EXPENSIVE

It is wise to reserve a table at the more expensive restaurants.

A Commenda
Centro Cultural de Belém, Praça do Império
Tel: 21 361 2613
Sophisticated restaurant with extensive views of the river and the city serving Portuguese and international cuisine. Famous for its Sunday brunch; serves late suppers after any shows at the Cultural Centre. Closed Sunday (dinner). €€€

A Confraria
Rua das Janelas Verdes 32
Tel: 21 396 2435
Set in the tranquil gardens of the York House Hotel, this is a peaceful place to enjoy an exceptional meal. Open daily. €€€

Bachus
Largo da Trinidade 9, Bairro Alto
Tel: 21 342 2828
Sophisticated food and decor. Closed Sunday. €€€

Casa da Comida
Travessa das Amoreiras 1
Tel: 21 385 9386
Attractive setting around an internal courtyard. Delicious, unusual cuisine. Closed Saturday lunch, Sunday. €€€

Casa do Leão
Castelo de São Jorge
Tel: 21 887 5962
Smart place with the best view in town. Open daily. €€€

Conventual
Praça das Flores 45
Tel: 21 390 9196
One of the most renowned restaurants in Lisbon reflecting ancient convent cuisine. Closed Saturday lunch and Sunday. €€€

Gambrinus
Rua das Portas de Santo Antão 25, near Restauradores
Tel: 21 342 1466
A popular place for Lisboetas splashing out. Noted for fish and seafood. Open daily. €€€

Pabe
Rua Duque de Palmela 27A, near Praça Marquês de Pombal
Tel: 21 353 5675
Haunt of politicians and journalists. Portuguese and international dishes. Open daily. €€€

Taveres Rico
Rua da Misericórdia 37, Bairro Alto
Tel: 342 1112
The best-known luxury restaurant in town. Gilt-edged and glittering. Cold buffet lunch on the first floor. Closed Saturday and Sunday lunch. €€€

Terreiro do Paço
Lisboa Welcome Centre, Praça do Comércio
Tel: 21 031 2850
Excellent Portuguese cuisine, made with the freshest ingredients, with good service in relaxed surroundings. Closed Sunday. €€€

Torre Vasco da Gama
Cais das Naus, Parque das Nações.
Tel: 21 893 9550
A luxury restaurant on top of the Vasco da Gama Tower with sweeping views over the Tagus estuary. Portuguese and international cuisine. Closed Monday. €€€

MODERATE

Adega da Tia Matilde
Rua de Beneficencia 77, near the Gulbenkian Foundation
Tel: 21 797 2172
Regional Portuguese dishes. Closed Saturday dinner and Sunday. €€

Café Martinho da Arcada
Praço do Comércio 3. Baixa
Tel: 21 886 6213
Supposedly the city's oldest surviving café, where the literati of

Drinking Notes

Wine in Portugal is very drinkable and invariably you can do little better in restaurants than simply ask for the house wine (*vinho de casa*), which is nearly always available in half bottles as well as bottles. Red is *tinto*, white is *branco* and *vinho verde* is a refreshing young white wine which is slightly sparkling (it can also be red, but usually is white).

There are 10 demarcated wine regions in the country. The principal ones are the Douro in the north, where port also comes from, the Dão, Bairrada and Alentejo. There are four small regions close to Lisbon:
Carcavelos, on the road to Estoril, is a small vineyard producing an amber-coloured, fortified wine. **Bucelas**, 32 km (20 miles) north of Lisbon, produces a white wine under the Caves Velhas label.
Colares is about 5 km (3 miles) from the coast on the edge of the Sintra hills. It produces a small quantity of whites and reds.

Setúbal is the main growing region in the area and it produces reds, whites, rosés and moscatel. The main house is Fonseca, which can be visited (*see page 219*).
Madeira: these islands' fortified wines come in various guises. In whites there is Verdelho and the drier Sercial, both pleasant aperitifs. Malmsey (*Malvasia*) and Boal are sweeter, dessert wines.
Port: this product of the lava-rich soils around the Duoro valley is synonymous with Portugal. Vintage port takes up to 20 years to mature and dusty old bottles in Baixo food shops sell for more than €400. It's worth trying a dry white as an aperitif. There is no better place to try them than the Solar do Vinho do Porto – **The Port Wine Institute**. This is in Rua São Pedro de Alcântara 45, opposite the top of the Gloria funicular. Open 2pm–midnight Monday–Saturday, it is not as intimidating as it sounds and it is a good place to meet.

the *Belle Epoque* met. Portuguese and international cooking. Closed Sunday. €€
Doca Peixe
Doca de Santo Amaro, Armazém 13, Alcântara
Tel: 21 397 3565
Esplanade restaurant overlooking the marina at the Santo Amaro docks, serving fresh fresh and seafood. Closed Tuesday. €€
Dom Sopas
Rua de São Bento 107
Tel: 21 396 4037
Near the São Bento palace. As the name suggests, soup is the speciality but it also serves traditional Portuguese dishes. Closed Sunday. €€
Mercado de Santa Clara
Campo do Santa Clara 7
Tel: 21 873986
In the heart of the Alfama, with a view of the Tejo. Traditional Portuguese food. Closed Sunday dinner and Monday and all of August. €€

Nariz de Vinho Tinto
Rua do Conde 75
Tel: 21 395 3035
Located in Lapa in an old atelier. High standard of classic Portuguese cuisine with an impressive list of 200 wines and 80 ports. €€
Pap'Açorda
Rua da Atalaia 57, Bairro Alto
Tel: 21 346 4811
In a remodelled bakery, this restaurant has an excellent reputation. Popular, and difficult to get into on a Friday or Saturday night. Closed Sunday and Monday. €€
Porta Branca
Rua Teixera 35. Bairro Alto
Tel: 21 342 1024
Serves good traditional Portuguese food. Closed Sunday. €€
São Jerónimo
Rua dos Jerónimos 12, Belém
Tel: 21 364 8797
Excellent Portuguese and French

cuisine and 1930s decor. Closed Saturday lunch and Sunday. €€
Sua Excelencia
Rua do Conde 34. Lapa
Tel: 21 390 36 14
A small, personal restaurant serving immaculate traditional Portuguese dishes. Closed September, Wednesday, Saturday and Sunday lunch. €€

INEXPENSIVE

Bomjardin
Travessa de Santo Antão 11, near Restauradores
Tel: 21 342 4389
Some say it's the best roast chicken in town. Quick turnover. Open every day. €
Bota Alta
Travessa da Queimada 35.
Bairro Alto
Tel: 21 327959
Pretty, popular, red-checked tablecloth restaurant. Closed Saturday lunch and Sunday. €
Cervejaria da Trindade
Rua Nova da Trindade 20C,
Bairro Alto
Tel: 21 342 3506
Very ordinary food but popular for the former convent's decor of classical wall-to-wall tiles. Go early at weekends. Open daily until 2am. €
Forno Velho
Rua do Salitre 42
Tel: 21 353 3706
Traditional food including goat roasted in the wood stove. Open every day. €
Malmequer Bemmequer
Largo de São Miguel 25
Tel: 21 887 6535
In the heart of the Alfama. Closed Monday. €

Price Guide

The restaurants are divided into the following price categories based on a meal for one, including wine:
€€€ above €40
€€ €20–40
€ below €20

Pateo Bagatella
Rua da Artilharia Um, Loja L
Tel: 21 386 2670
Specialises in grilled steaks and
fresh fish. Open every day. €

Primeiro de Maio
Rua Atalia 6–10
Tel: 21 342 6840
Typical Portuguese restaurant in the
Bairro Alto. Popular and trendy;
great fish dishes. €

Solar dos Presuntos
Portas de Santo Antão 150
Tel: 21 342 4253
Hearty Minho food in the street-of-
many-restaurants. Closed Sunday.
€

Sol Dourado
Rua Jardim do Regador 19–25 (off
Restaudores)
Tel: 21 347 2570
Tasty local food in a cheerful
setting. €

VEGETARIAN

Vegetarians get a bit of a rough
deal in Lisbon – unless they eat
fish. There are a few vegetarian
restaurants but they tend to be a
bit spartan and usually self-
service. Most of them are only
open at lunch time, too. If you
want to eat in comfort in a
restaurant with atmosphere, you
may have to settle for salads and
omelettes. Otherwise, try the
following:

Celeiro
Rua 1º de Dezembro 65
A self-service restaurant in the
basement of a health food
supermarket, behind Rossio
station. Open 9am–7pm.

**Centro de Alimentaçao e Saude
Natural**
Rua Mouzino da Silveira 25
Tel: 21 315 0898.
Self-service, more imaginative than
most, and has a nice courtyard.
Near Praça Marquês de Pombal.
Open 9am–2.30pm, 3.30–6pm.

Espiral
Praça Ilha do Faial 14, Largo do
Estefânia.
Tel: 21 357 3585.
Self-service; average macrobiotic
food. Open noon–9.30pm.

Let Them Eat Cake

"Let them eat cake!" may sum
up Lisboetas' attitude to
vegetarians, whose refusal to eat
meat they regard as distinctly
odd. This is somewhat strange,
perhaps, for people who once
had the nickname "*Alfacinhas*" or
"little lettuce eaters". But things
will no doubt change, if the
demand is there. In the
meantime, the cakes are very
good indeed.

Cafés

**Antiga Fábrica dos Pastéis de
Belém**
Rua de Belém 84, Belém
Famous for it's pastries, served
warm and topped with cinnamon.
Good coffee.

Brasileria
Rua Garret 120, Chiado
Established in 1922 this is one of
the best-known and most
atmospheric cafés in the city. Open
till 2am.

Café Nicola
Praça Dom Pedro IV 26
One of the oldest and most popular
cafés in Lisbon. Art Nouveau decor.

O Chá do Carmo
Largo do Carmo, 21
Home-made cakes, light lunches,
coffee and a choice of 50 teas.

Pastelaria Suiça
Praça Dom Pedro IV 100
A popular meeting place, so be
prepared to wait for an outside table.

NET CAFÉS

Ciber-Bica
Rua dos Duques de Bragança 7.
Chiado
The first "virtual" café in Lisbon,
where you can surf along with
partaking of light refreshments and
a drink. Open: noon–2am. Closed
Sunday.

Café.Com
Costa do Castelo 75. Castelo
A lovely view. Serves tapas and
drinks. Open 2pm–midnight. Closed
Monday.

MUSEUM CAFÉS

Many of Lisbon's museums have
excellent cafés and restaurants
where you can get a light lunch for a
reasonable price, often with a view.
The restaurant at the **Museum of
Ancient Art**, with its terrace
overlooking the River Tejo, is very
popular. A bit more formal, and with
views from the terrace overlooking
the Parque Monteiro-Mor, is the
restaurant at the **National Costume
Museum**. Food is sold by the kilo at
the **Chiado Museum**, and in the
restaurant at the **National Tile
Museum** you can admire the re-laid
tiles, depicting food. which were
originally from a 19th-century
kitchen. The restaurant at the
Calouste Gulbenkian Museum is
particularly popular on Sunday.
    For details of where to find all
the above museums, see the
appropriate chapter in the *Places*
section of the book.

Culture

Information

Lisbon council puts out a monthly booklet called *Agenda Cultural* which is worth having for up-to-date information and listings of events. You should be able to pick up a copy at the Tourist Office, hotel or travel agent. It's partly in English and easy to follow. Daily papers, such as *Público* and *Diario de Noticias*, also carry listings of the following week's events or you can pick up a copy of *What's on in Lisbon* from some hotels.

Museums

Most of the major museums are described in the Places section of the book so no detail will be given here. In brief, most museums are open from 10am–5pm, closed on Monday and public holidays. Exceptions to this are noted in the main text. If a museum is closed for lunch there is usually a good self-service restaurant on the premises. Museum admission averages at around €2.50. Students get in free.

Cinema

Lisbon is a great place for movie fans: not only are there so many cinemas – the Amoreiras, Colombo and Vasco da Gama shopping complexes all have multiple screens – but the films are all shown in their original language. The older cinemas such as the Mundial, the King Triplex and the quaint Quarteto, show films by lesser-known directors. The Ávila specialises in showing old films.

Sadly, the Animatógrafo do Rossio in the Baixa, opened in 1907 and one of the oldest in Europe, no longer functions as a cinema but is interesting architecturally.

Art Galleries

The galleries showing contemporary art in Lisbon are not clustered around a single area but are dispersed throughout the city. In addition to the more firmly established galleries are numerous new spaces that have opened over the past decade showing the younger generation of Portuguese artists. Several of the larger commercial centres and hotels increasingly exhibit collections of works by up-and-coming artists. **Galeria 111**, Campo Grande 111–113. One of the few older galleries to have survived the 1974 revolution, it continues to thrive. Its "stable" includes members of the older generation of established and well-known Portuguese modern artists who fetch high prices at home and abroad.

Among them are the lyrical painter António Dacosta (who died in 1990), the vigorous work of Júlio Pomar, and Menez, who has turned from her earlier abstractions to haunting evocations of figures in empty interiors or garden settings.

Galeria 111 has shown the work of Maria Helena Vieira da Silva, the great Portuguese abstract painter, who lived in Paris for many years and died in 1992.

Undoubtedly the most highly acclaimed living Portuguese artist to be exhibited regularly at a gallery is Paula Rego, now resident in Britain who, in 1990–91, became the first Associate Artist at London's National Gallery. **Módulo**, Calçada dos Mestres 34, Campolide. Another gallery that managed to survive the turbulence of the 1970s. Its policy has been to discover young artists and put them on the map.

Cómicos, Rua Tenente Raul Cascais 1, near the British Institute, is a space that opened in the early 1980s. Of all the galleries in Lisbon, this is the one with the highest international profile, bringing together avant-garde artists of different nationalities, including Joel Fisher, Joseph Kosuth and Cristine Iglesias.

Galeria Garça Fonseca, Rua da Emenda 26, near Chiado, opened in the late 1980s with a similar programme. Several artists from other galleries moved here in the early 1990s, including Leonel Moura, Pedro Portugal and Pedro

Proença, all of whom are in the forefront of contemporary art.

Alda Cortes, Largo de Santos, is another interesting gallery. Here, watch out for the hauntingly evocative paintings of Miguel Branco and the sculpture of José Pedro Croft, undoubtedly one of the more interesting sculptors working in Portugal today.

Other galleries to look out for: **Galeria Lisboa 20**, Calçada da Estrela. Exhibitions of paintings, sculptures, drawings and photographs by Portuguese artists. **EMI Valentim de Carvalho**, Rua Cruz dos Poiais 111, down the road from the British Institute. This beautiful space overlooking a garden has a mixed programme of mostly Portuguese artists. **Palmira Suso**, Rua das Flores 109. A new gallery with occasionally interesting shows. **Diferença**, Rua S. Filipe Neri 42, near Lago do Rato; and **Monumental**, Campo Martires da Patria 101, show mainly younger and sometimes less-known Portuguese artists. **Galeria de São Franciso**, Rua Ivens 40, Chiado. Exhibitions promoting young Portuguese artists.

Theatre

The great bulk of the Teatro Nacional Dona Maria II in Praça Dom Pedro IV (Rossio Square), tel: 21 342 2210 is unmissable. Another major venue is the Teatro Trindade, Rua Nova Trinidade 9, Bairro Alto, tel: 21 342 0000. There are also a number of smaller theatres and there are often visiting companies.

Obviously, most productions are in Portuguese, so are not of great interest to the majority of visitors, unless they speak the language.

However, the city has a tradition of musical revues, which can be appreciated even if you don't speak Portuguese. Parque Mayer (currently being renovated) by the Avenida Metro station on Avenida da Liberdade has fringe theatres and other entertainments.

The Teatro Politeama, Rua Portas de Santo Antão 109, tel: 21 343 0327/96, stages a musical called simply *Amália* about the Portuguese *fado* diva that looks set to run and run for the forseeable future.

Occasionally large-scale events are staged at the Pavilhão Âtlantico in the Parque das Nações.

The ABEP kiosk at the bottom of Praça do Restauradores has information and tickets for all entertainments, and charges a small commission.

Music & Opera

The Teatro São Luis, Rua António Maria Cardoso 40, Chiado, tel: 21 346 1260, and the beautiful Teatro Nacional de São Carlos, Rua Serpa Pinto 9, Chiado, tel: 21 346 8408, are the city's opera and ballet houses, though their seasons do not extend through the summer.

The Fundação Calouste Gulbenkian, Avenida de Berna 45, Praça de Espanha, tel: 21 793 5131, has both indoor and outdoor facilities and is an active year-round cultural centre. Its huge auditorium has wonderful acoustics. The foundation has its own choir, orchestra and ballet company.

The exciting Centro Cultural de Belém, Praça do Imperial, Belém, tel: 21 361 2400, stages a wide variety of events, from classical concerts and ballet, to jazz and modern and classical drama, as well as art exhibitions. Among the internationally known names that have performed here during 2001 are the Royal Shakespeare company and the Harlem Gospel Singers.

In the summer there is music all around the city, particularly in the cathedral and other attractive churches, such as São Roque and the ruined Carmo convent in the Bairro Alto.

Lisboa Card

The Lisboa Card is sold at all the main tourist offices *(see page 230)* and offers free transport, free entry to the major museums and discounts on other sites and attractions (such as river trips) for 48 hours – well worth it if you are going to be doing a lot of sightseeing and travelling around the city.

There is also a Lisboa Shopping Card, which offers up to 20 percent discount in a number of shops, and the Lisboa Restaurant Card, which gives you a discount in a number of restaurants.

Nightlife

The Lisbon Scene

Lisboetas are night owls, but a night out means different things to different people. For some it's a jug of wine with friends and a traditional night of *fado* in the Bairro Alto. For others it's visiting one of the flashy discos nearby, or enjoying the lively atmosphere at the Doca de Santo Amaro. Or it may be just an evening in the neighbourhood café.

Much of the city's nightlife, from *fado* to disco, takes place in the Bairro Alto where the traditional seems to mix easily with the trendy. Wander its streets on a Friday or Saturday night and you will be spoilt for choice of places to go.

For an update of what's in, what's out and who's playing where, consult the daily papers or monthly *Agenda Cultural* published by Lisbon City Council.

Discos & Music Bars

Bars with live music and dancing are called *boites*, or "dancing". Discos sometimes have live music as well. Many are within strolling distance around the Bairro Alto and the neighbouring Rato district. Bars have free entry: *boites* and discos have an entrance fee of a few euros. Several new discos have become popular in the west of the town, in the Alcântara district, near the Ponte 25 de Abril and the Santo Amaro docks. The Campo Pequeno in the north-east of the city also has popular discos. "In" places can be "out" very quickly, as fashions change, so it is impossible to give a truly accurate list. Try to check what is still open and still popular when you visit.

Frágil, Rua da Atalia 126, tel: 21 346 9578. The best-known nightspot in the Bairro Alto, where the fashionable go to see and be seen. Minimalist interior. Closed Sunday.

Hot Club de Portugal, Praça de Alegria 39 (just above Avenida da Liberdade), tel: 21 346 7369. The best place in town for jazz. Closed Sunday and Monday.

Lux, Rua Gustavo Mato Sequeira 42, Santa Apolónia, tel: 21 882 0890. Very trendy and popular, this club in a converted dockside warehouse near Santa Apolónia station has great sounds and an easy-going atmosphere. You can eat here, too. Open till very late; closed Monday.

Plateau, Travessa das Escadinhas da Praia 7, Alcântara, tel: 21 396 5116. The most prestigious disco and current attraction. Closed Sunday and Monday.

Ritz Club, Rua da Gloria 57, Avenida da Liberdade, tel: 21 342 5140. Good African music. Closed Sunday and Monday.

Salsa Latina, Gare Marítima de Alcântara, tel: 21 395 0555. As its name suggests, it has a Latin American flavour. Closed Sunday.

W, Rua Maria Luísa Olstein 13, Alcântara. Dancing all through the night. Closed Sunday and Monday.

Fado

Not surprisingly, many of the larger *fado* houses are tourist haunts, but that doesn't mean the singers are inferior. The genuine article has to be hunted out. These are the places where anyone gets up to sing, even the bar staff, and often the places have no visible name. They are mainly around Rua Atalaia in the Bairro Alto, and around the Largo do Chafariz in the Alfama. There are also *fado* houses in Alcântara and Lapa.

Larger Houses

These are marked by their uniformed doormen. They usually serve dinner and have a high entrance fee or minimum consumption charge. Singing starts around 9.30 or 10pm and there is sometimes additional "folkloric" music and dancing. It is best to make a reservation, especially in summer or at weekends.

Adega Machado, Rua do Norte 91, Bairro Alto, tel: 21 322 4640.

Lisboa a Noite, Rua das Gáveas 69, Bairro Alto, tel: 21 346 8557.

Sévera, Rua das Gáveas 51–61, Bairro Alto, tel: 21 342 8314.

More Traditional

Dragão de Alfama, Rua Guilherme Braga 8-loja, tel: 21 886 7737.

Parreirinha de Alfama, Beco do Espírito Santo 1, Alfama, tel: 21 886 8209.

Senhor Vinho, Rua Meio à Lapa 1, Lapa, tel: 21 397 2681.

Taverna do Embuçado, Beco dos Costumes 10, Alfama, tel: 21 886 5088.

It is usually possible to buy CDs and tapes of *fado* music in the restaurant. Otherwise, one of the best places is either Valentim de Carvalho or FNAC in Baixa Chiado.

House of Fado

Information about recommended places to hear *fado* can be obtained from the House of Fado, Largo do Chafariz de Dentro 1, Alfama, tel: 21 882 3470, open 10am–6pm, except Tuesday. This is a good place to find out about the origins and history of *fado*, through audio-visual events, exhibits and shows.

Excursions

City Tours

Tours of the city and its environs are easy to find out about. Hotels, travel agents and tourist offices have brochures of all tours. A few well-established ones are:

Cityrama, Avenida Praia da Vitória 12-B, Lisbon, tel: 21 319 1091. Terminal and information, Marques de Pombal, tel: 21 386 4322. Daily city tours, royal palace tours, sunset-with-*fado*-show tours.

Gray Line, Avenida Praia da Vitória 12-B, Lisbon, tel: 21 352 2594. Terminal and information, Marques de Pombal, tel: 21 386 4322. Tours of Lisbon by day and night, a mini-cruise, and day trips out of Lisbon.

Carristur specialises in three different sightseeing routes, leaving from the Praça da Comércio and lasting up to two hours. The Eléctrico das Colinas, a renovated tram car, goes around the city and has a night-time trip, too. Tickets, which must be booked, cost around €15.

Circuito Tejo (Tagus Tour) tours the main attractions of the city in an open-top bus, including the Gulbenkian Museum, Amoreiras shopping centre, and out to Belém. You can leave and board the bus at any point you wish. The same conditions apply with the **Expresso Oriente (Orient Express)**, which includes the botanical gardens, the bullring and Parque das Nações. Tickets (which are valid on the Carris public network throughout the day) cost around €15, on board. Tel: 21 358 2334.

Cruzeiros no Tejo Two-hour cruises on the River Tejo mainly take place from April to October, at 11am and 3pm. Prices are between €10–16.

They are also operated by Gray Line *(see above)*. Information can be obtained from the Terminal Fluvial do Terreiro do Paço, the ferry terminal from which they depart, tel: 21 882 0348.
Combois Turistícos de Belém. The mini-train touring around Belém is a relaxing way to enjoy the main tourist sites. Departs from in front of the Jeronimós monastery. (There is also a mini-train at the Parque das Nações).

Out-of-Town Tours

Historic Sintra and the resorts of Cascais and Estoril should be the first places to think of for a day away from the city *(see page 195)*. Queluz and Mafra are also a short distance to the north *(see page 201)*; Batalha and Alcobaça further north still *(see page 207)*; Arrábida, Setúbal and Sesimbra to the south; and Evora three hours to the east *(see page 215)*.

Details of these destinations can be found on the relevant pages in the text. It is obviously easier and more convenient if you have a hire car, but you can go by train. For Cascais and Estoril, trains leave Cais do Sodré station about every 15 minutes; for Sintra, take one of the frequent trains from Rossio station; for Mafra, Batalha and Alcobaça and all points north, take a train from Santa Apolónia; for all the southern destinations, you cross the river by ferry from Terreiro do Paço or Cais do Sodré as a foot passenger, then take a train from the other side. There are also bus links with the ferries that will take you to the Costa Caparica.

There are tour companies who make day trips by coach to Batalha and Alcobaça; enquire at one of the main tourist offices for details.

Activities for Children

Aquário Vasco da Gama is in Dafundo near Algés station just beyond Belém. The aquarium's main attraction are the live seals and sharks. Open daily 10am–6pm.

Feira Popular Amusement Park (Metro: Entrecampos) is the city's permanent fun fair with big wheel and other rides. It is not just for children and stays open late into the night.
Funcenter, Centro Colombo, is an in-door amusement park and includes bowling alleys, a giant wheel, bumper cars and many more. Not only for the children! Open daily noon–midnight.
Jardim Zoológico: (Metro: Jardim Zoológico) with its 2,000 live animal species, offers a wide variety of entertainment, including the dolphin spectacular and feeding the sea lions. You can visit a small farm or take the cable car. There is also an amusement park. Open in the summer from 10–8pm.
Oceanário de Lisboa, at the Parque das Nações, houses the largest oceanarium in Europe and is open daily from 10am–7pm in the summer.
Parque Recreativo do Alto da Serafina, Alto da Serafina, is an adventure park for children. Open daily from 9am–8pm in the summer.
Planetarium: Belém, beside the Jerónimos monastery. Another philanthropic arm of the Gulbenkian. Open Saturday and Sunday, with sessions at 3.30 and 5pm. Sunday morning at 11am.

Shopping

Where to Shop

All the shopping most people need can be done downtown in the Baixa, where there are many small, specialist shops, and the Bairro Alto, where the Chiado district around Rua Garrett has numerous smart shops. There are small malls throughout the city, including a high-class one at the Ritz and a small exclusive one at the Tivoli Forum in the Avenida da Liberdade.

For those who like their retail experiences on a large scale, shopping in Lisbon has never been easier with its abundance of large shopping centres. There is Colombo, Iberia's largest shopping mall, to the north of the city; Amoreiras, Lisbon's first; the sleek Vasco da Gama in the Parque das Nações; the medium-sized Chiado Shopping in the Baixa; and Via Veneto up-town in Avenidas Novas. Smart shops can be found around Avenida da Liberdade and Avenida de Roma. See *Shopping* chapter for general notes about what to buy.

ANTIQUES

Antique shops can be found in various parts of the city, but the biggest concentration runs for about a mile from Cais de Sodré station. Start up Rua do Alecrim and continue up Misericórdia, along São Pedro de Alcântara and Dom Pedro V to Escola Politécnica.
Alberquerque & Sousa Lda, Rua do Dom Pedro V 145. Beautiful antique tiles from the 17th–20th century.
Manuel Henriques de Carvalho, Rua da Escola Politécnica 89–99. Ceramics in a lovely old tea shop.

ARRAIOLOS RUGS

Casa Quintão, Rua Ivens 30. Off Rua Garrett in Chiado. This is one of the best-known stores of its kind. **Casa dos Tapetes de Arraiolos**, Rua do Imprensa Nacional, 116E. Beautiful, customised rugs, made to any shape, style or size.

BOOKS

Antiquarian and collectors' books, as well as old prints, are found in the Bairro Alto around Largo Trindade Coelha.
Livraria Barateira, Rua Nova da Trindade 16C. Antiquarian and second-hand, including foreign books.
Livraria Británica, Rua de São Marçal 83, Principe Real. English bookshop. Specialises in academic titles but has a good range of novels, etc.
Livraria Buchholz, Rua Duque de Palmela 4, Praça Marquês de Pombal. Has an English-language section (as well as French, Spanish, German and Italian). Coffee shop in the basement.
Livraria Camões, Rua da Misericórdia, 139. Antiquarian books.
Livraria Olisipo, Largo do Trindade Coelha. A large selection of prints.

CERAMICS, TILES & HANDICRAFTS

Fábrica Sant'Anna, Rua do Alcrim 95. Ceramic tiles *(azulejos)* of every type, price and size and lots of pottery, all hand-painted. Fun for just browsing. Visitors are also welcome at their factory at Calçada da Boa Hora 96, in Belém.
Fábrica Céramica Viúva Lamego, Largo do Intendente 25. Viúva also has its own factory. The quaint shop, near the Intendente Metro stop, has some pottery and a wide choice of tiles.
Vista Alegre, Largo do Chiado 18. The makers of the country's best-known porcelain have half a dozen outlets in the city. They are also

Women's Dresses/Suits

US	Italy	UK
6	38/34N	8/30
8	40/36N	10/32
10	42/38N	12/34
12	44/40N	14/36
14	46/42N	16/38
16	48/44N	18/40

Women's Shoes

US	Italy	UK
4½	36	3
5½	37	4
6½	38	5
7½	39	6
8½	40	7
9½	41	8
10½	42	9

Men's Suits

US	Italy	UK
34	44	34
—	46	36
38	48	38
—	50	40
42	52	42
—	54	44
46	56	46

Men's Shirts

US	Italy	UK
14	36	14
14½	37	14½
15	38	15
15½	39	15½
16	40	16
16½	41	16½
17	42	17

Men's Shoes

US	Italy	UK
6½	—	6
7½	40	7
8½	41	8
9½	42	9
10½	43	10
11½	44	11

represented in all the main shopping centres and at the international airport.
Loja dos Descobrimentos, Rua dos Bacalhoeiros 12-A. Right next to the Casa dos Bicos, selling a wide variety of Portuguese crafts – *artesenato* – with a workshop where

you can watch tiles being painted and order your own personal choice.
Regional Portuguese Goods, Praça dos Restauradores 64. Next to the post office in one of the oldest artisans' shops in Lisbon. Sells all types of regional handicrafts.

CLOTHING

Many leading designers such as Benetton, Stefanel, Manoukian, Rodier, Lacoste and Pierre Cardin have franchises in the city. Spanish high street fashion houses such as Massimo Dutti (for men) and Don Algodón and Zara (both for women) are doing well. And from Brazil comes Mr Wonderful.
Loja das Meias, Rossio 1; Rua Castilho 39; and Amoreiras shopping centre. Lisbon's leading men's and women's wear store.
Ana Salazar, Rua do Carmo 16E; and Avenida de Roma 87. Portugal's most famous designer.

EMBROIDERY & LACE

Casa Regional da Ilha Verde, Rua Paiva de Andrada 4. Near the Chiado, this shop has a beautiful selection of handmade items, primarily from the Azores.
Madeira Gobelins, Rua Castilho 40. Lots of embroidered works in a rather touristy setting. Plus needlepoint kits to take home and make your own.
Tito Cunha, Rua do Ouro 246. Embroidered work from Madeira.

JEWELLERY & SILVERWORK

Eloy de Jesus, Rua Garrett 45. Beautiful, high-quality silver filigree.
Sarmento, Rua Aurea 251. Good selection of traditional filigree in both silver and gold.
Torres, Rua Aurea 202, 253, 255; and Rua Augusta 257. Five generations of the family have run this jeweller's, selling items antique and modern.

Markets

Mercado da Ribeira, the main morning market, is behind the Cais de Sodré station. Try to catch, too, the frantic flower market at 6pm Monday, Wednesday and Friday. **Feira da Ladra** (Thieves' Fair), Campo Santa Clara. The great Alfama flea market takes place on Tuesday morning and Saturday. **Feiras do Parque**, Parque das Nações. Every Sunday the Park of Nations holds a different fair. On the first Sunday of the month it specialises in books, stamps, coins and collectable items; on the second Sunday, Portuguese handicrafts; on the third, antiques; the fourth, paintings and other art works; and the fifth, CDs and records. It is open from 10am to 7pm during the summer.

Hypermarkets

Hypermarkets – *hipermercados* – are generally to be found in the larger commercial shopping centres. **Continente** is in Centro Columbo and the Centro Comercial Vasco da Gama. **Carrefour** is in the Avenida das Nações Unidos at Telheiros and **Jumbo** is on the Estrada Nacional at Alfragide. **Pingo Doce** is a very popular *supermercado* and is to be found all around the city including one in Rua 1º de Dezembro, just behind Rossio station and another in the Tivoli Forum in Avenida da Liberdade. **Celeiro** in Rua 1º de Dezembro a vegetarian and health food supermarket, is also behind Rossio station. It has a self-service vegetarian restaurant (almost!).

Convenience stores (*lojas de conveniência*) are to be found dotted around the city. Look out for **Lojas Select** and **Lojas Smart**. They are open (purportedly) 24 hours a day.

Tax-Free Shopping

Visitors from non-EC countries spending more than €58 in any shop with a Tax Free sign may fill out a form and hand it in at the relevant desk at the airport or other point of departure and reclaim the tax paid.

Sport

Bullfighting

The bullfighting season lasts from Easter to October and the city's bullring is the Praça de Touros do Campo Pequeno (Metro: Campo Pequeno), where fights generally take place on Thursday and Sunday, often in the evening.

There is also a ring at Cascais, but the most famous in the area is at Vila Franca de Xira, a suburb some 32 km (20 miles) north of the capital. Trains go from Santa Apolónia and Oriente stations. Tickets for bullfights are on sale at the arenas or from the ABEP ticket kiosk in Restauradores square.

Football

Football dominates sporting life in Portugal. The three most important teams are FC Porto and Lisbon's two clubs, Benfica and Sporting Club de Portugal. The season runs from September to July. Games are usually held on Sunday afternoon. Benfica play at the Estádio da Luz (Metro: Colégio Militar; bus: No 41), Sporting at Estádio de Alvalade (Metro: Campo Grande; bus: Nos 1 and 36). Tickets aren't usually hard to get. Try buying them at the ABEP kiosk in Restauradores, or at the gate.

Portugal will host the European Championships in 2004 and by then Sporting should have a brand new stadium, while Benfica's ground is due for a complete overhaul.

Golf

The nearest golf courses are in Estoril:
Clube de Golf do Estoril, Avenida da Republica, Estoril. Tel: 21 468 0176.

Has 18 plus 9 holes, with restaurant bar swimming pool and golf shop managed by the Palácio Hotel.
Golf Estoril Sol, Estrada da Lagoa Azul, Linhó. Between Estoril and Sintra. Tel: 21 923 2461. With 9 holes, plus a restaurant, bar, an open-air café and a golf shop.
Quinta da Marinha, Quinta da Marinha, Cascais. Tel: 21 486 0100. Has 18 holes. There are restaurants, bars, tennis courts, two swimming pools, golf shop and hotel.
Lisbon Sports Club, Casal da Carregueira in Belas. Near Queluz. Tel: 21 431 0077. With 18 holes. The club also has a restaurant, bar, tennis courts, swimming pool and golf shop.
Quinta da Beloura Golfe, Quinta da Beloura, Rua Sesmarias, 3, Estrada de Albarraque, Sintra. Between Cascais and Sintra. Tel: 21 910 6350. With 18 holes and a restaurant.

Horse Riding

Centro Hípico da Costa do Estoril, Estrada da Charneca, 2750 Cascais (bus from Cascais station). Lessons and rides available. Open Tues–Sun.
Quinta da Marinha, Cascais. Tel: 21 486 0100. The golf and sports club mentioned above also has stables where you can have lessons or rides. Open Tues–Sun.

Tennis

Apart from the **Quinta da Marinha** and **Lisbon Sports Club** mentioned above, try the **Clube VII** in the Parque Eduardo VII, tel: 21 384 8300; the **Clube Ténis Estoril** in Av. Conde Barcelona, Estoril, tel: 21 466 2770; the Lisbon municipal **Centro de Ténis de Monsanto**, tel: 21 364 8741 in Parque Monsanto or the **Complexo Desportivo do Jamor**, Estadio Nacional, Praça da Maratona, Cruz Quebrada-Dafundo, tel: 21 419 7212, which has 37 courts. Take the train from Cais do Sodré to Algés from where there's a bus.

Watersports

The sea is not clean enough to swim in until reaching the Atlantic beaches around Cascais. The best place to obtain information about watersport activities is at the **Marina de Cascais**.

Atlantic Charter, tel: 21 483 6188, arranges boat hire; you can hire a surf board at Aerial, tel: 21 483 6745 and if you contact Planeta Azul, tel: 21 483 7305, they may be able to arrange a sailing trip.

There are several municipal indoor pools in Lisbon that operate all year round, including the **Piscinas Municipais da Areeiro** in Avenida da Roma and the **Piscinas Municipais do Campo Grande** at Campo Grande. There is a heated swimming pool (with removable canopy) at the **Clube VII**, Parque Eduardo VII. Swimming pools can also be found a short distance from the centre of Lisbon: near Algés is the **Complexo Desportivo do Jamor**, Estádio Nacional, Praça da Maratona, Cruz Quebrada-Dafundo. Take a train from Cais do Sodré to Algés from where there's a bus. And there's even a pool on the top floor of the **Colombo Shopping Centre**.

Language

Useful Words & Phrases

Portuguese is a Romance language, similar in some respects to Spanish, though with quite different pronunciation. It is spoken in Portugal and Brazil and is the *lingua franca* of the former colonies, which in turn have introduced some of their words into Portuguese. Lisboetas are formal and polite. "Please" is *faz favor*, pronounced "fash favOOR" and is used to get people's attention. "Thank you" is *obrigado* if you are a man, *obrigada* if you are a woman.

Useful expressions include:

Basic Communication

Yes *Sim*
No *Não*
Thank you *Obrigado/a*
Many thanks *Muito obrigado*
Alright/Okay/That's fine *De acordo/Está bem*
Please *Faz favor/por favor*
Excuse me (to get attention) *Faz favor*
Excuse me (to get through a crowd) *Com licença*
Excuse me (sorry) *Desculpe*
Wait a minute *Espere um momento*
Can you help me? *Pode ajudar-me?*
Certainly *Com certeza*
Can I help you *Posso ajudá-lo/a?*
Can you show me...? *Pode mostrar-me...?*
I need... *Preciso...*
I'm lost *Estou perdido/a*
I'm sorry *Desculpe-me*
I don't know *Não sei*
I don't understand *Não compreendo*
Do you speak English/French/German? *Fala Inglês/Francês/Alemão?*

Please speak slowly? *Faz favor de falar devagar*
Please say that again *Diga outra vez, se faz favor*
Slowly *Devagar*
Here/There *Aqui/ali*
What/When/Why/Where? *O quê/Quando/Porquê/Onde?*
Where is the toilet? *Onde é a casa de banho?*

Greetings

Hello (good morning) *Bom dia*
Good afternoon/evening *Boa tarde*
Good night *Boa noite*
See you tomorrow *Até amanha*
See you later *Até logo*
See you soon *Até já*
Goodbye *Adeus*
Mr/Mrs/young lady/girl *Senhor/Senhora/Menina*
Pleased to meet you *Muito prazer em conhecê-lo(la)*
I am English/American *Sou Inglês(a) / Américano(a)*
I'm here on holiday *Estou aqui de férias*
How are you? *Como está?*
Fine, thanks *Bem, obrigado*

Questions

Where is...? *Onde é...?*
When...? *Quando...?*
How much...? *Quanto custa...?*
Is there...? *Há...?*
Do you have...? *Tem...?*
At what time...? *A que horas...?*
What time is it? *Que horas são?*
Do you have a...? *Tem um...?*

Telephone Calls

I want to make a telephone call *Quero fazer uma chamada*
The area code *O indicativo*
The number *O número*
Can you get this number for me? *Podia fazer-me uma chamada para este número?*
The line is engaged *Está ocupada*
There's no reply *Ninguém atende*
The operator *A telefonista*
Hello *Está lá?*
May I speak to... *Posso falar com...*
Hold the line please *Não desligue, faz favor*

Who is that? *Quem/Onde fala?*
May I leave a message? *Posso deixar um recado?*
I will phone later *Ligarei mais tarde*

At the Hotel

Do you have a room available? *Há algum quarto disponível?*
I have a reservation *Tenho uma reserva*
Single/double room *Um quarto individual/duplo*
Twin/double bed *Camas individuais/cama casal*
With bathroom *Com casa de banho*

For one night *Para uma noite*
Two nights *Para duas noites*
How much is it per night? *Qual é o preço por noite?*
With breakfast? *Com pequeno almoço incluindo?*
Does it have air conditioning? *O quarto tem ar condicionado?*
It's expensive *É caro*
Can I see the room? *Posso ver o quarto?*
What time does the hotel close? *A que horas fecha o hotel?*
Dining room *Sala de jantar*
What time is breakfast? *A que horas será o pequeno almoço?*
Please call me at... *Acorde-me às...*

The bill please *A conta por favor*
Can you call a taxi please? *Chame um táxi por favor*
Key *A chave*
Lift *Elevador*
Towel *Toalha*
Toilet paper *Papel higiénico*
Pull/push *Puxe/empurre*

Eating and Drinking

Bar snacks and drinks
We'd like... *Queríamos...*
coffee (small, black and strong) *Um café*
coffee with milk *Um café com leite*

Menu Decoder

Entradas (starters)
Amêijoas ao natural clams with butter and parsley
Camarão shrimps
Caracois com alho snails with garlic
Gambas prawns
Melão com presunto melon with smoked ham

Sopa (soup)
Caldo verde finely chopped cabbage and potato soup
Canja chicken broth
Creme de marisco seafood soup
Sopa de coentros coriander, bread, and a poached egg

Peixe (fish)
Arroz de marisco seafood rice
Atum tuna
Bacalhau dried codfish
Caldeirada de peixe fish stew
Enguias eels
Lagosta lobster
Lampreia lamprey
Linguado sole
Lulas squid
Pescada whiting
Polvo octopus
Robalo sea bass
Rodovalho halibut
Salmão salmon
Salmonete red mullet
Sardinhas sardines
Sável shad
Truta trout

Carne (meat)
Bife steak
Cabrito kid
Cozido à portuguesa variety of boiled meats and vegetables
Coelho rabbit
Frango chicken
Fígado liver
Javali wild boar
Leitão suckling pig
Pato duck
Peru turkey
Porco pork
Vitela veal

Cooking methods
Assado roast/baked
Churrasco barbecued
Cozido boiled
Espetada kebab
Estufado braised
Frito fried
Grelhado grilled
Guisado stewed
Na brasa grilled on hot coals
Recheado stuffed

Salada (salad)/Vegetables (legumes)
Alface lettuce
Alho garlic
Batatas potatoes
Cenoura carrot
Cebola onion
Cogumelos mushrooms
Couve cabbage
Feijão beans

Pepino cucumber
Pimentos peppers
Tomate tomato

Sobremesas (sweets)
Arroz doce sweet rice with cinnamon
Gelado ice cream
Leite creme crème brulee type of custard
Mousse de chocolate chocolate mousse
Natas (Chantilly) cream
Pudim Flan crème caramel
Queijo Cheese
Marmelada Quince marmalade

Fruta (fruit)
Ananas pineapple
Banana banana
Maça apple
Melão/Meloa melon
Morangos strawberries
Pera pear
Pêssego peach
Laranja orange
Uvas grapes

Basic foods
Açucar sugar
Azeite olive oil
Azeitona olive
Pão bread
Manteiga butter
Pimenta pepper
Sal salt
Vinagre vinegar

large, weak coffee with milk *Um galão*
tea (with lemon) *Um chá (com limão)*
orange juice (fresh) *Sumo de laranja (natural)*
mineral water (fizzy) *Agua sem gás (com gás)*
beer *Cerveja*
milk *Leite*
cakes *Bolos*
sandwich (ham/cheese/ham & cheese) *Sande de fiambre/queijo/mixta*
toasted sandwich (cheese/ham & cheese) *Tosta de queijo/tosta mixta*
cheers *Saúde!*
Toilets (ladies/gents, men/women) *Casa do banho/w.c./(Senhoras/ senhores, homens/mulheres)*

In a Restaurant

Can we have lunch/dinner here? *Podemos almoçar/jantar aqui?*
A table for two/three... *Uma mesa para dois/três...*
May we have the menu? *A ementa se faz favor*
What do you recommend? *Que recomenda?*
What is this? *O que é isto?*
Do you know what this is in English? *Sabe o que é isto em Inglês?*
What wine do you recommend? *Qual é o vinho que recomenda?*
Red/white wine (mature/'green') *Vinho tinto/branco (maduro/ verde)*
Bottle/half bottle *Garrafa/meia garrafa*
Not too expensive *Não muito caro*
Is it good? *É bom?*
I'll have that *Quero aquilo*
Well cooked/rare *Bem passado/mal passado*
Would you like some more? *Deseja mais?*
No thank you – no more *Obrigado – não desejo mais*
Yes, please *Sim, faz favor*
I enjoyed that *Gostei muito*
We have finished *Acabámos*
The bill please *A conta se faz favor*

Sightseeing

What should we see here? *O que podemos ver aqui?*
What is this building? *Que edifício é este?*
Where is the old part of the city/town? *Onde é a zona antiga da cidade/vila?*
When was it built? *Quando foi construída?*
What time is there a Mass? *A que horas há missa na igreja?*
When is the museum open? *A que horas está aberto o museu?*
Is it open on Sunday? *Está aberto no domingo?*
How much is it to go in? *Quanto custa a entrada?*
Admission free *Entrada gratuita*
Can I take pictures? *Posso tirar fotografias?*
Photographs are prohibited *É proibido tirar fotografias*
Follow the guide *Siga o guia*
We don't need a guide *Não precisamos de guia*
Where can I get a plan of the city? *Onde posso obter um plano da cidade?*
How do I get to...? *Como se vai para...?*
Can we walk there? *Podemos ir a pé?*

Shopping

What time do you open/close? *A que hora abre/fecha?*
Can I help you? *Posso ajudar?*
I'm looking for... *Procuro...*
We are just having a look around *Queremos ver o que há*
How much does it cost? *Quanto custa?*
Do you take credit cards? *Aceitam cartões de credito?*
Have you got...? *Tem...?*
Can I try it on? *Posso experimentá-lo?*
This is not my size *Não é a minha medida*
Too small/big *É muito pequeno/muito grande*
It's expensive *É caro*
I like it/don't like it *Gosto/Não gosto*
I'll take this *Levo isto*
Bakery *Padaria*

Barber *Barbearia*
Bookshop *Livraria*
Butcher *Talho*
Chemist *Farmácia*
Department store *Armazém*
Dry cleaner *Lavandaria a seco*
Fishmonger *Peixaria*
Grocer *Mercearia*
Optician *Oculista*
Post office *Correios*
Shoe shop *Sapataria*
Shopping centre *Centro comercial*
Stationer *Papelaria*
Tobacconist *Tabacaria*

Travelling

Airport *Aeroporto*
Arrivals/departures *Chegadas/ partidas*
Boat *Barco*
Bus *Autocarro*
Bus station *Centro camionagem*
Bus stop *Paragem*
Car/hire car *Automóvel/automóvel de aluguer*
Customs *Alfândega*
Driving licence *Carta de condução*
Flight *Voo*
Motorway *Auto-estrada*
Railway station *Estação de comboio*
Return ticket *Bilhete de ida e volta*
Single ticket *Bilhete de ida*
Smokers/non smokers *Fumadores/ não fumadores*
Taxi *Taxi*
Ticket office *Bilheteria*
Toll *Portagem*
Train *Comboio*

Health

Is there a chemist's nearby? *Há uma farmácia aqui perto?*
Where is the hospital? *Onde é o hospital?*
I feel ill *Não me sinto bem*
It hurts here *Tenho uma dor aqui*
I have a headache *Tenho dor de cabeça*
I have a sore throat *Doe-me a garganta*
I have a stomach ache *Tenho dores de estômago*
I have a fever (temperature) *Tenho febre*

Call a doctor *Chame um médico*
Take this prescription to the
chemist *Leve este receita para a
farmácia*
Take this note to the hospital *Leve
esta carta para o hospital*
Danger! *Perigo!*
Look out! *Cuidado!*
Help! *Socorro!*
Fire! *Fogo!*

Days of the Week

Sunday	*Domingo*
Monday	*Segunda-feira*
Tuesday	*Terça-feira*
Wednesday	*Quarta-feira*
Thursday	*Quinta-feira*
Friday	*Sexta-feira*
Saturday	*Sábado*

Numbers

1	*um/uma*
2	*dois/duas*
3	*três*
4	*quatro*
5	*cinco*
6	*seis*
7	*sete*
8	*oito*
9	*nove*
10	*dez*
11	*onze*
12	*doze*
13	*treze*
14	*catorze*
15	*quinze*
16	*dezasseis*
17	*dezassete*
18	*dezoito*
19	*dezanove*
20	*vinte*
30	*trinta*
40	*quarenta*
50	*cinquenta*
60	*sessenta*
70	*setenta*
80	*oitenta*
90	*noventa*
100	*cem*
200	*duzentos*
1000	*mil*

Further Reading

Portuguese Literature

There is not a great deal of literature in print. Classics such as William Beckford's *Recollections* and Fernando Pessoa's poems have to be sought out. The rush of political books published on the fall of Salazar now seem a little out of date.

Two well-known 19th-century Portuguese authors have been translated: Almeida Garrett (*Travels in my Homeland*, Peter Owen) and Eca de Queiroz (*The Maias*, Dent). Modern writers to look out for in translation include Fernando Namora, Mario Braga, Ferreira de Castro and Antonio Lobo Antuines. Jose Sartamago's historical novel, *Balthasar & Blimunda*, has been published by Cape.

Books on Portugal

Os Lusíadas (The Lusiads) by Luís de Camões, first published in 1572. The epic poem of Vasco da Gama and the history of Portugal by the country's best-known writer. Penguin.
They Went to Portugal by Rose Macaulay. A lively account of Lisbon's vistors, mainly British, and including Beckford's stay in the city. Penguin.
A Visit to Portugal by Hans Christian Andersen. Impressions of a visit in the 1860s by the fairy-tale teller. Peter Owen.
The Portuguese by Marion Kaplan. A thorough, affectionate, finely drawn and extremely welcome portrait of the country. Penguin.
Lisbon by Manfred Hamm and Werner Radasewsky. Beautiful pictures of the city with informative text. Available in three languages in Lisbon. Nicolaische Verlagsbuchhandlung, Berlin.
A Concise History of Portugal by David Birmingham. An interesting historical account of the country. Cambridge University Press.
The Taste of Portugal by Edite Vierira. Gives all the flavour of the country's traditional food.
The Wines of Portugal by Jan Read. A clear and comprehensive study of the country's wines. Faber.
Jancis Robinson Tastes the Best Portuguese Table Wines by Jancis Robinson. A useful and well-informed guide to the best wines. Edições Cotovia Lda, Lisbon. English edition.

Other Insight Guides

There are around 190 Insight Guides to countries, cities and regions of the world including books to Portugal and its neighbours.

Insight Guide: Portugal is the perfect companion to **Insight Guide: Lisbon**. With the same fine photography and lively text, it looks at the country beyond the capital. Madeira is also the subject of an Insight Guide.

Travellers who like to be looked after will appreciate Insight Pocket Guides. Each one is written by a specialist host author who gives itineraries for every day of your stay. Titles include **Insight Pocket Guide: Algarve** and **Insight Pocket Guide: Portugal**.

Compact Guides are user-friendly mini-encyclopedias that will go everywhere with you, to give you on-the-spot information about services and sites. Titles include: **Compact Guide: Lisbon, Compact Guide: Portugal** and **Compact Guide: Madeira**.

ART & PHOTO CREDITS

66 I was first drawn to the
Insight Guides by the
excellent "Nepal" volume.
I can think of no book
which so effectively
captures the essence of
a country. Out of these
pages leaped the Nepal
I know – the captivating
charm of a people and
their culture. I've since
discovered and enjoyed
the entire Insight Guide
series. Each volume deals
with a country in the
same sensitive depth,
which is nowhere more
evident than in the
superb photography. 99

Sir Edmund Hillary

New Insight Maps

Maps in Insight Guides are tailored to complement the text. But when you're on the road you sometimes need the big picture that only a large-scale map can provide. This new range of durable Insight Fleximaps has been designed to meet just that need.

Detailed, clear cartography
makes the comprehensive route and city maps easy to follow, highlights all the major tourist sites and provides valuable motoring information plus a full index.

Informative and easy to use
with additional text and photographs covering a destination's top 10 essential sites, plus useful addresses, facts about the destination and handy tips on getting around.

Laminated finish
allows you to mark your route on the map using a non-permanent marker pen, and wipe it off. It makes the maps more durable and easier to fold than traditional maps.

The first titles
cover many popular destinations. They include Algarve, Amsterdam, Bangkok, California, Cyprus, Dominican Republic, Florence, Hong Kong, Ireland, London, Mallorca, Paris, Prague, Rome, San Francisco, Sydney, Thailand, Tuscany, USA Southwest, Venice, and Vienna.

✵ INSIGHT GUIDES

The world's largest collection of visual travel guides

Lisbon Metro

Linha Gaivota - Seagull Line (Blue)
Linha Girassol - Sunflower Line (Yellow)
Linha Caravela - Caravel Line (Green)
Linha Oriente - Orient Line (Red)

Lines under construction

Interchange station

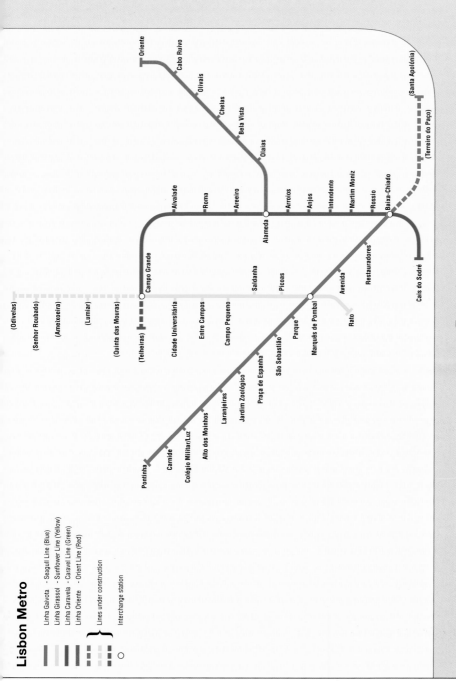